THE BEST OF
ORANGE COUNTY
CALIFORNIA

A Guide to Scenic, Recreational
& Historical Attractions

THE BEST OF
ORANGE COUNTY
CALIFORNIA

*A Guide to Scenic, Recreational
& Historical Attractions*

SECOND EDITION

Gregory Lee

JOHNSTON
ASSOCIATES
INTERNATIONAL
P.O. Box 313
MEDINA, WASHINGTON 98039
(206) 454-7333

The Best of Orange County, California
Second Edition
©2001 by Gregory Lee

ISBN 1-831409-26-0

ISSN 1535-623X

Cover art and book design by Kate Kilpatrick

Frontistpiece: Fishing at Seal Beach Pier

All photos by the author with the exception of the following: Page 150, Photos courtesy of Knott's Berry Farm. The author wishes to thank David Lee for his research and tireless fact checking.

JASI

Post Office Box 313
Medina, Washington 98039

Printed in the United States of America

Contents

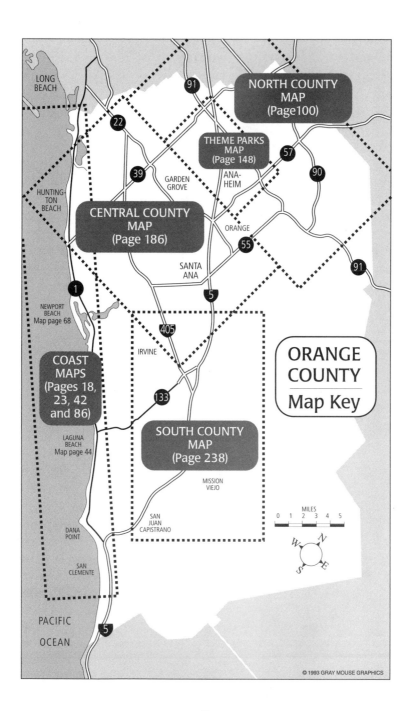

LONG
BEACH

**NORTH COUNTY
MAP
(Page100)**

91

22

**THEME PARKS
MAP
(Page 148)**

57

39

GARDEN
GROVE

ANA-
HEIM

90

HUNTING-
TON
BEACH

**CENTRAL COUNTY
MAP
(Page 186)**

ORANGE

SANTA
ANA

55

91

1

5

NEWPORT
BEACH
Map page 68

405

IRVINE

**ORANGE
COUNTY**

Map Key

**COAST
MAPS
(Pages 18,
23, 42
and 86)**

133

LAGUNA
BEACH
Map page 44

**SOUTH COUNTY
MAP
(Page 238)**

MISSION
VIEJO

DANA
POINT

SAN
JUAN
CAPISTRANO

MILES
0 1 2 3 4 5

SAN
CLEMENTE

N
W   E
S

PACIFIC

OCEAN

5

© 1993 GRAY MOUSE GRAPHICS

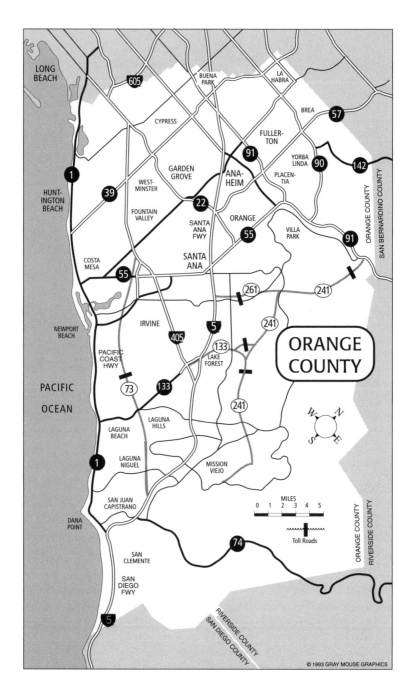

Introduction to the Second Edition

Orange County has long lived in the shadow of Los Angeles. The sprawling metropolis to the north is really one of the world's biggest counties, with more than 100 cities and seven million people. The greater Los Angeles area, as the visitors' bureaus call it, is so vast that it surpasses the population and gross national product of most countries. Because "L.A." includes such famous mythical places as Hollywood, Rodeo Drive and Malibu Beach, many travelers tend to lump all of Southern California under this one metropolitan umbrella. As a result, they often overlook the distinct pleasures to be found in the areas south of L.A. I should know. I grew up here.

When I was a boy, Orange County still had plenty of orange groves, but in the late 1950s and '60s, the suburban growth was explosive; sizable chunks of prime sun-soaked real estate were being turned into new housing tracts, schools and shops. Orange County experienced an explosion of growth that has barely abated. The desire to live in this region south of L.A. is evident everywhere, as more and more of the remaining canyons, hillsides and flatlands are built over by houses, townhomes and apartments for every style and taste.

Orange County was once known principally as a citrus farming region, sandwiched between the South Bay region of L.A. County to the north and San Diego County to the south. The Santa Ana Mountains form the eastern boundary, the Pacific Ocean is on the west. The county is shaped like a rough diamond, with the mountains paralleling the coastline. Foothills divide it into smaller areas, such as

Saddleback Valley, Laguna Canyon, and Yorba Linda in the northeast corner of the county.

When looking at a map of Southern California and comparing the size of the region's counties—Orange, Los Angeles, Riverside, Ventura, San Bernardino and San Diego—you can be deceived and think Orange County is rather small. But California counties tend to be much larger than those in many other states, and when you begin exploring Orange County, you'll discover that it can take a good hour's drive to get from one end to the other, providing the traffic's not too heavy. The amount of time it takes to travel from Point A to Point B will vary with the destination, the roads or freeways that lead to it, and the time of day. This may sound obvious, but trust me, looking at a map makes some destinations appear much closer than they are in actual travel time. So allow enough time to make it to your destination, and prepare to be frustrated by continual road improvements and freeway-widening projects and other roadside nuisances that are the legacy of a once-justly famous freeway system that is now 50 years old and showing its age.

Orange County is often passed over by tourists who think it is just one giant suburb between Los Angeles and San Diego, with one place—Disneyland—the only worthwhile stop. Disneyland remains one of the best tourist attractions on Earth, but there is certainly much more to Orange County. There are several lovely harbors where you can pass a pleasant day just watching the sailboats glide in the sunshine. There are large tree-filled parks where you'd swear the urban surroundings have vanished. The Cleveland National Forest in the Santa Ana Mountains is full of wildlife, wildflowers, and wild experiences for those who love to hike, ride horseback, or just peer at birds through binoculars. For locals and tourists alike, Orange County has some wonderful annual events, such as Laguna Beach's popular Pageant of the Masters, that defines summer in that lovely seaside community.

One of the nicest things about visiting or living in Orange County is the weather: the temperatures are usually milder than in the midst of Los Angeles, and there is generally less smog due to the proximity of the ocean. Meteorologists classify our weather as "Mediterranean." This is rarer than you might think. Unless you live in a narrow latitude near the French Riviera, California is one of the few places on the whole globe where you can enjoy mild temperatures year-round, and where you don't have to shovel your car out of a snowdrift three months of the year. Maybe that's why more than three million people now live in Orange County's 786 square miles of sunshine.

This guide is *not* the yellow pages of Orange County. For instance, it doesn't attempt to cite each and every place where you might enjoy a great meal. I've highlighted things I would want every new resident or traveler to discover. But exploring on your own is one of the pleasures of traveling to a new place. A guide like this can help the first-time visitor or new resident quickly spot places that they'll want to return to, and having a guide does maximize your visiting time. Whether you are just passing through, have just moved to Orange County, or consider yourself a "native," as I do, I hope this guide will help you appreciate the special place that makes me cherish Orange County, my home.

Welcome to Orange County!

Using This Guide

This guide is designed for easy reference, with the county divided into five geographic sections: the Coast, North County, Central County, South County, and "Wild" Orange County. Specific communities are detailed within each section. Disneyland and Knott's Berry Farm—the two largest tourist attractions in Orange County—are grouped in a separate section called Theme Parks. Entries that have something in common are grouped together, such as Outdoors (beaches, parks, and trails), Attractions and Special Events (such as festivals), Museums and Galleries, Historical Sites, Shopping, Restaurants and Lodging (mentioned only if there is an unusual opportunity to consider). Addresses, phone numbers, hours (if pertinent) and directions are given beneath each individual entry.

Area Codes

Orange County is not immune to the proliferation of area codes throughout the United States. In 1998, the county was split into two area codes: 714 and 949. I have tried to indicate which is which throughout this guide, but there may be a few that I've missed. Communities on the Orange - Los Angeles County border often share the 310 and 562 area codes, further complicating matters. When in doubt, check with directory assistance (dial 411).

The blossoming of the World Wide Web has made online research an obvious tool, and wherever I feel the information might be useful, I have listed the Website addresses of places and events in this guide for your convenience.

Beach & Park Activities

The Harbors, Beaches and Parks division of he County of Orange has a pre-recorded information line about current special events scheduled at all of the county's harbors, beaches and parks. Dial (714) 834-2400, 24 hours a day.

The state of California has placed some convenient "Coastal Access" signs along Pacific Coast Highway so that visitors know whether a certain side street or sidewalk will allow them to reach the beach. Look for the brown signs with the white silhouette of bare feet. Parking at municipal, county and state beaches is not free, but it's cheap; free parking along city streets and Pacific Coast Highway is scarce, and usually restricted in duration.

To obtain camping information for the state parks located along Orange County's coast, call 1-800-444-PARK to reach the California State campground reservation system. Folks with campers and RVs can reserve a campsite at any beach state park up to eight weeks before arrival.

Pets

If you're traveling with your dog, it is often hard to find a place where your family member is welcome. There are a few places on or near Orange County's coastline where pooches can find respite:

Costa Mesa Bark Park. This is near the Orange County Fairgrounds at the corner of Newport Boulevard and Arlington Drive. Hours: 7 a.m.-dusk, every day except Tuesdays. (949) 754-5041.

Huntington Beach City Beach. This dog beach, located from 22nd Street to Seapoint Avenue near lifeguard station No. 22, is definitely dog friendly. You can let your pal off the leash as long as he or she is frolicking in the water and tide line area; otherwise, dogs need to be on a leash. Between 5 a.m.-10 p.m. (714) 536-5281.

Huntington Beach Dog Park. On Edwards Street between Ellis and Slater avenues, adjacent to Central Park West. (714) 536-5672.

Laguna Beach. A bit more restrictive than the others, this beach allows leashed dogs at least on the main before 6 a.m. and after 6 p.m. (prime jogging time, I suppose) from mid-

June to mid-September (prime tourist time); the rest of the year, it's all day.

Laguna Beach Bark Park. Open dawn to dusk at 20654 Laguna Canyon Road, about 1/2 mile south of El Toro Road. (949) 458-9663.

Laguna Niguel Dog Park. Located on Golden Lantern between Sardina and Beacon Hill Way. Hours: 7 a.m.-dusk Tuesdays, Thursdays and Saturdays; 8 a.m.-dusk on Sundays; and noon-dusk on Mondays and Fridays. (949) 362-4350.

Newport Beach. Keep your dog on a leash and he or she can enjoy this beach year-round before 9 a.m. and after 5 p.m.

San Onofre State Beach. This campground has an area just for leashed dogs, between Trails #4 and #6. From I-5 southbound, exit at Basilone Road, go west, then follow the signs to San Onofre State Beach. Call (714) 492-4872 for more information.

Fishing

It is permissible to fish off any Orange County pier without a fishing license from the California Department of Fish and Game. Anywhere else in the county where you might fish—on a boat offshore or at a park lake—you must have a permit. Juveniles under age 16, however, are not required to have a license. Permits may be purchased in many places, from sporting goods stores to the concessionaires who are on-site at the county's parks. For more details on Fish and Game regulations in California, call (310) 590-5132.

Historic Sites

For thousands of years Native Americans inhabited the area we now call Orange County, and the first European visitors trekked through here more than 200 years ago. In that time a lot of historical interest has accumulated. The combination of Indian, Mexican and European influences on the architecture and agriculture of Orange County has produced cities and towns with a wonderful diversity of sights, sounds and smells. In this guide I've listed some of the more prominent historical structures still standing that you may visit; however, there are many more historical sites not listed. Many of them are only marked by a plaque or historical marker, and consequently make them less interesting than sites where you can at least see and feel what the surroundings may have been like for the original inhabitants.

Restaurants

Southern California is a gastronomic dream. Thanks, in part, to the many different ethnic groups that have settled here, the available cuisine in Orange County is nicely varied. No matter what type of food you crave (or miss from your homeland), it's probably available here.

Orange County has a great number of immigrants from many Southeast Asian countries such as Thailand and Vietnam, and their native dishes offer a spicier alternative than other, more familiar types of Asian cuisine; Orange County has several fine restaurants featuring French and Belgian cooking; Cuban, English, German, Greek, Indian, and Persian food graces menus from Anaheim to San Clemente.

Don't be surprised to find many excellent restaurants located in small, nondescript shopping centers at countless corners throughout Orange County. It is not at all unusual for these neighborhood restaurants (usually family run) to offer some of the best in Orange County eating. The exteriors may be unimpressive, but it's what goes on in the kitchen that counts. I have mentioned a mere handful in this guide; don't be shy about asking the locals where they like to eat.

Southern California is also full of chains, of course, and the restaurant chains are many. The fact that a restaurant is part of a chain doesn't make it any less worthy of your consideration, however. El Torito is found throughout the county, and offers some of the best California-style Mexican food around; Souplantation is really one long soup and salad bar that's a haven for people on a vegetarian diet; and for those who crave red meat, Southern California's most famous hamburger chain, In 'n Out, remains one of the best places for fries and a milkshake. For your fix of cafe latte or double espresso, be sure and try Orange County's homegrown coffeehouse chain, Diedrich. At last count, there were at least two dozen Diedrich Coffee locations in Southern California (www.diedrich.com).

Smoking is now banned in all restaurants in California, so you no longer hear the question, "Smoking or non-smoking?" However, you'll often be asked, "inside or patio?" The weather is so spectacular here year-round that it's no wonder that many restaurants—good and ordinary—offer outdoor dining. These are usually the most popular tables, however, so it's not unusual to have to wait for outdoor seating. Diners are typically asked to wait in the bar. If you have children, don't worry. Children are allowed to sit in the area of a restaurant where alcoholic beverages are served provided that food is served in the same establishment.

Dining in most Orange County restaurants is casual; that is, as long as you have shoes and a shirt on, most places will serve you without a second glance. Restaurants that require formal evening dress certainly do exist, especially in the swankier parts of OC, such as Newport Beach. But such places are usually easy to pick out. If you're uncertain, call ahead first and ask while you make your reservation. It's rare to pick a restaurant by chance while you're just "out and about" and find yourself inappropriately attired.

Safety

Orange County, like any major metropolitan area, has crime. But there's no need to be paranoid about crime—just use common sense. When you park your car, always lock it even if you're just leaving it for a couple of minutes. Don't leave tempting packages or personal items visible—put them in the trunk. If you're going to be returning to your car after sunset, make sure you've parked in a well-lighted place near other cars.

Shopping and Entertainment

For current entertainment information, the two local newspapers, the *Times Orange County* and the *Orange County Register* are full of details to movies, concerts, and more. OCNOW.com is an engaging web site with lots of currnt information about Orange County.

Tickets to Concerts and Other Events

Many Orange County events are available for advanced ticket purchase from local Ticketmaster outlets. Call 740-2000 for information.

Traffic

Orange County, like all of Southern California, has notoriously busy traffic both on freeways and surface streets at any time of day. If you are a little unfamiliar with the freeways, tune into any local radio station. Most give regular traffic reports on Southern California freeways.

If you want to leave the driving to someone else, there are metropolitan buses run by the Orange County Transportation Authority (OCTA), covering most of the county. Call 636-RIDE for information on routes and rates.

Accuracy

The author has tried to make sure the information contained in this guide is current and accurate. But Orange County is a dynamic place, and neither the author nor the publisher can assume responsibility for changes in information. We happily welcome your comments and suggestions for additions to our next edition. If there is anything you would like to see in the way of additional categories and new entries, please write to Greg Lee in care of: JASI, P.O. Box 313, Medina, WA 98039. Fax: (425) 462-1335.

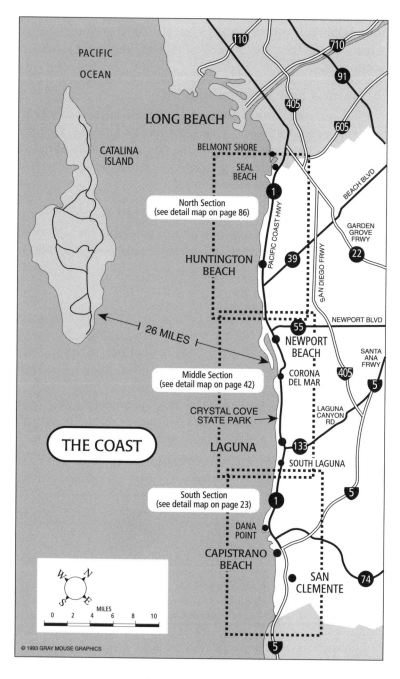

THE COAST

PACIFIC OCEAN

CATALINA ISLAND

LONG BEACH

BELMONT SHORE

SEAL BEACH

North Section
(see detail map on page 86)

HUNTINGTON BEACH

⊢ 26 MILES ⊣

Middle Section
(see detail map on page 42)

CRYSTAL COVE STATE PARK

LAGUNA

South Section
(see detail map on page 23)

NEWPORT BEACH

CORONA DEL MAR

SOUTH LAGUNA

DANA POINT

CAPISTRANO BEACH

SAN CLEMENTE

PACIFIC COAST HWY

BEACH BLVD

GARDEN GROVE FRWY

SAN DIEGO FRWY

NEWPORT BLVD

SANTA ANA FRWY

LAGUNA CANYON RD

110 710 91 405 605 22 39 55 405 5 133 5 1 74 5 1

MILES
0 2 4 6 8 10

© 1993 GRAY MOUSE GRAPHICS

18

The Coast

It's hard to find a more attractive region to recommend to first-time visitors than the shoreline of Southern California. The weather is so good year-round that it is rare to find a day at the beach that is anything less than pleasant. True, there are days when the shore remains cloaked in low clouds, and there are days when the inland dust and smog are blown out to sea by the Santa Ana winds, leaving an unsightly brown shroud hovering over the water. And occasionally the heat of summer makes even the beaches toasty. But the vast majority of the year, the weather from Seal Beach to San Clemente is great. Bring a jacket for nighttime, bring some sun block for the days, and plan to enjoy the many pleasures of Orange County's coast.

There is plenty of variety to the beaches and neighboring amenities, so if one setting isn't to your liking, just move down the road a bit and find another. All the beaches can be recommended, but some are nearer shopping and other niceties that might make a day at the beach more pleasant. You can get away from the sensation of buildings crowding you at the beaches of Capistrano, Doheny, and Huntington State. On the other hand, Newport Beach, Corona del Mar, and Laguna Beach are very much a part of the popular towns for which they are named.

Overlooking Laguna Beach

There are eight separate coastal camping parks in Orange County. If you want to be guaranteed a spot upon arrival, you must make reservations for campsites through the state's Mistix phone system (800-444-7275). There is a non-refundable fee of $3.95 per campsite in addition to the per night fee. Reservations can be made between eight weeks and 24 hours before the date of your arrival.

One special artery connects all of Orange County's coastline, from Long Beach in the north to Camp Pendleton in the south. It is Pacific Coast Highway, or Coast Highway, or Highway 1, or just "PCH." One short portion in downtown San Clemente is known as El Camino Real, but don't let that fool you. It's all PCH, and if we slip occasionally and call it PCH in this book, you'll know we mean: the one and only Pacific Coast Highway. PCH provides wonderful views of the Pacific Ocean 24 hours a day (even the fog can make the coastline eerily beautiful), but sometimes the traffic can be slow. The most congested stretches are through Corona del Mar just south of MacArthur Boulevard, Laguna Beach near Broadway (where the Main Beach begins), and Dana Point near the Interstate 5 turnoff.

We'll begin our tour of the coastline at the southernmost point of Orange County at the San Diego County line and work our way up Pacific Coast Highway all the way to Los Angeles County. The top coastal portion of San Diego County belongs to Camp Pendleton, a Marine Corps Reservation that is off limits to the public. As a result, traffic traveling north from San Diego has to skirt the ocean via the San Diego Freeway (I-5). You can see the ocean, but there is only one viewpoint where you can stop (south of the San Onofre Nuclear Power Plant). After passing San Onofre State Beach, the San Diego Freeway (I-5) crosses into Orange County.

Our Orange County journey starts in the city of San Clemente. Use the Avenida Magdalena exit off I-5 and head north on El Camino Real. This is also Highway 1 and will soon be called Pacific Coast Highway when you leave San Clemente headed north.

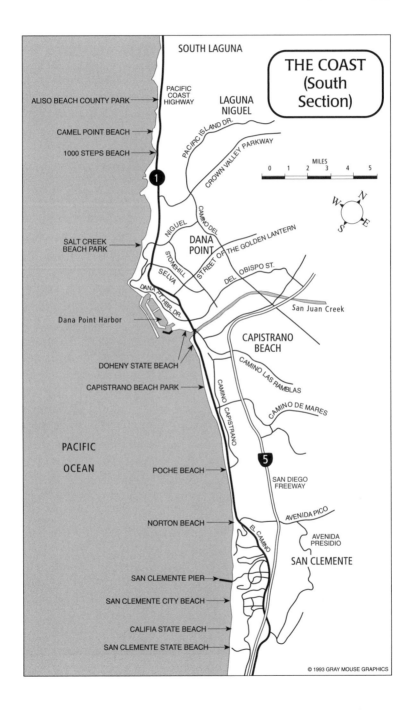

THE COAST
(South Section)

SOUTH LAGUNA

PACIFIC COAST HIGHWAY

LAGUNA NIGUEL

ALISO BEACH COUNTY PARK

CAMEL POINT BEACH

1000 STEPS BEACH

PACIFIC ISLAND DR.

CROWN VALLEY PARKWAY

MILES
0   1   2   3   4   5

N
W   E
S

NIGUEL

CAMINO DEL

DANA POINT

STONEHILL

SELVA

STREET OF THE GOLDEN LANTERN

DEL OBISPO ST.

SALT CREEK BEACH PARK

DANA PT. HBR. DR.

San Juan Creek

Dana Point Harbor

CAPISTRANO BEACH

DOHENY STATE BEACH

CAMINO LAS RAMBLAS

CAPISTRANO BEACH PARK

CAMINO CAPISTRANO

CAMINO DE MARES

PACIFIC

OCEAN

POCHE BEACH

5

SAN DIEGO FREEWAY

AVENIDA PICO

NORTON BEACH

EL CAMINO

AVENIDA PRESIDIO

SAN CLEMENTE

SAN CLEMENTE PIER

SAN CLEMENTE CITY BEACH

CALIFIA STATE BEACH

SAN CLEMENTE STATE BEACH

© 1993 GRAY MOUSE GRAPHICS

San Clemente

The swaying palm trees and glistening ocean visible from the San Diego Freeway give travelers the obvious clue that this is the land's end. The Pacific Ocean beckons, and San Clemente is a prime spot to enjoy it. Here's your chance to visit a relatively unspoiled California beach town. No wonder former president Richard Nixon chose this as the site of his "Western White House."

Unlike Dana Point to the north, with its natural harbor, or San Juan Capistrano, the inland site chosen by the missionaries as their first home here, San Clemente is perched along seaside bluffs that attracted little attention until this century. San Clemente was the vision of Ole Hansen, who founded the town in 1925. He created his version of a coastal paradise along this stretch of hills that slope gently down to the sea (although periodic storms produce mud slides that have ruined many a seaside home). When you survey the town from the freeway, you'll see residences ringing the hillsides above the town's center, and palm trees scattered among Spanish tile roofs.

Most of the action in San Clemente is along El Camino Real and the old heart of town, Avenida Del Mar. Park anywhere near Del Mar and you will be right in the center of its shops and cafes. This avenue doesn't pretend to have the boutique variety of Laguna Beach because San Clemente doesn't try to rival the tourist scene. That's why coming here is so pleasant.

As you walk down the brick sidewalk of Avenida Del Mar toward the ocean, you'll discover that this is where San Clemente's residents actually do their shopping. You can congratulate yourself on avoiding the economic pitfalls of shopping in resort gift shops. If you truly enjoy window shopping, you have the additional satisfaction of knowing that you're avoiding the pallor of shopping-mall-itis. Who would want to browse indoors when the weather is forever pleasant in San

Clemente? On most days the gentle slope of Avenida Del Mar affords you a great view of the Pacific.

The shops of San Clemente—and especially those along Avenida Del Mar—are many and varied. There are yarn, fabric, craft, boutique and toy shops, as well as numerous delis and sidewalk cafes offering great, inexpensive food. Several establishments serve fresh ground coffee and pastries. There's a sort of reggae/tie-dye/head shop, a Thai restaurant, a used book shop, and a health food store. Avenida Del Mar is clean, tidy and unpretentious.

On your way north out of town note the quaint architecture of the Ole Hansen Beach Club located one-half block west of El Camino Real on Avenida Pico. This bathing club dates from the early part of this century, when it was the site of the U.S. Olympic swimming trials for the 1932 Olympics held in Los Angeles. The swimming pool is still in use, and the club's seaside vista makes it a popular spot for weddings and receptions. Directly below the beach club is Norton Beach, where cookouts and fishing are permitted. Call (949) 492-1011 (San Clemente lifeguard) for surf and weather information.

A nifty way to get to San Clemente (if you have the time) is to catch the morning Amtrak train southbound from Fullerton, Anaheim or Santa Ana in the northern part of Orange County. This ride is inexpensive (less than $30), depending upon your point of departure. One possible itinerary: take the train down at around 8:30 in the morning and disembark at the pier; camp out on the beach for some morning rays; stroll up Avenida Del Mar and through San Clemente's quiet neighborhoods; enjoy lunch on the pier or in town; put on some more suntan oil for a sunny siesta, and then roll up your towel and head home around 4 p.m. It is also possible to travel up from San Diego and Oceanside (in San Diego County) and enjoy the same lazy day. Check with Amtrak for exact schedules, because they change often. Call 1-800-872-7245 for Amtrak information.

Outdoors

San Clemente Pier

End of Avenida Del Mar
Information: (949) 361-8219

The gem of San Clemente is its municipal pier, set on beautiful San Clemente City Beach and reaching out over the Pacific. It's a quiet viewpoint, as compared to the hustle farther north in Laguna Beach, Newport Beach and Huntington Beach. You could walk all the way from Del Mar's shopping district to the pier, but it's an uphill return, so you might want to drive down to the parking lot near the pier instead. Fishing is permitted from the pier.

A popular surfing spot ("T Street") is located just south of the pier. You'll be amazed to see surfers vying for waves at virtually any time of day or night.

San Clemente State Beach/Calafia State Beach

Avenida Calafia and Avenida Del Presidente
Lifeguard station: (949) 492-5172
Camping information: (949) 492-3156

Just south of San Clemente City Beach is San Clemente State Beach, home of the surfing spot affectionately known as "Toads"—a surfing acronym for "take off and die." Toads is for daredevils only. But if you're not surfing, you can still enjoy the overnight camping and cookout facilities here. There are 157 sites; 72 of those are RV hookups. The Amtrak railroad line passes along the shore here on its way from Los Angeles to San Diego.

San Clemente Municipal Golf Course

150 E. Avenida Magdalena
Information: (949) 361-8384

According to connoisseurs, this is still one of the best—and oldest—golf courses in the state of California. There is a view of the Pacific Ocean from every hole, including the stunning 15th hole (par 2). Located just above El Camino Real and I-5 (bisected by Avenida Magdalena), this municipal golf course is open to everyone. Be sure to book your desired starting time seven days in advance. Call for green fees and rentals.

A slightly more expensive course in San Clemente is the Shorecliff Golf Course, located higher up the town's Pacific Ocean slopes at 501 Avenida Vaquero (949-492-1177). *The Golf Trekker*® (see Recommended Reading at back of book) describes Shorecliffs as "a very tight course with a lot of water throughout. Ocean view on seven holes." Originally built in 1962, this course weaves in and out of a canyon, so the changes in course elevation are quite a challenge.

Attractions and Special Events

Cabrillo Playhouse

202 W. Avenida Cabrillo
Information: (949) 492-0465

Broadway plays and musicals, such as *Deathtrap* and *Stop the World, I Want To Get Off*, are performed regularly at this community playhouse, one of several around Orange County. Call for current program and show times. Cabrillo is located one block north of Avenida Del Mar.

Selected Restaurants

Fisherman's Restaurant

San Clemente Pier
Information: (949) 498-6390
Hours: Monday through Thursday, 11 a.m. to 9 p.m.;
Friday and Saturday, 8 a.m. to 10 p.m.; Sunday 9 a.m. to
9:30 p.m. Serving: Breakfast, lunch, dinner; Sunday
brunch

Both cocktails and food are served inside and outside at this seafood restaurant perched right above the surf at San Clemente City Beach. Heat lamps around the tables keep the chill away on cold nights. This is an excellent place to come for a cocktail at sundown. Even foggy days look picturesque from here, where you can see Dana Point curving into the ocean to the north, and the occasional fishing vessel or Navy ship cruising by in the distance.

Capistrano Beach

Capistrano Beach is hardly more than a strip of sand between the cliffs and the sea, with PCH and the Amtrak right-of-way sharing the narrow gap between Dana Point and San Clemente. This strip of beach and cliffside homes is actually part of the city of Dana Point. The Coast Highway and the I-5 freeway parallel the beach and then turn inland at San Juan Creek. It's easy to get confused about which direction to choose. There's a freeway overpass with on-ramps and off-ramps on either side. If you proceed past the overpass, you will pass several blocks of businesses that represent what is left of the old village called Capistrano Beach. Then the road changes its name to Camino Capistrano and will take you to San Juan Capistrano (*see* Chapter 5).

In order to continue heading north on Pacific Coast Highway, take the on-ramp that indicates Highway 1 north. You'll do a 270-degree turn onto the overpass and cross a bridge over San Juan Creek heading into the town of Dana Point.

Outdoors

Capistrano Beach Park
Pacific Coast Highway and Beach Drive
Information: (949) 661-7013

The main attraction of Capistrano Beach is Capistrano Beach Park, where cookouts, surfing and volleyball are popular. It is definitely less crowded here than either Huntington Beach or Laguna Beach.

Pines Park
Calle Loma & Camino Capistrano

On the bluff directly above Capistrano Beach sits this lovely little park with a great view of the Pacific. But Pines Park is a bit tricky to find. As you drive north out of San

Clemente on PCH, turn right at Camino Capistrano about one mile north of Avenida Pico (this is before PCH turns inland and hooks up again with Camino Capistrano on the other side of the bluffs). Follow Camino Capistrano uphill and stay with it until you reach Calle Loma. Pines Park is a well-kept secret, so don't tell just anyone about it. It is beautifully landscaped with pine trees, and its steep walking paths are equipped with hand rails. There are picnic tables and playground equipment. There is no path directly down to the beach, and you should not attempt to reach the beach from here. Try stopping here to picnic with the family and enjoy a view that many visitors miss. You can return to PCH the way you came, taking Camino Capistrano back down the hill and continuing north toward Dana Point.

Selected Restaurants

Olamendi's Mexican Cuisine

34660 Coast Highway
Information: (949) 661-1005
Hours: Tuesday through Thursday, 11:30 a.m. to 9 p.m.;
weekends, 11 a.m. to 10 p.m.; closed Monday. Serving:
Lunch, dinner

Along Pacific Coast Highway, opposite the beach, is a small Mexican cafe that serves Margaritas and cerveza (that's Spanish for "beer"). It's very casual and inexpensive, and authentically south-of-the-border in food and decor.

Dana Point

Dana Point is named after its ocean promontory, which in turn was named for an early California visitor, sailor Richard Henry Dana (1851–82). Dana's book, Two Years Before the Mast, is required reading in California schools. He chronicles his days sailing and trading in animal hides off California's coast during the 19th century. Dana loved the headlands here, returning to this beautiful, sheltered spot many times. It was known in his day as Capistrano Point because of its proximity to the mission. The point was used to extend a jetty in modern times, converting this part of the coast into a small marina. Dana's likeness is depicted in a tall statue on Dana Island (the small island in the middle of the harbor) at Island Way and Dana Drive.

Outdoors

Doheny State Beach
25300 Dana Point Harbor Drive
Information: (949) 496-6171

From PCH turn left at Del Obispo and you will come to Doheny State Beach, one of several immortalized by the Beach Boys' song Surfin' U.S.A. Will fishing, swimming, surfing, riding, camping, barbecuing and diving be enough for you? Doheny may be Orange County's most popular beach camping spot. There are showers, barbecues and picnic tables, as well as beach front campsites for both RVs and tents. The campsites are level with the beach, but they are closely packed together. There's a small interpretive center that showcases the wildlife you may encounter in Doheny State Marine Life Refuge—an underwater park for divers. The center has a 400-gallon tide pool touch tank. Doheny is also the terminus for the five-mile San Juan Creek Bike Trail and an equestrian trail that links with another trail heading inland to San Juan Capistrano.

Surfers, incidentally, call the northernmost reef at Doheny the "Boneyard"—a reference to the shallow rock bottom where the waves break. Those rocks and spiny sea urchins can, well, hurt your bones.

Historical note: Doheny, in case you're wondering, is a name that crops up quite frequently around Southern California. The Dohenys were one of the prominent families of boom town Los Angeles. Edward L. Doheny (1856–1935) was the first person to discover oil in Southern California, which means he was also one of L.A.'s original millionaires. Oil wells are still found all over the L.A. Basin (and, as you'll see, farther up north along Huntington Beach). The Doheny family became big-time patrons in this area; hence their name appears in many places.

Dana Point Harbor

Dana Point Harbor Drive

The busiest section of Dana Point is on PCH between the Street of the Blue Lantern and Del Obispo Street, and contains the usual proliferation of fast food stops and shops. To avoid them, continue past Doheny State Beach and then turn left on Del Obispo to Dana Point Harbor. This excellent marina holds 2,500 boats and includes a wharf area with numerous shops and restaurants. The marina is smaller than those of Huntington Harbor or Newport Harbor, but that's one reason it is so appealing. For one thing, the other harbors do not have the beautiful headlands that created Dana Point.

Dana Wharf Sportfishing & Parasailing

34675 Golden Lantern
Information: (949) 496-5794

At the southern end of the wharf, you'll find many fishing vessels waiting to whisk you out to sea to enjoy your own ocean fishing excursion. Everything you need for a day or evening of fishing is supplied: bait and tackle, rod and reels, and expert assistance in catching and cleaning your fish. You can go for half a day, an entire day, even two days.

For those angling enthusiasts who prefer to stay completely dry, there's a small fishing pier at the west end of Dana Point Harbor Drive below Cove Road (a short, windy cliff-climber that takes autos straight out of the harbor and up onto the bluffs). Children can enjoy the small beach to the left of the pier, where there are no waves, and parents can watch their young ones play in shallow water. Both spots are good places to watch the windsurfers, boaters and kayak paddlers who form a constant maritime parade.

If you've ever wanted to try parasailing, now's your chance. You can embark from this same location and enjoy a breathtaking tow outside the jetty—no experience required. If you prefer to stick closer to the water, you can always rent a stand-up or sit-down jet-propelled water ski vehicle. Renting these exciting water vehicles includes instruction, wetsuit and life preserver (call Capo Beach Watercraft at 949-661-1690). Oh, and don't forget to ask about whale watching by boat.

Aventura Sailing Association
24650 Dana Point Harbor Drive
Information: (949) 493-9493

Surely the ultimate in challenging the sea is to be your own captain. The Aventura Sailing Association, with 24 hours of instruction, will introduce you to the fun of sailing without the necessity of owning a boat. Even if you've never set foot on a boat before, this club can teach you to sail one. Once you're certified, you can charter the club's boats, which come in many different sizes and rent for very reasonable hourly rates.

Overview Park

Terminus of Blue Lantern

To get a better perspective on this lovely yacht harbor, you should find this small overlook at the end of Blue Lantern. From the wharf village, take Dana Point Harbor Drive west, turn right on Cove Drive and proceed up the hill to the Street of the Green Lantern. Make a right and then another right on Santa Clara Avenue, then right again and you're there. If you're traveling north on PCH, turn west toward the ocean at the corner of Blue Lantern, and proceed to the end of the street.

Whale Watching

Whale watching, for the uninitiated, is one of the more awesome opportunities to witness nature that you can imagine. This may sound like a grandiose statement, but in fact, most animal migrations are something that people can't witness very easily. Yet every year, the California gray whales (recently taken off the Endangered Species list) travel from their summer feeding waters in the Bering Sea and head for their breeding lagoons off Baja California. The whales travel in small groups called pods — females with young calves, mature and immature males — hugging the shore (that is, they stick close to the coast, but "close" in whale terms can mean five miles out to sea). The whales surface to breathe because they are mammals, needing to take air into their lungs. They can stay underwater for minutes at a time (even up to half an hour), but generally while traveling it is possible to follow them for several miles as they undulate their great bodies through the water.

During a two- or three-hour whale watching cruise, the boat's captain scans the sea for signs of the whales

This is the finest spot for overlooking Dana Point's harbor. A gazebo perched right on the cliff affords a great view to the south and west. The majestic schooner Pilgrim is usually docked beneath this lookout, next to the Orange County Marine Institute (described under Attractions and Special Events). These headlands were a prominent navigation marker for early sailors, Indians and, apparently, migrating gray whales. Biologists have identified more than 100 species of plants on these bluffs, and the California gnatcatcher (a threatened bird species) resides here. This combination of rare flora, fauna and unusual rock formations makes this

and then brings the boat as close as possible to the migrating grays, but not so close as to disturb or stress them. Those who take these cruises are always armed with their cameras and camcorders, hoping the whales will hurl their bodies out of the water, or "breech," as it is called. Marine mammal scientists are still not certain why whales do this, but the effect is spectacular.

Whale watch cruises are generally offered from January through the end of March at several concessions in both Dana Point and Balboa Peninsula:

Catalina Passenger Service
Balboa Pavilion; information: 673-5245

Dana Whale Sportfishing
34675 Golden Lantern, Dana Point; information: 831-1850

Davey's Locker
400 Main Street, Balboa Peninsula; information: 673-1434

Newport Landing Sportfishing
309 Palm Street, Balboa Peninsula; information: 675-0550

headland one of the most distinctive in Southern California. It's also an especially nice place to catch a spectacular Southern California sunset.

Hide Trail

Between Amber and Violet Lantern Streets

After visiting the lookout point mentioned above, head back to PCH, turn right for a few blocks and then right again on Amber Lantern. At the end of the block is the beginning of a quarter-mile-long walking trail by the edge of the bluffs. Follow this trail to Violet Lantern, and you will come upon the "hide drogher statue" which depicts the way sailors used to fling cowhides off the cliffs so they could be loaded onto their waiting vessels below. Hides were one of the commodities traded with merchants on the East Coast. Occasionally the heavy, tanned skins would lodge in the crevices midway down, forcing the sailors to climb up and retrieve them. Also along this trail are the ruins of a hotel from 1930 that was never completed, due to the Great Depression.

Salt Creek Beach Park

West of Pacific Coast Highway off Ritz-Carlton Drive
Information: (949) 661-7013

Tide pools, surfing, and cookout facilities make this a really good beach stop. Working on your tan here is also a great way to see the elegant Ritz-Carlton hotel from the beach. It is described under Lodging. There is a nice picnic area above the beach that is good for kite flying and affords a pleasing view of the waves and the distant horizon.

The Links at Monarch Beach

23841 Stonehill Drive, Laguna Niguel
Information: (949) 240-8247

The entrance to this fine golf course may be in Laguna Niguel (an inland community), but the greens are in the midst of Dana Point and reach right to the beach. Expensive green fees ($50 on weekdays, $75 weekends) reflect the quality of the outstanding views. Two holes are played right alongside the Pacific Ocean. You can pretend you're at Pebble Beach, only you won't be as cold. The course was designed by Trent Jones, and, in the words of one Los Angeles Times golfing expert, the 16th hole is "extremely treacherous." Is it true that golfers are masochists?

Attractions and Special Events

Nautical Heritage Society & Museum

24532 Del Prado
Information: (949) 369-6773
Hours: Monday through Friday, 9 a.m. to 5 p.m.

This is the headquarters of the tall ship Californian, which travels between Northern and Southern California throughout the year, offering day sailing programs to school children. The ship is also open to the general public for day sails on weekends whenever it is docked at Dana Point. When she's in town, Californian docks next to Pilgrim, the Orange County Marine Institute's resident tall ship.

If Californian is not around, you can still visit the society's small museum dedicated to nautical history of the sailing "tall ship" variety. They have ship models, sailing art, artifacts salvaged from shipwrecks, antiques and displays about the sailing life from the late 18th and early 19th centuries.

You can spot the museum by the "lighthouse" protruding from its rooftop and the one-ton cannon (taken from a Spanish galleon) outside. The museum is located between Amber and Violet Lantern streets.

Orange County Marine Institute

35502 Dana Point Harbor Drive
Information: (949) 496-2274
Hours: Weekends only, 10 a.m. to 4:30 p.m.
Admission: Donation

This small research and nature center is located along the west basin of the marina at the end of Dana Point Harbor Drive. Kids love the displays of tidepool life and nautical sailing gear, and there's a huge replica of a California gray whale skeleton suspended from the ceiling. There's also a small gift shop that helps support the educational programs at the center.

Marine research workshops are regularly scheduled, and on weekends visitors can step aboard Pilgrim. This replica of the 1830 schooner that Richard Henry Dana sailed on is docked alongside the marine institute year-round. Lucky schoolchildren get to spend overnight field trips on board to experience what it was like to be a sailor in the 19th century.

Every September volunteer sailors take Pilgrim out as part of the Tall Ships Festival. Arts and crafts are on display during the festival weekend, and volunteers don period costumes and stand watch. In February, the institute is also the site of the Festival of the Whales, celebrating the annual winter migration of California gray whales from Arctic waters to the lagoons of Baja California. Exhibits, arts and crafts, lectures, and a 5K run are part of the fun. Regular whale watching cruises are offered here in February and March.

Shopping

Hobie Sports Shop
24825 Del Prado
Information: (949) 496-2366

Dana Point is home to another famous legend, surfing pioneer Hobie Alter. Alter developed the light, foam-core boards for surfers which replaced the heavier and longer wooden varieties. Surfing was never the same, and Hobie designs led to the early '60s explosion in the sport's popularity. But Alter didn't stop with surfboards. He also built catamarans, and the Hobie Cat bears his name.

You can view a collection of classic surfboards at the Hobie Sports shop in Lantern Bay Village, a Cape Cod-style center at the corner of Del Prado and Golden Lantern in the heart of Dana Point.

Selected Restaurants

Wind & Sea Restaurant

34699 Street of the Golden Lantern
Information: (949) 496-6500
Hours: Daily, 11:30 a.m. to 2:30 p.m. (lunch);
5:30 to 9:30 p.m. (dinner); bar open until midnight

This is a fine spot to watch the yachts enter and leave Dana Point Harbor, because it is located at the eastern end of the marina. Sit outside on the deck under the heat lamps and enjoy some peace and quiet. The menu is abbreviated — salads and hamburgers, mainly — but there is a full bar.

Chart House

34442 Street of the Green Lantern
Information: (949) 493-1183
Hours: Daily, 5-10 p.m. Sunday-Thursday, until 10:30 p.m.
Friday-Saturday

Yes, this is a familiar surf-and-turf chain to residents of California, but the view from this particular location is outstanding, atop a cliff above Dana Point Harbor, which is why it rates a mention here. Visitors enter through a "crow's nest" and walk down a spiral staircase to enter the restaurant. A window table is a must where you can enjoy a magnificent 180-degree view of the coastline, yachts and waves. The salad bar here is more like a gigantic buffet, where you can gorge yourself quite nicely.

Lodging

Marriott Laguna Cliffs Resort

25135 Street of the Park Lantern
Information: (949) 661-5000

A comfy hotel crafted in neo-Victorian/Cape Cod style, the Laguna Cliffs Resort is located just above the marina. This makes it convenient to all the aquatic sports nearby, and provides lovely views of the Pacific from beautifully manicured grounds. Rooms with terraces and balconies are available, and prices are variable depending upon the season.

The Ritz-Carlton Hotel

33533 Ritz-Carlton Drive
Information: (949) 240-2000

This is simply one of the finest hotels in the United States. If you can't afford to stay at this seaside resort, you can at least stroll inside for a glance at the posh interiors and relax in the lounge that overlooks Salt Creek Beach Park. It's a perfect spot to enjoy a sunset while sipping a cocktail. High tea is served daily between 2:30 and 5 p.m. (from 2 to 6 p.m. on weekends) in the hotel library.

If you want to dine in elegant style, make reservations for the Club Grill, a five-star restaurant with all the amenities: superb, formal service (yes, gentlemen wear jackets), delicious food, old wines, rare liqueurs, and equestrian decor.

South Laguna

When the shoreline gets steeper and the cliffs get rockier, you're in South Laguna. You can no longer see the ocean openly—you glimpse it through gaps in the bluffs. The higher elevation makes this area particularly popular for those seeking a Pacific Ocean view out their living room window, so there are many old (and new) residences on the hillsides.

Outdoors

Camel Point Beach

Access at West Street, Bluff Drive, and 5th Avenue
1000 Steps Beach Access at 9th Avenue

These beaches are accessible in several spots directly off the highway, but you have to park where you can and make your way to the beach down steep stairs anchored to the hillsides. Look for the state "coastal access" signs to make sure you don't park too far away from one of these paths. The tide pooling here is especially good.

Aliso Beach County Park

31000 block of Pacific Coast Highway

Aliso Beach is popular with some residents because of its cookout pits and relatively small, cozy size. The once popular fishing pier, alas, was razed after being repeatedly battered by winter rainstorms. The beach survives, however, nestled in a large cove bisected by Aliso Creek. There's plenty of room to fling the Frisbee, play volleyball, cook some hot dogs, and explore rocky areas on the southern end of the beach.

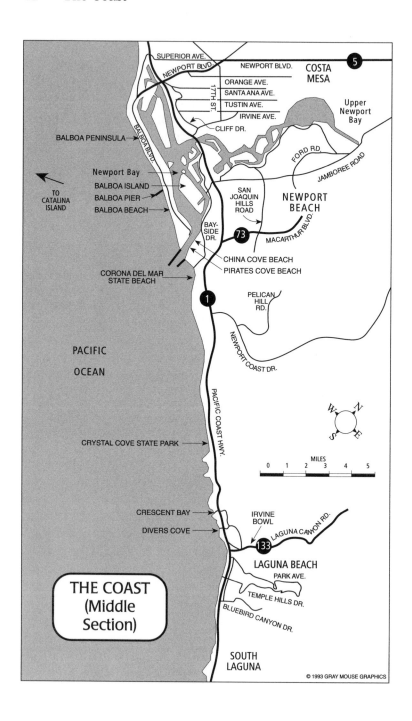

THE COAST
(Middle
Section)

© 1993 GRAY MOUSE GRAPHICS

Selected Restaurants

Dizz's As Is Restaurant

2794 Pacific Coast Highway
Information: (949) 494-5250
Hours: Open at 5:30 p.m. Tuesday through Sunday; seating
begins after 6 p.m. Serving: Dinner

Dizz's As Is is a casual restaurant with a small, choice menu that offers delicious food within a cute, beach-cottage atmosphere. Located off busy PCH, Dizz's has only a few tables. The atmosphere is dark but humorous, with black-and-white photos of old Hollywood movie stars and funky murals of some indistinct paradise. The cuisine is continental; entrees are $16.95 and up. This is a place to go for fine food, and also to relax for a few hours (seating is first-come, first-served). The service is unpretentious; it's like dining in someone's house.

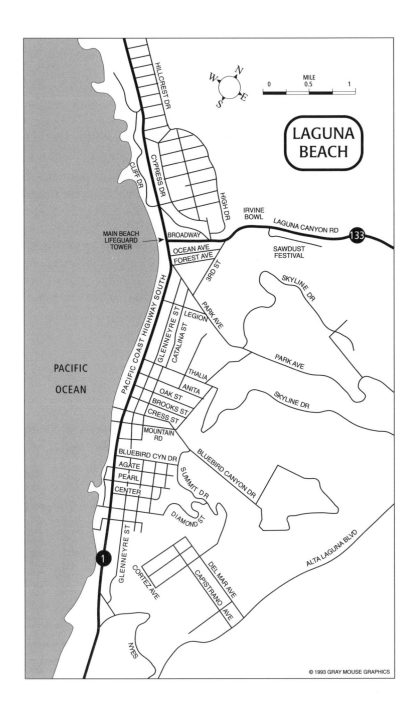

PACIFIC OCEAN

LAGUNA BEACH

MAIN BEACH LIFEGUARD TOWER

IRVINE BOWL

SAWDUST FESTIVAL

HILLCREST DR
CYPRESS DR
CLIFF DR
HIGH DR
BROADWAY
OCEAN AVE
FOREST AVE
3RD ST
PARK AVE
LEGION
GLENNEYRE ST
CATALINA ST
THALIA
ANITA
OAK ST
BROOKS ST
CRESS ST
MOUNTAIN RD
BLUEBIRD CYN DR
AGATE
PEARL
CENTER
SUMMIT DR
DIAMOND ST
GLENNEYRE ST
CORTEZ AVE
CAPISTRANO AVE
DEL MAR AVE
NYES
BLUEBIRD CANYON DR
PARK AVE
SKYLINE DR
SKYLINE DR
ALTA LAGUNA BLVD
LAGUNA CANYON RD
PACIFIC COAST HIGHWAY SOUTH

133
1

MILE
0   0.5   1

© 1993 GRAY MOUSE GRAPHICS

Laguna Beach

Laguna Beach has always attracted artists who were inspired by the sea, so it's no surprise that it became known as an artist's colony. In 1917 there was a resident community of some 40 artists. Their interest in capturing the shifting California colors along the bays and cliffs produced a style that is now labeled California Impressionism. The result of this active artist community is the number of art galleries that fill the town. Both the novice and serious collector can view new works by artists who aren't old masters yet, but give or take a hundred years and who knows? Walk anywhere along Pacific Coast Highway or Forest Avenue in the heart of town, and you'll find art for sale to suit every taste and decor. You might even enhance your personal art collection with a future Hockney or Pollack!

Stand anywhere on Main Beach in the heart of downtown and face the cliffs — you will see the variety of beautiful beach housing perched precariously along the slopes on either side of the canyon that connects Laguna Beach with the interior of Orange County. The early Hollywood screen legends discovered the scenic beauty of Laguna and many kept houses here: Mary Pickford and Douglas Fairbanks, Judy Garland, Bette Davis, and Rudolph Valentino.

However, Laguna Beach is best known as home to the Pageant of the Masters, a unique art festival that features recreations of works by famous painters using live models—volunteers from the community (see listing below under Attractions and Special Events).

The heart of town—known locally as "the village"—is Broadway and PCH. This T-intersection is also the center of Main Beach, recognizable by its distinctive lifeguard tower (immortalized in many of the local paintings that you will see). This is the one spot where you don't have to climb down steep stairs set into cliffs to reach the real Laguna Beach. A short boardwalk winds around some basketball and volleyball courts (which are in constant use year-round). If you start here, you can walk south along the beach for more than a mile, and be treated to a beautiful view of both the sea and the homes, apartments and hotels perched on the edge of the cliffs.

Laguna is a friendly and attractive town, so it draws considerable traffic on weekends in all months of the year. During the summer, Pacific Coast Highway through Laguna is always busy with a nonstop parade of vehicles and pedestrians who have come to see or be seen. With the weather so consistently mild, it's no wonder. Even business travelers who favor hotels nearer Irvine and John Wayne Airport for convenience take time to come to Laguna Beach, if only for an evening's dinner.

For years Laguna Beach had an official welcoming committee—a committee of one, that is. "The Greeter," as he was affectionately known around these parts, was a bearded old gentleman named Eiler Larsen, a Dane with hair below his shoulders and a great, gray beard. He usually stood around the corner of Forest Avenue and PCH, waving to everyone as they zipped past along the highway. Eventually, the city council proclaimed Larsen as the Official Greeter. He is gone, but not forgotten, as he is now immortalized in two statues, one at the Greeter's Restaurant at Main Beach, and another in front of the Pottery Shack just south along PCH. The Greeter symbolizes the earthy, welcome feeling that people sense when they come to Laguna Beach.

Laguna Beach is best seen on foot, so park on any handy side street near the village and plunge into the walking tide as it makes its way to and fro along PCH. Check out the shops, restaurants, and galleries until your feet can't take it any more. Then rest awhile on Laguna's wonderful, sandy beach.

Outdoors

"Dog Park"
Laguna Canyon Road

Directions: From PCH in Laguna Beach, take Broadway inland (which becomes Laguna Canyon Road) for two miles and look for the park behind a chain link fence on your right; from Irvine or Laguna Hills, take Laguna Canyon Road toward PCH and the park will be about one-half mile past El Toro Road.

This is just what its name says—a park for your dog. A local utility company loaned two grassy acres to the city for this purpose, so now people come here daily so their dogs can run and romp with their four-legged friends. It's a great opportunity to let your pooch off the leash to just go wild doing what dogs like to do. The sociability of dogs is readily apparent—most of them love playing with each other, and the contrast in sizes and breeds is fun to see. Rarely do the dogs get in scrapes, but you should keep a leash handy in case someone else's dog doesn't like yours.

Everyone cleans up their own dog's mess, and litter bags and receptacles are handily provided at the entrance gate.

Friends of the Sea Lion Marine Mammal Center
20612 Laguna Canyon Road
Information: (949) 494-3050
Hours: Daily 10 a.m. to 4 p.m.
Admission: Donations welcome

This is a hospital for sick and injured marine mammals and birds. If you take your family, be aware that some of these animals have been harmed by fishing activity and other man-caused events, so they may be maimed and sad to see. The good news is that you can witness how animals are nursed back to health. Tours are given to groups of five or more, if you call ahead first.

Hortense Miller Garden

505 Forest Avenue
Information: (949) 497-0716
Hours: Tuesday through Saturday, 10 a.m. By appointment only

This three-acre garden is located on private property and is therefore only open to special tours arranged two weeks in advance. The many varieties of plants here include native ones such as coastal sage, poppies and bougainvillea. The beautiful pride of Madeira (Echium fastuosum) is plentiful as well. The garden is located above town on the slopes of Boat Canyon with a great view of the Pacific Ocean. Because it is planted on a steep slope, the tour is not open to children and has no wheelchair access. For details about the tour, call the information number.

Divers Cove

Foot of Cliff Drive

Just below Cliff Drive near Main Beach is Divers Cove, the most popular of several offshore spots for divers. Divers claim this is one of the best places in all of Southern California to see the beautiful coastal shelf environment. This area is now an ecological reserve, and nothing may be disturbed or taken.

Laguna Coast Wilderness Park

20101 Laguna Canyon Road
Information: (949) 494-9352

In this large, unspoiled section off Laguna Canyon you can enjoy views of the Pacific Ocean and browse among the natural shrubbery and wildflowers that drape these undulating hills. Because the area is protected, access is limited to specific trails open from 8 a.m. to 3 p.m. every first and third Sunday of each month. Docents give tours along a three-and-a-half mile section every Saturday. Call ahead for specific times and information about the current hiking conditions.

Attractions and Special Events

Laguna Beach has not one, not two, but three art festivals for which it is justly famous. The visual arts provide the appropriate focal point for Laguna's celebration of summer.

Festival of Arts/Pageant of the Masters

Irvine Bowl
650 Laguna Canyon Road
Information: (949) 494-1145
Hours: Festival of Arts, 10 a.m. to 11 p.m.; Pageant of
the Masters, 8:30 p.m. to 10:30 p.m.
Admission: $10 to $50

This internationally famous event is held from the second week in July through August in Laguna Canyon. Founded in 1933, the Festival of Arts celebrates Laguna Beach's dedication to all artistic pursuits, and its most dramatic element is the Pageant of the Masters. The pageant presents tableaux vivants—real, live models posing in the midst of life-size recreations of famous art. Months are spent preparing the magnificent three-dimensional scenes that the artists pose within. Each model wears elaborate makeup and costume to make them appear exactly as their counterparts in the original work. The Last Supper is a perennial favorite.

The tradition of placing real people in recreations of beloved works of art is actually an old one, reputedly dating back to the Middle Ages. The volunteers, who stand still under the gallons of latex and yards of fabric, are seen in paintings by da Vinci, Erte, Michelangelo, Degas and even Norman Rockwell.

Before the evening Pageant shows, visitors enjoy the arts and crafts of more than 100 exhibitors on hand during the daily Festival of Arts. Here artisans offer all manner of jewelry, fine art, and photographs, as well as classes for children and adults.

The Irvine Bowl, where the festival is held, is a short

distance from Main Beach up Laguna Canyon Road. The bowl is also host to outdoor concerts during the summer.

Sawdust Festival

935 Laguna Canyon Road
Information: (949) 494-3030
Fee: $4 adults, $3 seniors, $2 children, children under 6 free
Hours: Daily 10 a.m. to 10 p.m.; to 11 p.m. Friday and Saturday. Held from the beginning of July through the end of August (in tandem with the Festival of Arts/Pageant of the Masters)

The Sawdust Festival is Laguna's version of a community swap meet. This outdoor festival of handmade arts and crafts is just a little farther up Laguna Canyon from the Irvine Bowl. Artists set up a customized booth where they will make, display and sell their creations to customers who amble along the sawdust path. There are usually around 200 exhibitors, so you're bound to see the full range of creative arts and crafts: sculpture, jewelry, musical instruments, pottery, dolls, glassblowing, leather, printmaking, and even metalworking and stonecutting. Besides demonstrating their particular crafts, many of the artists design and create pieces especially for you.

The Sawdust Festival grounds, despite the name, have been turned into a patchwork of theme gardens with waterfalls and exotic plants. Musicians play everything from bluegrass to Hawaiian and New Age music, while jugglers and magicians keep the crowds amused. Food and beverages are also sold.

Art-A-Fair

777 Laguna Canyon Road
Information: (949) 494-4514; (www.art-a-fair.com)
Hours: 10 a.m. to 9 p.m. (Sun.-Thurs.); until 10 p.m. (Fri.-Sat.)
Admission: $5.00

The third art festival held in Laguna Beach during the summer is the Art-A-Fair, a co-op of professional artists offering free workshops in painting, as well as beautiful sculpture, ceramics and even digital art items for sale — unique creations with which to furnish your home. This fair runs concurrently with the Festival of Arts and the Sawdust Festival. The Tivoli Too restaurant, a recent addition to the fairgrounds, provides elegant dining year-round.

Art Institute of Southern California

2222 Laguna Canyon Road
Information: (949) 376-6000
Hours: Monday through Friday 8 a.m to 5 p.m.;
Saturday 9 a.m. to 4 p.m.

If you can't get enough art at the Pageant of the Masters or in Laguna Beach's numerous galleries, stop by this community art center to view its gallery of new works and the sculpture garden. The Art Institute is a fully accredited college of art and design, but it also offers education classes to the local community.

Orange County Museum of Art, Laguna Beach

307 Cliff Drive
Information: (949) 494-6531
Hours: Tuesday through Sunday, 11 a.m to 5 p.m.
Admission: Adults, $5; students and seniors, $4;
children under 12, $3

It's hard to miss the California-pink exterior of this museum located at the corner of Cliff Drive and PCH, just north of Main Beach. Even though it looks brand new, this museum has actually existed in one form or another for more than 70 years. Inside, the rotating exhibits of modern art and photography are distinctive and handsomely displayed. This is a nice way to get a respite from the busy traffic on PCH while checking out tomorrow's art horizons.

The Laguna Playhouse

606 Laguna Canyon Road
Information: (949) 497-9244

The Laguna Playhouse is the home of the oldest continuously operating theater company on the West Coast. Founded in 1920, the Laguna thespians offer up a consistently excellent mix of comedy, musicals and dramas by the big names of American theater, such as Neil Simon and Stephen Sondheim. The Moulton Theater has 12 orchestra rows and three mezzanine rows, providing great sight-lines and acoustics for the entire audience. The playhouse is just a short walk from Main Beach and all the restaurants, shops and galleries of downtown Laguna Beach, so leave yourself some time either before or after the performance to combine your theatrical enjoyment with the sights of this charming town. The Laguna Playhouse season runs from September to June.

Shopping

Pottery Shack

1212 South Coast Highway
Information: (949) 494-1141
Hours: Open daily 10 a.m.-7 p.m. (for 64 years!)

In the center of the Pottery Shack courtyard is a huge piece of jade, set on a pedestal and—get this—they want you to touch it. This giant green rock jellybean is supposed to bring you good luck when you rub it.

The Pottery Shack is a favorite place to shop for new tableware, from southwestern style to old English patterns. Mugs, plates, serving dishes, salt-and-pepper shakers and all sorts of glassware are sold here. The courtyard is just the beginning: the rest of the store is a series of interconnected rooms where it's easy to lose your companions. This place is always crowded. You'll recognize the Pottery Shack because a statue of Laguna Beach's famous Greeter stands on the sidewalk outside the entrance, waving to one and all.

Laguna Village

Corner of Legion Street and PCH

Besides its cluster of open-air arts and crafts shops, the Laguna Village is highly recommended as a food and beverage break with a great view of the Pacific Ocean. Time your arrival before noon, or in mid-afternoon, and you can usually find a table right on the cliff for a spectacular view overlooking the beach. Share a glass of wine, some coffee, or a plate of nachos; you will never get bored with this view. The menu also features good sandwiches, beer and smoothies.

The little shops clustered next to this cliffside view feature pottery, sculpture, paintings, jewelry and other gifts. There's also a flower stand next to the tiny gravel parking lot. It's easiest to park on one of the side streets off Pacific Coast Highway and just walk to the village. You're also within handy walking distance of the main Laguna Beach shops and restaurants near Forest Avenue.

Forest Avenue/Lumberyard Mall

Two blocks south of Broadway, in the heart of Laguna, you will find everything from souvenirs to paintings. Some galleries offer more than paintings and sculptures, while other shops feature imported crafts and gifts from all around the globe. This is for those who love to stroll and shop.

Near the eastern end of Forest Avenue is the Lumberyard Mall (384 Forest Avenue), with several interesting shops, such as Fawn Memories (949-494-2071), which features decorative seashells, plants, and baskets.

Sherwood Gallery

460 Pacific Coast Highway
Information: (949) 497-2668

One of the funniest art galleries in all of Laguna Beach, the Sherwood contains a riotous collection of art that's impossible to describe. What's more, as you gaze at some sculpture or painting, you may find someone looking over your shoulder—but it's not a someone, it's a something. The gallery is loaded with life-size characters resembling stuffed animals, but their attire and demeanor seem more lifelike than the average mannequin—especially out of the corner of your eye.

Selected Restaurants

Laguna Beach has a plethora of fine eateries, with fare and prices for every taste. Those listed below are just a tiny sampling. Maybe the best part of exploring this seaside village is finding your own special place.

Aegean Cafe

540 S. Coast Highway
Information: (949) 494-5001
Hours: Tuesday through Thursday, 5 p.m. to 10 p.m.;
Saturday, 5 p.m. to midnight; Sunday, 5 p.m. to 10 p.m.;
also Friday to Sunday 11:30 to 4 p.m. (lunch only); closed
Mondays. Serving: Lunch, dinner

Authentic Greek cuisine served by the sea, with a diverse wine menu (featuring Greek, Italian, French and American wines) and live entertainment. Souvlaki, shish kabobs, and vacalaos skordalia are just a few of the homeland specialties. (Entrees range from $13.95 to $22.95.) If these recipes don't conjure up Mediterranean images, what will?

The Cottage

308 N. Coast Highway
Information: (949) 494-3023
Hours: Monday through Friday, 7 a.m. to 4 p.m. (breakfast,
lunch) and 5 to 9:30 p.m. (dinner); Saturday and Sunday,
7 a.m. to 10 p.m.

This restaurant is also an historic home—more than 100 years old—and features "homestyle" cooking of traditional favorites, from chicken marsala and scallops amandine to top sirloin and prime rib. Moderately-priced and casual. Great breakfasts, too.

Las Brisas

361 Cliff Drive
Information: (949) 497-5434
Hours: Monday through Saturday, 8 a.m. to 10:30 p.m.
(breakfast), 11 a.m. - 3:30 p.m. (lunch); Monday through
Thursday, 5 p.m. to 10 p.m. (dinner); Fridays and
Saturdays until 11 p.m.; Sundays, champagne brunch from
11 a.m. to 3 p.m., dinner from 4:30 p.m. to 10 p.m.

Just behind the Laguna Art Museum is Las Brisas, one of the most popular restaurants in Laguna Beach. Las Brisas features Sonoran-style seafood entrees, which are vastly different from the standard Cal-Mex food you'd expect in any number of chain-owned cantinas. You can sit outside in the patio after a visit to the museum and enjoy a Margarita, but dinner and Sunday brunch reservations are a must. Parking in Las Brisas' parking lot is limited, and nearly impossible along adjacent Cliffs Drive. Try parking along the side streets on the north side of PCH.

Romeo Cucina

249 Broadway
Information: (949) 497-6627
Hours: Tuesday through Sunday, for lunch and dinner

This fine Italian restaurant is just a short block from Main Beach, and features excellent wood-fired pizzas, pastas, seafood and salads. The service is generally excellent. Come early or call for reservations, because this is a popular place on any evening.

San Shi Go Japanese Restaurant

1100 S. Coast Highway, Suite 303
Information: (949) 494-1551
Hours: Tuesday through Friday, 11:30 a.m. to 2 p.m.
(lunch), 5 p.m. to 10 p.m. (dinner); Saturdays, 3 p.m. to
11 p.m., Sundays until 10 p.m.

Traditional Japanese cuisine, from tempura to sushi, is served on the second floor of the Village Faire shopping complex. The restaurant affords a nice view of the Pacific. Prices for entrees are fairly inexpensive.

The White House Tavern And Restaurant

340 S. Coast Highway
Information: (949) 494-8088
Hours: Monday through Friday, 7 a.m. to 2 a.m., Saturday
and Sunday, 8 a.m. to 2 a.m. Serves breakfast, lunch and
dinner

"Est. 1918" it says on the outside, and you will believe it when you walk in and see the rich, dark wood bar and decor. This is a cozy place to have a drink while you rest your feet from all the gallery tours. The White House is a Laguna Beach institution. Music is offered nightly, featuring Motown, rock 'n roll, blues, and reggae.

Splashes (in the Surf & Sand Hotel)

1555 S. Coast Highway
Information: (949) 497-4477
Hours: 7 a.m. to 10 a.m. (breakfast); 12 to 4:30 p.m. (lunch);
5 to 10 p.m. (dinner), Friday and Saturday until 11 p.m.;
also Sunday brunch, 10 a.m. to 4 p.m.; reservations
strongly recommended

In Laguna Beach you can dine well, or you can watch the Pacific Ocean up close. You can do both at Splashes. The "Mediterranean cuisine" is first rate, and the Surf & Sand, by the way, is a first-class hotel with great romantic rooms for weekend getaways.

Lodging

The Hotel Laguna

425 S. Coast Highway
Information: (949) 494-1151
Reservations: 800-524-2927 (within California)

This venerable landmark was one of the first commercial buildings in Laguna Beach. There wasn't much else around here in the '20s except for some beach cottages, so this became a popular retreat and quiet getaway for Hollywood celebrities. The Hotel Laguna is still a nice place to stay, with smaller old-fashioned hotel rooms and views of the sea at prices that aren't outrageous.

Weddings often take place in the courtyard, and lunch and dinner are popular in Claes' restaurant (with an ocean view, naturally). The Hotel Laguna has a beautiful Rose Garden that you may visit even if you're not planning to spend the night.

Other Hotels

Most of Laguna's seaside hotels include the customary resort amenities such as spas, continental breakfasts and rooms with kitchenettes for extended stays. Since summer usually presents "no vacancy" signs, it's a good idea to reserve in advance, especially during the art festival season. Here are a few:

By The Sea Motel

475 N. Coast Highway. Information: (949) 497-6645

Capri Laguna Inn On The Beach

1441 S. Coast Highway. Information: (949) 494-6533;
reservations: 800-225-4551 (North America)

The Carriage House

1322 Catalina Street. Information: (949) 494-8945

Crescent Bay Inn

1435 N. Coast Highway. Information: (949) 494-2508

Eiler's Inn

741 S. Coast Highway. Information: (949) 494-3004

Inn At Laguna Beach

211 N. Coast Highway. Information: (949) 497-9722 or reservations: 800-544-4479 (United States)

Laguna Riviera

825 S. Coast Highway. Information: (949) 494-1196

Surf & Sand Hotel

1555 S. Coast Highway. Information: (949) 497-4477

Vacation Village

647 S. Coast Highway. Information: (949) 494-8566

Crystal Cove

Crystal Cove State Park
8471 Pacific Coast Highway
Information: (949) 494-3539

Between Corona del Mar and Laguna Beach lies Crystal Cove State Park. This is a wonderful, three-mile stretch of unspoiled beach sheltered from PCH by distinctive headlands. Tide pooling is excellent, especially during a minus tide. The offshore area is designated an underwater park; the entire shoreline park purposely remains undeveloped, with minimal signs or trail maintenance.

The park also encompasses El Moro Canyon, permanently protecting this natural area from the creeping encroachment of the housing and resort developments to the north. Crystal Cove is nearly 2,800 acres in size, and is a bonanza of preserved outdoor beauty for picnickers, hikers, and bird watchers. There are 23 miles of trails.

Parking lots on both sides of the Coast Highway provide access either to the beach, or to trails in El Moro Canyon (part of the San Joaquin Hills that separates the coast from the Saddleback Valley inland). Either way, it's about as natural as things get in Southern California. Crystal Cove is the largest park situated along the Orange County coast, and provides visitors with the best uninterrupted look at the topography that separates the ocean from the county's Saddleback Valley.

If you want a delightful, albeit rustic, outdoor experience, there are three areas where overnight camping is permitted, provided you don't burn fires or use your automobile to get there. For $9 (which you pay at the ranger station) you can park and hike or bike into El Moro Canyon, Deer Canyon, or Lower Moro Ridge, and select a campsite in a remote and beautiful spot. The Pacific and the stars are yours. Pit toilets are the only facilities here, so you have to be able to cope without your basic amenities.

Selected Restaurants

Crystal Cove Shake Shack

7408 Pacific Coast Highway
Information: (949) 497-9666
Hours: Weekdays, 10:30 a.m. to 5 p.m.; weekends,
10:30 a.m. to 6 p.m. (varies with the seasons)
Serving: Lunch

Blink and you'll miss this yellow hut, perched on a cliff and tucked into a curve on PCH between Laguna Beach and Corona del Mar. This tiny institution offers smoothies, sandwiches and shakes, including their famous date shake. Good view, too.

Corona Del Mar

Literally translated as "crown of the sea," Corona del Mar, like Laguna Beach to the south, began as a collection of beach cottages perched on and around the coves in this area. It was, and still is, a popular vacation getaway for folks in Los Angeles, and if you travel its streets south of PCH you will see some of the quaint, sardine-packed charm of California-style beach town life. Many of the properties here are delightfully landscaped, so just touring the side streets makes a pleasant excursion if you're interested in architecture and gardening.

The coves in Corona del Mar are among my personal favorite beach spots, because this is where my folks used to take me as a kid. Digging in the sand and playing "chicken" with incoming waves is one of the great pleasures of being five years old in California.

Corona del Mar is really just the southern extension of Newport Beach, but it is distinctly different from the rest of Newport. There are many upscale boutiques, most located south of where PCH meets MacArthur Boulevard.

Outdoors

Corona del Mar State Beach/Pirates Cove/ China Cove

Between Ocean Boulevard and Iris Avenue
Information: (949) 644-3047

If you take the steps at the northern end of the Corona del Mar Beach parking lot, you descend to Pirates Cove, a great place for tide pooling and beachcombing. Depending upon the time of day, the tide reveals rocky outcroppings for you to explore and hunt for seashells. If you take the stairs on Ocean Boulevard at Fernleaf Street, you will reach China Cove (there's no lifeguard here, however). Both are especially appealing for families, because you get a great view of the yachts and boats sailing in and out of Newport Harbor. Corona del Mar State Beach has surfing, diving, fishing, volleyball nets and fire pits for barbecues.

Sherman Library and Gardens

2647 E. Pacific Coast Highway
Information: (949) 673-2281
Hours: Daily 10:30 a.m. to 4 p.m.
Fees: $3 (Mondays free)

Everyone needs an oasis in their lives: a place to relax away from the many demands of life. The Sherman Library and Gardens, located right on the busy Pacific Coast High-

Grunion Runs

A grunion *(Leuresthes tenuis)* is a small fish about six inches long. It is related to the topsmelt, and is the only fish on earth that spawns on land. During the spring and summer, millions of them swim ashore at night during the highest tides (known as peak tides). The females bury their tails in the sand in order to lay their eggs. The males wrap themselves around the female and spread milt (fish sperm) in the same spot. The fertilized eggs will remain in the sand, undisturbed, for about two weeks. When the next high tide arrives, the newly hatched grunion are washed out to sea. The evolutionary advantages of having its incubating eggs hidden in the sand away from predators has kept the grunion flourishing along Southern California beaches for, well, no one knows how long. Scientists only know that the beaches of Baja and Southern California are the only places in the world where you can see this amazing natural event.

The bodies of these greenish fish shimmer and glimmer in the moonlight. Because they're flapping around in mass ritual profusion, their sudden appearance on the beach is mystical for some. Many people used to think their friends were putting them on about "grunion runs" (there was an episode of *The Beverly Hillbillies* that poked fun at this natural phenom-

way, in this "happening" beach town, offers a remarkably tranquil retreat. Begun in 1966 by Arnold D. Haskell, who wanted a cultural center devoted to the Pacific Southwest, the gardens are mini-portraits of different botanical habitats. Brick pathways and sculptured animals guide you around this lovely setting, planned with the care typical of an English country garden (with hints of Japanese garden formality here and there).

The Sherman Library and Gardens is located at the corner of Dahlia Avenue and takes up a small city block. The entry fee for this quaint collection of gardens is a mere $3. More than 1,000 species are on display—what the Sherman

enon). But it truly does happen, from Point Conception north of Santa Barbara to Point Abreojos down in Baja, so there are plenty of sites to witness this event. The tricky part is, grunion may or may not emerge at specific beaches on a specific night. The local newspapers can tell you the exact dates and times of the peak tides when grunion will be running (usually for three or four nights in a row; the time is generally from 11 p.m. to nearly 3 a.m.), but they can't tell you exactly where they will run. You just have to be lucky.

When the grunion are exposed on the beach they make a tempting target for humans. With all these fish just lying about, the local Native Americans knew a good thing when they saw it. They regularly collected the grunion. Grunion, it turns out, are tasty — bony, but tasty. Modern grunion hunters come to the beach with a pail, flashlight, some warm clothes and a fishing license (it is illegal to hunt grunion with any other equipment — the state cracked down when too many people were using large nets to rake them up). Bare hands only, folks. Hunting squirming grunion by hand in the dark along muddy beaches is quite an art. Once you clean them, place them in a shallow, greased baking pan and brown them for a few minutes.

Library likes to call a "museum of living plants"—set amid sculpture, fountains, courtyards and manicured lawns. Hanging plants, vines, and flower beds are in profusion, separating the various gardens: Shade, Rose, Cactus & Succulent, a Discovery Garden (designed especially for touching and smelling by blind visitors), and a tropical conservatory enclosing exotic vegetation. The Sherman Gardens is really a small-scale arboretum, and one you can enjoy in just half an hour— although you should take advantage of this oasis and not rush the experience.

Many of the garden's flora displays are of plants not native to California. There is staghorn fern from New Guinea, cacti from Mexico, and an amazing moosehorn fern (it grows on the bark of a tree) that is at least thirty years old. The greenhouse contains some species of huge vines and towering, broad-leafed plants.

The various buildings are representative of California style architecture. A small room is devoted to early Orange County memorabilia. The Sherman Library, which is reserved for those researching the Pacific Southwest, contains thousands of books, photographs, maps and other documents about the history of this region. The library contains more than 20,000 books, pamphlets, maps and documents on microfilm.

When you've finished exploring the gardens, take a seat in the Tea Garden for a light snack; fruit, cheese, sandwiches, soups and desserts are available to enjoy in this placid setting, and the prices are reasonable. On your way out, duck into the Garden Shop—a surprisingly good gift stop.

Roger's Gardens

2301 San Joaquin Hills Road
Information: (949) 640-5800
Hours: Daily 9 a.m. to 6 p.m., until 9 p.m. during December

Roger's Gardens is one of the largest and most beautiful nurseries in Orange County. If you want a taste of the variety and vegetation that makes California so lush, come wander along the many paths at Roger's. A large garden and gift shop is on the premises.

To reach the gardens from PCH, turn right at MacArthur Boulevard and head inland for a few blocks to San Joaquin Hills Road. Roger's Gardens is on the corner to your right. From the San Diego Freeway (I-5), take the MacArthur Boulevard exit and proceed to San Joaquin Hills Road.

Selected Restaurants

The Five Crowns

3801 E. Pacific Coast Highway
Information: (949) 760-0331
Hours: Daily from 5 p.m. Serving: Dinner

This is a famous old Orange County restaurant, modeled after one of England's oldest inns. The atmosphere is warm and cozy and the service and food first rate. With dining rooms on two stories, the Five Crowns is also expensive and dressy. Look for the British-style phone booth out in front. Reservations are recommended.

Newport Beach

Like its Rhode Island cousin, Newport is a notoriously well-heeled community, and there's lots to see and do here. For starters, Newport Harbor is jam-packed with yachts of every variety—more than 10,000—with some of the largest running more than 100 feet from bow to stern. Newport Beach's yacht harbor is its most visual commodity, offering nautical pleasure to those who can afford the astronomic upkeep. Renting a boat slip, maintaining a boat, insuring it, fueling it—all of these add up to stiff bills every month (the largest yachts can cost as much as $40,000 a month to sustain). Yet other locals maintain tiny sloops (the kind that can barely hold two people) and take them out every weekend. The freedom of boating is a pleasure that Newport Harbor denizens will never give up.

The annual Christmas Boat Parade of Lights is probably the biggest single event at Newport Harbor, merging one of the year's biggest holidays with the citizens' love for their salty pastime.

Balboa Peninsula & Harbor Highlights

Balboa Peninsula provides a wonderful day excursion that shouldn't be rushed. The Peninsula and Balboa Island in Newport Bay are havens for summer beach rentals, and during the summer a perpetual party atmosphere pervades this part of town. The fun is infectious and spills over to visitors as well.

The Peninsula was created partly by the shifting outflow of the Santa Ana River, eventually producing the sand spit that sheltered what was once just called the "new port" between San Pedro and San Diego. As the boom in population turned this town into a resort, the relatively small bay was converted into one of the world's largest yachting harbors.

Begin your tour by taking the Balboa turnoff from Pacific Coast Highway. Before heading down the peninsula, turn left on either 31st Street or 28th Street/Lafayette Avenue and walk around the Cannery Village area. This used to be a cannery row during the 1940s, but now it's been converted to a charming shopping district.

Outdoors

Newport Beach/Balboa Beach

West of Balboa Avenue between 61st Street and
Island Avenue
Information: (949) 644-3047
Surf and weather: (949) 673-3371

Yes, there is a "beach" in Newport Beach: one long, uninterrupted stretch of white sand extending the entire length of the peninsula, with not one but two piers, Balboa and Newport. The main beach path between the beach cottages and the sand has been a favorite with roller skaters, bicyclists and walkers for years. If you pedal or walk up and back, from 32nd Street to West Jetty Park, you'll have covered seven miles.

If this is your first stop of the day, and you like fresh fish, head for the fish market in McFadden Square at the foot of Newport Pier (between 20th and 22nd Place). Every morning from dawn until around 9 a.m., fishermen using small boats bring their early morning catch directly to this open air market. Seafood doesn't get any fresher than this.

If you love body surfing, you have to visit the infamous "Wedge" at the end of the Peninsula. The Wedge is one of the best spots in all of Southern California for body surfing—if you're an expert, that is. The waves sometimes get as high as ten feet. Even if you don't want to take the plunge yourself, you'll enjoy a great show watching others attempt it, while you relax and work on your tan.

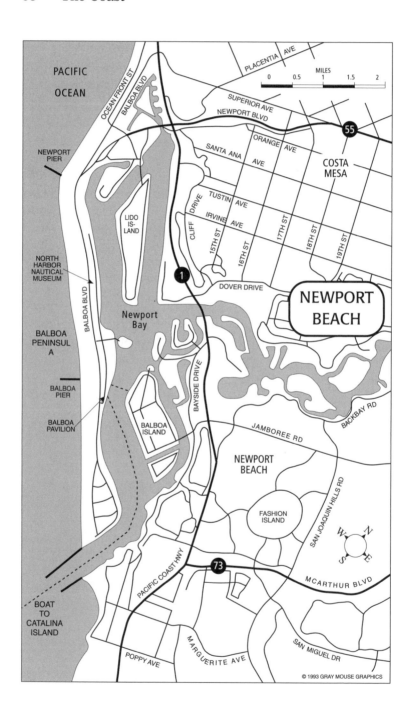

Balboa Village
Balboa Boulevard between Palm and A Streets

The district near the end of Balboa Peninsula has been home to California seaside recreation since the turn of the century. Balboa Village is nearly three miles from the mainland turnoff. It consists of three square blocks of eating and window shopping—not to mention the site of many local attractions. As you head southeast on Balboa, turn right on Palm Street and use the municipal parking lot just one block down. The lot borders the beach and Balboa Pier. It's best to explore the district on foot. If you head toward the mainland via Palm Street, Washington Avenue, or Main Street, you will find many attractions. At the foot of Main is the Balboa Pier, a hardy pier that has outlasted many violent storms. From this location an aviator named Glenn Martin flew to Avalon on Catalina Island and back in his own, home-built hydroplane. The flight took just 37 minutes (the longest and fastest over-water flight in its day).

At the corner of Main Street and the parking lot is the Balboa Inn, one of the oldest hotels along Orange County's coast. Built in 1929, it has gone through many renovations but is still open for business.

At Main Street and Bay Avenue is the home of the Balboa Pavilion (400 Main Street, 949-673-5245). You can catch the Catalina Flyer from here to—where else?—Santa Catalina Island. Catalina is a beautiful and unusual getaway that is worth adding to your itinerary if you can spare an entire day (or day and night) of your itinerary. (See page 82 for more about Santa Catalina Island.) There are also a number of other harbor concessions located here.

The Balboa Pavilion, a Victorian structure that was originally a bath house and a terminal for the Pacific Electric Red Car line, dates back to 1906. Long before the days of freeways and fast cars, bathers used to disembark here for a day of fun at the beach. Later, big bands entertained folks during the 1930s and '40s. The Pavilion is listed in the National Register of Historic Places.

Catalina Passenger Service

400 Main Street
Information: (949) 673-5245
Summer: Tours depart every half hour from 10 a.m. to
7 p.m. Winter: Once every hour from 11 a.m. to 3 p.m.
Fare: 90-minute cruise: Adults $8, children $1; 45-minute
cruise: Adults $6, children $1

From the Pavilion you can take harbor cruises aboard Pavilion Queen (which resembles a Mississippi river boat) and Pavilion Paddy. Both are double-deck boats providing narrated cruises of Newport Harbor—one of the largest small boat harbors in the world (with about 15 miles of waterfront). The homes and the yachts are spectacular. Many celebrities have their homes right along the water, which the tour guides are only too willing to point out. These boats are available for private parties, and special brunch cruises are conducted in season. Every year, for instance, Newport Harbor sponsors a Christmas Boat Parade from December 17 to 23, and you can catch an evening cruise to see the festivities from the water instead of the shore.

Fun Zone Boat Company

700 Edgewater
Information: (949) 673-0240

This outfitter offers the same type of cruises as Catalina Passenger Service, and also has a sunset cruise that leaves at 7 p.m.

Newport Landing Sportfishing

400 Main Street
Information: (949) 675-0550

If a guided tour of the harbor isn't stimulating enough for you, perhaps you'd like to try marine fishing. Fishing for that big time ocean catch is something you can tell your grandchildren about. But you must have a fishing license if you're over age sixteen (licenses are readily purchased at sporting goods shops and many of the fishing concessionaires). This outfitter offers trips in half-day, three-quarter day and twilight versions. Groups too. And they are equipped with some fancy fish-locating gear that makes finding the best spots more predictable.

Parasailing/Water Sports International at Davey's Locker

400 Main Street
Information: (949) 673-3372
Season: Daily (weather permitting) March through August
Fee: $45 per person
Flight time: 8 to 10 minutes

So you've always wanted to be suspended 300 feet above the ocean hanging from nothing but a sail and being dragged by a boat? Here's your chance. It's called parasailing, and it's much more fun if you do it over the Pacific. While you enjoy a nice boat ride outside the harbor, you and your fellow adventurers are instructed in this fine art, and then zip—it's up, up and away! You take off and land inside the boat, so you don't have to be a water skier and you don't have to get wet. No experience needed. C'mon, you know you want to— I did! They offer a $75 price if you go in tandem with something (such as a child), but there are weight limitations.

Attractions and Special Events

Adventures at Sea Yacht Charters

3101 W. Coast Hwy., Suite 209
Information: (949) 650-2412

I suggest you take a cruise around Newport Harbor on one of these quiet, electrically-powered gondolas, lubricated with champagne and a catered meal. The gondolier provides some romantic background music and stories of the gondola's place in history. Newport Harbor is ideal for this charming mode of transportation.

Christmas Boat Parade of Lights

Held from December 17 through the December 23 between 6:30 and 8:45 p.m., this annual boat parade is a major event in and around Newport. Hundreds of decorated boats cruise the harbor in a literal parade of lights celebrating the holiday. You have to find a spot early, because thousands of visitors crowd the harbor's edge from every available sidewalk, beach and dock. Harbor-view restaurants are booked well in advance for large parties. It's really a beautiful sight.

Balboa Fun Zone

Next to the Balboa Pavilion
Hours: Summer and weekends, 11 a.m. to 11 p.m.;
off season, 12 to 8 p.m. daily.

The Balboa Fun Zone is next to the Balboa Pavilion on the shore side of the Peninsula. Since 1936 folks have enjoyed some old fashioned fun while visiting the beach. There's a ferris wheel, a carousel, bumper cars, a scary ride in the dark, arcades and food.

There are also several outfitters along Edgewater Avenue that offer small electric boats, paddle boats and kayaks for rent by the hour. Paddle Power (949-675-1215) provides you with kayaks so you see the bay and work out at the same time. Or try Electric Boat Rentals (949-673-7200) for spacious crafts that are big enough to hold up to 12 people, perfect for a marine picnic with family and friends. You can bring your own goodies or let them cater for you.

Newport Harbor Nautical Museum

Aboard Pride of Newport, 151 Pacific Coast Hwy.
Information: (949) 673-7863
Hours: Tuesday through Sunday, 10 a.m. to 5 p.m.

Here is a 13,000-square-feet museum devoted to the life of the sea, and of course, it is on board a paddle-wheeler,

Pride of Newport. Navigation instruments, ship models, and other nautical exhibits and antiques are on permanent display, as well as aerial photographs of the area taken in the 1920s. The boat's large salon is devoted to art and photography of the nautical life. What's more, after you've indulged in all these things maritime, you can go next door to the Riverboat Restaurant for breakfast, lunch or dinner.

Balboa Island

When you decide to leave the simple attractions of the Fun Zone, you must take your car or your feet onto the Balboa Island Ferry, a family-run business since 1919. Two small rafts (big enough for three autos and some passengers) journey back-and-forth between the Peninsula and Balboa Island. You can ride across on foot or in your car for less than the cost of a cheeseburger. In about two minutes you have arrived at Balboa Island, a little crowded paradise for people who want to pay mucho dinero to live in tiny houses so close together they can hear their neighbor sneeze. Yes, I'd live here in a second. When you see these streets and neo-doll house cottages, you'll understand why the owners stay here even though it's like living in a goldfish bowl. It's unabashedly cute. There's a funky avenue of small shops along Marine Avenue (at the east end of the isle) that's fun to explore and where you can grab a bite to eat before driving across the bridge that takes you back to the mainland of Newport Beach.

The Opal Street dock is a good place to take youngsters. You can sit and fish while watching all the boats laze by. Stores are just one block away, and there's a small beach next to the dock.   ·

When you decide to leave Balboa Island (if you decide to leave), take Marine Avenue north and follow the signs to PCH, then continue heading north to our next destination.

Outdoors

Upper Newport Bay State Ecological Reserve
Back Bay Drive and Jamboree Road
Hours: Daily, sunrise to sunset
Information: (949) 640-1751

Among the more natural endeavors you can enjoy in Newport Beach are kayaking, canoeing, hiking or cycling around the Upper Newport Bay State Ecological Reserve. These wetlands are the largest in coastal Southern California, and have survived despite their proximity to some of the highest-priced real estate in Orange County. This 892-acre preserve is so close to Newport Beach's financial district that you can see many high-rises nearby. Aircraft taking off from John Wayne Airport fly directly over this area.

The bay is open to water craft as long as they travel five miles per hour or less. This estuary is home to cormorants, grebes, ducks, and herons—nearly 200 species of water birds. Key among them is the light-footed clapper rail; more than half of its remaining U.S. population uses this reserve as their home. This protected wilderness helps supply food to these birds as well as dozens of fish species. There's plenty of marine life, of course, which—aside from the nesting space—is the principal attraction for the birds. So if you watch closely you'll see some of the marine creatures: anchovies, killifish and even halibut in the shallow water. The vegetation is much the same as it was centuries ago along this part of the coast — mostly black sage, California sagebrush, pickleweed and cordgrass.

To reach this natural preserve, take Pacific Coast Highway to Jamboree Road, turn inland, then turn left on Back Bay Drive. From the San Diego Freeway, take the Jamboree Road exit west to Back Bay Drive and turn right. Then make a left turn on Back Bay Drive and follow the road until you see one of several dirt parking areas. You can enjoy this lovely area on foot if you don't want to venture onto the water.

Bird lovers note: the best month for touring this reserve is November, when migrating bird populations are at their peak. But the birds are plentiful through March, according to the California Department of Fish and Game. Wading birds and other waterfowl are most prominent from October through March, terns and songbirds in spring and summer.

To explore this unique natural reserve on the water, you can rent a canoe or a kayak for $10 an hour ($15 for a double) at the Newport Aquatic Center (949-646-7725). Rowing lessons are offered on Saturdays. Kayak tours are available from the nearby Newport Dunes RV Park (see next entry). They sign people up and leave around 10 a.m. on Sundays only. The cost is $10 per person ($12 for a two-person canoe).

Author Jerry Schad in his fine book, Cycling Orange County, recommends taking a bike tour clockwise, beginning at Bayview Way (just off Jamboree Road near the junction of Highway 73 and the Bristol Street exit). All of the marshy areas of this reserve are easily seen from the bike paths. Along the way you'll notice the changes in elevation that this area has experienced over geologic time as flood waters and sea level combined to erode the nearby cliffs.

Bicycles are available for rent on weekends at Newport Dunes RV Park.

Newport Dunes RV Park

1131 Back Bay Drive
Information: (949) 729-3863
Reservations: (800) 765-7661
Hours: Daily, 8 a.m. to 10 p.m.

You can learn to sail, paddleboat and kayak around the 15-acre lagoon that is part of the Newport Dunes Aquatic Park. This is a large RV park with all the amenities: a convenience store, freshwater swimming pool and spa, clubhouse and banquet rooms, open-air pavilions, showers, laundry—

even tennis courts. There are more than 400 RV spaces, and a boat launch area. Marine repair and equipment sales are also available at this full-service park.

Overall, there are 100 acres of sun'n fun here: volleyball, biking, horseshoes, barbecues, windsurfing, boat rentals and lessons for practically everything. You can take tours of the ecological reserve from here as well. The price reflects the amenities: between $25 and $50 per night, depending on the size and location of your space.

Pelican Hill Golf Club

22651 Pelican Hill Road S.
Information: (800) 529-6553, (949) 760-0707

Located near PCH and Newport Coast Drive, this is actually a pair of courses opened in the early 1990s. Pelican Hill is probably the most breathtaking (and expensive) golf experience in Orange County. The 6,634-yard and 6,856-yard tournament layouts, designed by Tom Fazio, are truly a duffer's paradise. The landscaping alone rivals that of the prestigious Pebble Beach, and there's a view of the Pacific Ocean and Catalina Island from every hole.

Attractions and Special Events

Orange County Museum of Art

850 San Clemente Drive
Information: (949) 759-1122
Hours: Open daily except Monday, 11 a.m. to 5 p.m.
Admission: Adults, $5; students and seniors, $4;
under 16 free (Tuesdays are free to all)

Formerly known as the Newport Harbor Art Museum, this institution merged in 1997 with the Laguna Beach Art Museum and has a reputation for showing modern and avant garde works. Check out the cube on the southwest corner of the building. The museum is located in the heart of the Newport Beach civic center. Call ahead for the current exhibits.

Newport Theatre Arts Center

2501 Cliff Drive
Information: (949) 631-0288

This is a nice, cozy community theater overlooking the beautiful harbor of Newport Beach. Attending a performance here is rewarding just for the view you get during intermission. Call for current production, showtimes and admission.

Shopping

Fashion Island Shopping Center

401 Newport Center Drive
Information: (949) 721-2022
Hours: Monday through Friday, 10 a.m. to 9 p.m.;
Saturday 10 a.m. to 7 p.m.; Sunday, 11 a.m. to 6 p.m.

Set on a bluff overlooking Newport Beach/Corona del Mar, Fashion Island is certainly one of the prettiest settings in Orange County for shopping. It sits in the center of a circle of office buildings that radiate around it like the spokes of a wheel. Palm trees are abundant in and around this complex of shops and office buildings.

Distinctive shops mingle with the more familiar chain stores, and the Atrium Court features a Farmer's Market that has a scrumptious deli. You can get all types of food to carry out, from salads and mashed potatoes and gravy to imported cheeses and fancy pate.

Some of the glitzier, famous designer stores are found in this mostly outdoor mall. Unique and more quiet than South Coast Plaza, Fashion Island is a nice place to sample some of the latest shopping fashions, catch a movie, and enjoy a touch of elegance without going near Rodeo Drive. Each year at Christmas time, Fashion Island boasts the tallest decorated tree anywhere in Orange County.

Near Fashion Island is the Four Seasons Hotel (690 Newport Center Drive (949-759-0808), and as you'd expect, it is top-drawer and is not for the timid of wallet. The hotel is located along the same drive that circles Fashion Island itself, at the intersection of Santa Cruz and Newport Center Drive.

Selected Restaurants

In such a well-heeled community, you can bet that dining out is a major pastime. Newport Beach has so many fine restaurants that they would fill a separate guidebook. My suggestion is to ask a few locals and you're bound to wind up with the food you want at a price you can tolerate. Be forewarned, however: too often visitors in an unfamiliar place succumb to the choice that's handiest when they're hungry, and that means you wind up with just another overpriced seafood and pasta restaurant. Newport Beach is full of them, and most offer views of the marina or the beach. Great views are everywhere in Newport Beach. If it's good, dependable cuisine you're after, I've listed some of the popular options below.

Amelia's

311 Marine
Information: (949) 673-6580
Hours: Daily, 11:30 a.m. (lunch); from 5 p.m. (dinner)

Amelia's has been an institution on Balboa Island for more than 35 years. It features a quaint atmosphere with pastel blue walls and Old World appointments. Pastas and seafood are the menu staples, ranging from $10 to $16 per entree. This is a good choice for family dining.

The Arches

3334 West Coast Highway
Information: (949) 645-7077
Hours: Monday through Friday, 11 a.m. to 3 p.m. (lunch); from 4:30 p.m. (dinner); the bar is open continuously until 1 a.m., and the full menu is served until 1 a.m. as well). Reservations strongly recommended.

This landmark has been around for more than 70 years. It began as a roadside gas station and cafe back in "the good old days," offering one of the few chances for travelers to fill up their Model-T and get a soda along some lonesome stretches of highway. The restaurant—painted in barn red—is easily spotted on the northeast corner of PCH and Newport Avenue, just south of the Newport Boulevard bridge (the same overpass that leads to Balboa Peninsula).

The building used to have real arches, but a fire destroyed the old structure. The wooden structure that replaced it is, at best, nondescript. The interior is dark and cozy, the way the locals prefer it. Many loyal patrons have been stopping by for generations. Longtime Newport Beach resident John Wayne used to come here for steak. Other Hollywood celebrities made this a popular spot in the '50s and '60s.

A dinner for two with wine from the Arches' extensive list can run upwards of $90.

The Hard Rock Cafe

451 Newport Center Drive
Information: (949) 640-8844
Hours: Daily, 11:30 a.m. to 11:30 p.m.; Friday to Saturday, until 1 a.m. Serving: Lunch, dinner

Fashion Island is also home to the ubiquitous Hard Rock Cafe, perhaps one of the most recognizable restaurant chains in world because of the owners' penchant for selling clothing with the names of other Hard Rock locations, such as New York, Aspen, Kona, etc. You can't miss the location of this one: there's a giant, 40-foot neon Fender Stratocaster guitar marking the entrance. Aside from shopping in the restaurant's boutique, you can chow down on burgers and fries, milk shakes, salads, and even grilled fish or chicken wings. It's a party atmosphere, suitable for families or for happy hour socializing. You come here to see and be seen, not necessarily to dine like a gourmand.

The Hard Rock is notable mainly for its name and logo, and the rock 'n roll memorabilia displayed at each location is from the personal collection of owner Peter Morton. Visitors can enjoy the bill of fare while admiring the surf-and-rock decor. This Hard Rock has a '59 Cadillac suspended over the bar, as well as a pair of Fender Strats courtesy off Dick Dale (Southern California's unofficial king of surf music).

JACKshrimp

111 21st Place
Information: (949) 723-1113
Hours: Tuesday through Saturday, 5 to 9 p.m.; Sundays from 3:30 p.m. Also, lunch on Fridays from 11:30 a.m. to 3:30 p.m.

Shrimp is the name of the game here, served in generous helpings on ice, over pasta or rice, and even between slabs of French bread. The shrimp are large and undisguised by batters and other extras that get in the way. The plates come in big and small appetite portions and the prices are real reasonable. JACKshrimp is located at the Newport Beach Pier on the Balboa Peninsula inside Lucy's Bayside Bar & Grill.

Pascal

1000 Bristol Street
Information: (949) 752-0107
Hours: Tuesday through Saturday, 11:30 a.m. to 2:30 p.m. (lunch), 6 to 9:30 p.m. (dinner); Sundays until 10 p.m.

A fine French bistro, rated as one of the best in Orange County by the Zagat Restaurant Guide. Seafood, lamb, chicken, venison, and duck are the staples on the menu. You can be casual or semi-dressy and still feel at home in this establishment. Next door is the Pascal Epicerie, where you can order gourmet food to go.

The Pleasant Peasant

4251 Martingale Way
Information: (949) 955-2755
Hours: Monday through Friday, 11:30 to 2 p.m. (lunch);
Monday through Thursday, 5:30 to 9 p.m. (dinner); Friday
and Saturday until 9 p.m.; closed Sundays

The owners describe the Pleasant Peasant as "French country dining." You will indeed enjoy the comfortable, Old World atmosphere. Pastas and entrees of game, chicken, lamb and shellfish are priced very reasonably (most under $15). Escargot and other delicacies are also on the menu.

The Quiet Woman

3224 E. Coast Highway
Information: (714) 640-7440

This Corona del Mar institution is more than 30 years old, and you'll find it by looking for the distinctive sign of a headless woman. It's a popular spot with the locals — dark and crowded, with old English decor. Besides a good basic menu and bar, there's music here of the loud variety from Thursday through Sunday.

The Ritz

880 Newport Center Drive
Information: (714) 720-1800

Readers of the popular publication OC Weekly voted this the "Best Ritzy" restaurant in Orange County, and it is. Conde Nast Traveler rated the service here as the best in the country — that's country, not county. The cuisine is mostly French, with some Germanic touches provided by German-born owner Hans Prager. Expensive? Yes. Delicious? You know it. Dress as if you're putting on the Ritz and you won't be disappointed.

Santa Catalina Island

Hotel & Tour Information: (310) 510-3000 Chamber of Commerce: (310) 510-1520
Catalina Passenger Service: (800) 830-7744

To be absolutely truthful, Santa Catalina Island isn't really in Orange County. It's 26 miles away, in fact. Because it's so easy to get to Catalina from Orange County, however, I would feel remiss in not mentioning what a fabulous place this is to visit if you've got an extra day in your itinerary. There aren't too many Catalinas in the United States. This offshore gem is a natural wonder, part of the Channel Islands National Park. Visitors may stay on the island for one night or a week in any of the hotels and bed and breakfast inns in Avalon, the only major town on Catalina.

Avalon is a cute village that you can tour in half a day, on foot or in little golf carts that you rent (the residents use them too—nobody drives a car through the narrow streets). There are shops with beautiful sea treasures like coral and seashells, and the more pedestrian gifts of T-shirts and paperweights. In between are some decent places to eat. There's parasailing in Avalon Bay, a glass bottom boat tour, fishing, hiking, scuba diving, golf and more.

If you tour Avalon by golf cart you get some fantastic, cliff-hanging views of the bay—definitely bring your camera. The best reason to go to Avalon may be to get a remarkably different perspective. Although you look back at California as it appears from across the channel, it is easy to imagine that you're in the Mediterranean, not the Pacific Ocean.

Romance tip: If you need a brief but intense second honeymoon, try fleeing to this island in the middle of January for two or three weeknights. There will be no one around and you will have the island to yourself. January provides blustery, but generally clear, conditions that provide spectacular ocean vistas. And because you can see Avalon in one day, you'll be forced to relax the rest of the time. Highly recommended for a romantic revival.

Bus tours of the islands take you through the wilderness and along cliff-hanging roads to the lone airstrip on the island which is near its highest point. One of the strangest sights on Catalina are the bison—stranded on the island after the filming of a Hollywood movie decades ago. The herd has survived and is pretty nonchalant about the tour buses.

Did I mention the famous Casino? No, you can't gamble there, but this elegant, circular structure dating back to the Swing Era is an architectural beauty even if you're not especially taken with buildings as a rule. You can tour the Casino and see it's lovely movie theater (still showing first-run movies) and the ballroom on the top floor. This building is so large that it is easily seen while you're still miles away at sea.

Catalina also has a fantastic garden worth visiting. Part of a memorial created by the Wrigley family of Chicago (as in spearmint gum and the Chicago Cubs), the Wrigley Memorial Garden is nestled in a canyon that slopes gradually uphill until you reach the family's monument. Mount the steps and you can look back toward the bay and the mainland. The garden contains thousands of interesting varieties of plants, including one of the finest cactus gardens anywhere.

You can catch the Catalina Flyer catamaran from Newport Harbor's Balboa Pavilion. You must reserve space in advance. The boat leaves promptly at 9 a.m. and departs Avalon at 4:30 p.m. This is generally a smooth way to get to the island (a 75-minute trip), but if you're bothered by even the slightest ocean swells, a little over-the-counter motion sickness remedy taken prior to departure should take care of it.

Huntington Beach

A bit farther north of Newport Beach, still on PCH, you come to Huntington Beach, the tenth largest city in the state. This city is a little schizophrenic. Inland there is a large population of nearly 200,000 suburbanites living in 1960s-era neighborhoods. Along Huntington Beach's waterfront, however, you discover an upstart resort area built on the remains of what was once a funky surfing area. The city of Huntington Beach wants to compete with the higher-born status of Laguna Beach and Dana Point to the south. Only time will tell. Meanwhile, enjoy the plentiful variety of oysters, sushi, and microbrewery malt brews that are available in the many eateries here. Remember, too, that there are two Huntington Beaches: the coastal community and the interior suburb. For more information about the inland Huntington Beach, see Chapter 4.

On the beach: it all starts when you reach the intersection of PCH and Main Street. Turn inland, and you are on a two-block stretch of beach, shops and sidewalk eateries known as Main Promenade. Whole city blocks along PCH were razed to create a new, more appealing and cohesive appearance. Once this was a mostly barefoot part of town that belonged to the young and the young at heart. The surfers and the young are still here, but the quasi-Mediterranean architecture is intended to bring in a more upscale visitor. Fortunately, the folksiness of the locals keeps things light, as does the reassuring sight of a mobile sidewalk pretzel stand. One can certainly still have a pleasant walkabout from the beach to the pier to one of the many bars. Be sure to check out all the second-floor walk-ups. If one looks too crowded, there's probably another one next door.

One good place to try is the Huntington Beach Brewing Co. (201 Main Street, 714-960-5343). It offers good pizza, pasta, and home brews, such as the HB blond ale.

The Huntington Beach Pier is new—or rather, it has been restored (several times) after withstanding many destructive Pacific storms during the 1980s. The original pier, constructed in 1904, was wood. A concrete pier, erected in its place in 1914, was the first of its kind in the United States. (It was also the longest and highest pier at the time, measuring 1,300 feet in length). The pier has been damaged and restored several times since then, the most recent restoration taking place after the pier sustained millions of dollars worth of damage in 1988. Now it's back and better than ever— four years and $10.8 million later. Residents were so happy to have their pier back that they held a big coming out party in July '92. There's a great statue of a surfer near the pier that commemorates the legend of what some locals call the original Surf City.

In case you're intrigued about lifeguard duty, you can arrange a tour of the lifeguard headquarters at 1st Street and PCH next to the pier. For details, call (714) 536-5285.

Outdoors

Bolsa Chica State Ecological Reserve
Pacific Coast Highway at Warner Avenue
Hours: Daily, sunrise to sunset
Information: (714) 846-1114

Bolsa chica is Spanish for "little pocket." These 500-plus acres of partially-restored salt marsh are exactly that: a pocket of wilderness in the large, increasingly urbanized coast of Orange County. Some 200 species of birds make their temporary homes here while traveling through on their yearly migrations. In general, you'll see shorebirds in the fall, waterfowl in winter, and songbirds and marine birds in spring and summer.

There are two places where you can park your car and enter the reserve on foot. One is on the south side of Warner Avenue just a few yards from the corner of Warner and PCH. The other lot is located about one mile south of Warner on PCH. From the latter there is a wooden walkway that

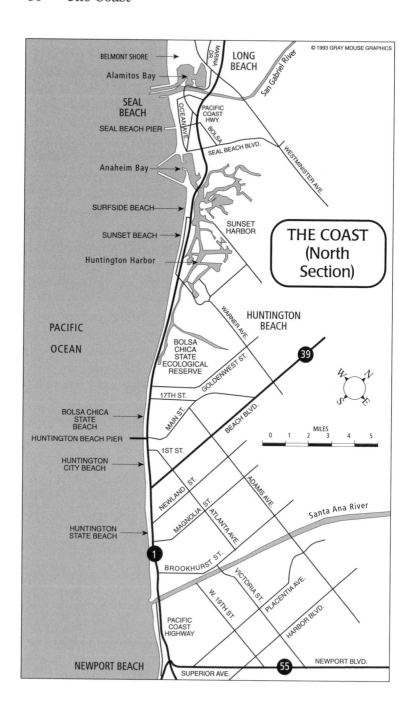

© 1993 GRAY MOUSE GRAPHICS

BELMONT SHORE

LONG BEACH

MARINA DR.

Alamitos Bay

San Gabriel River

SEAL BEACH

OCEAN AVE.

PACIFIC COAST HWY.

SEAL BEACH PIER

BOLSA

SEAL BEACH BLVD.

WESTMINSTER AVE.

Anaheim Bay

SURFSIDE BEACH

SUNSET HARBOR

SUNSET BEACH

Huntington Harbor

THE COAST (North Section)

PACIFIC

OCEAN

WARNER AVE.

HUNTINGTON BEACH

39

BOLSA CHICA STATE ECOLOGICAL RESERVE

GOLDENWEST ST.

17TH ST.

BOLSA CHICA STATE BEACH

MAIN ST.

BEACH BLVD.

HUNTINGTON BEACH PIER

1ST ST.

HUNTINGTON CITY BEACH

W   N

S   E

MILES

0   1   2   3   4   5

NEWLAND ST.

ADAMS AVE.

Santa Ana River

MAGNOLIA ST.

ATLANTA AVE.

HUNTINGTON STATE BEACH

1

BROOKHURST ST.

VICTORIA ST.

PLACENTIA AVE.

W. 19TH ST.

HARBOR BLVD.

PACIFIC COAST HIGHWAY

NEWPORT BEACH

NEWPORT BLVD.

55

SUPERIOR AVE.

stretches out across part of the marsh. Both lots are marked with signs that describe the evolution, disappearance, and restoration of these wetlands.

Bolsa Chica is divided into two bays, the Inner Bolsa Bay and Outer Bolsa Bay. There is a 1.5-mile loop trail that gives visitors a tour around the inner bay and its sand dunes, plus a view of the outer bay from a nearby bluff. The bluff is shaded with some of Orange County's distinctive eucalyptus trees. It is important that visitors stick to the marked trail, not remove anything, and not bring dogs (even on a leash). Many interpretive displays about the flora and fauna of Bolsa Chica are set along the path.

It's not hard to understand why bird watchers love this reserve. Some of the many species you may see include the black skimmer, Belding's savannah sparrow, the endangered least tern, and a variety of finches, towhees, ospreys, herons, egrets and peregrine falcons.

Many fowl aren't here just for the climate. There's lots of bird delicacies to eat under the waters of this estuary: California horn snails, jackknife clams, California mussels, mud crabs, and more than 50 species of fish. It's fun to watch the waterfowl dive for their meals—surf scooters actually dive to the bottom to find the tastiest mussels.

Two sand islands south of the boardwalk play host to least terns and snowy plovers. Aerial courtship displays are frequent in April and May.

The first inhabitants of Bolsa Chica were Gabrielino Indians who lived on bluffs overlooking this estuary more than 8,000 years ago. During what is known as the Milling Stone Period, these native Americans manufactured cogstones— round, flat discs three-to-five inches in diameter and one-inch thick. The edges of these stones were notched, and some had holes in the middle. Archaeologists do not know their purpose, but presume they were used during ceremonial rites.

The Indians did not inhibit the natural function of these wetlands. However, with the arrival of Europeans, the wetlands began to be affected by agriculture. As the practice of cattle ranching and farming increased inland, these activities harmed the natural runoff to Bolsa Chica. In 1899, a dam was built with tide gates causing the natural ocean entrance to eventually fill in with sand. This, and early twentieth-century oil production, took its toll on these wetlands. Fortunately, as the importance of this migratory way-station came to be understood, the state began to acquire some acreage to rescue, and now several hundred acres have been completely restored to salt marsh conditions (eventually, more than 1,000 acres will be restored). One hundred thousand traveling birds have not let this work go to waste. Since some 90 percent of all California wetlands have vanished, every acre helps.

Historical note: During World War II, this mesa was used for shore defense as Bolsa Chica Fort Command. Two big guns on rotating mounts were placed here, directed toward a possible enemy attack. The concrete turrets are still here.

This facility has restrooms and picnic tables. Tours are offered between 9 and 10:30 a.m. every first Saturday of the month.

Bolsa Chica State Beach

17851 Pacific Coast Highway. 1.5 miles south of Warner Avenue
Information: (714) 846-3460

Directly across from the Bolsa Chica wetlands is Bolsa Chica State Beach, a great site for a bonfire. The beach used to be called Tin Can Beach due to all the hobos who lived here in makeshift tents. When the state officially took charge, it was cleaned up and many concrete fire pits were installed. Now it's not unusual for 20,000 beach-goers to arrive on a single day and evening.

A relaxing night on the beach is a great way to get in some stargazing. At this particular beach, there are no city lights nearby to drown the sky in light pollution. Of course, the smoke from all those bonfires can sometimes obscure an otherwise great night for viewing. Try coming here in the middle of the week, particularly off season, when it's less crowded.

If you have an RV with your own facilities, overnight camping is available. There are no hookups here, and no sewage disposal. There are restrooms and outside showers. The fee is $14 per night.

Driftwood Golf Course
21462 Pacific Coast Highway
Information: (714) 969-8597

This is a really modestly priced course (green fees under $10) that's a par 67, excellent for beginners or for someone (you, perhaps?) who needs to work harder on their short game.

Huntington State Beach
Pacific Coast Highway at Brookhurst Avenue
Information: (714) 536-1454

This is probably the reason most people come to Huntington Beach in the first place. This beach in particular is the cookout beach in Orange County, with fire pits everywhere. And because it is 8.5 miles long, there's always room for one more. This broad expanse of sand has so many barbecue pits, that just by driving along PCH on a peak weekend you can smell the charcoal. The uninterrupted length of Huntington State Beach also makes its bike path one of the best in OC; whether you prefer rollerblading, jogging or cycling, here's a straightaway you can enjoy without negotiating through automobile traffic.

Huntington State Beach is a flat and friendly beach that gets mighty crowded on holidays and weekends, especially in summer. Yes, those big contraptions that keep bobbing up and down are oil wells. And the oil derricks you notice out at sea are offshore oil platforms. But don't let that deter you. The view is mostly marvelous, and this beach is worth a visit if you want to do your weenies and marshmallows the California way. Ten million visitors a year can't be wrong.

Beach barbecue tips: When you want to use a vacated fire ring, approach it carefully wearing sandals or thongs— sometimes lazy people leave roasting skewers in the sand around the pit, and you wouldn't want to step on one. Never walk inside the fire ring—it might still be hot from a previous fire. Don't let children play in them. Do not use water or sand to douse your fire after you're done, just let it burn itself out. Finally, use only wood that will fit inside the ring.

Huntington City Beach RV Facilities

103 Pacific Coast Highway
Information: (714) 969-5621

Between Main Street and Beach Boulevard is a parking lot that can be used by RV travelers. From June 1 to September 13—peak tourist season—the parking lot is reserved for RVs who are passing through. You can check in between 6 and 11 p.m., and you have to be out by 8 a.m. the next day. The intent is to keep travelers from parking alongside busy PCH—better for you, better for traffic. This overnight parking spot has sewage disposal, fire rings, outside showers (no privacy here) and fire rings. First come, first served. The price is $15 per night.

During the rest of the year, this same area is open to longer RV stays, but note the lack of all but minimal facilities. You can find this lot by driving north on PCH past Beach Boulevard, then turn left into the municipal parking lot at 1st Street.

Seacliff Country Club Golf Course

6501 Palm Avenue
Information: (714) 536-7575

Bent grass greens and long holes are the signature of this course. The club is private, but offers reciprocal restricted play to members of other clubs. The cart and green fee on a weekend will run you about $70.

Attractions and Special Events

Sand Castle Festival
First Street and Pacific Coast Highway

Every year Huntington Beach holds a Sand Castle Festival, generally the first weekend in October and located between the pier and the lifeguard headquarters near First Street and PCH. Participants help build an unbroken sculpture that reaches a mile in length by the time they're done.

Huntington Beach International Surfing Museum
411 Olive Ave.
Information: (714) 960-3483
Hours: Wednesday through Sunday, noon to 5 p.m.
Fees: $2 adults, $1 students, children under 6 free

Huntington Beach is still a surfer's town. If it's true that one of every five persons in Huntington Beach think of themselves as surfers, then it's only fitting that this should be the one and only home of the International Surfing Museum. You read it right: a museum dedicated to the preservation of this unusual sport's history, particularly its introduction to the mainland from Hawaii around 80 years ago.

Selected Restaurants

Sammy's No. 2
18011 Beach Boulevard
Information: (714) 847-7566
Hours: Monday through Friday, 10 a.m. to 9 p.m.;
Saturday, 11 a.m. to 8 p.m.; closed Sundays

The debate about where to find Orange County's finest chili dogs will probably never be settled, but the Times Orange County swears by the fare served at this eatery at Beach Boulevard and Talbert Avenue.

Sugar Shack

213-1/2 Main Street
Information: (714) 536-0355
Hours: Daily, 6 a.m. to 3:30 p.m. Serving: Breakfast, lunch

This three-decades-old institution is family-owned. It's located on the Main Street drag where Surf City was born. This is where locals come to eat and catch up on the day's events. The Sugar Shack is casual and inexpensive, and features homestyle cooking, such as mashed potatoes and gravy with turkey. Outdoor seating.

Lodging

Waterfront Hilton

21100 Pacific Coast Highway
Reservations: (714) 960-SURF

One block south of Main Promenade is the Waterfront Hilton, a 296-room resort hotel with all the trimmings. The hotel building itself is basic: a tall, rectangular tower that gives every room a view of the magnificent coastline. Good walking distance to the action along Main Street and the pier.

Huntington Harbor

This community, located north of the Bolsa Chica Ecological Reserve, is really part of Huntington Beach. It's mainly a residential marina. About the only place where you can take it in is from Peter's Landing (16400 Pacific Coast Highway), a small shopping center with some waterfront dining stops.

Attractions and Special Events

Huntington Harbor Cruise of Lights

Huntington Harbor Mall
Information: (714) 840-7542
Admission: Adults, $10, children, $6

The most popular event in Huntington Harbor is the annual Cruise of Lights, where the waterfront homes and a parade of boats are all lit up like Christmas trees. This beautiful electric pageant is on display every evening for nine days beginning in mid-December. This cruise works a little differently from the Newport Harbor Parade, because you can buy tickets to ride the boats that cruise Huntington Harbor. Boats make the circuit four times each evening, and the proceeds go to a good cause: the Huntington Harbor Philharmonic youth music programs.

Sunset Beach

If you blink, you might miss Sunset Beach, a bit of unincorporated county on the beachside of PCH opposite Huntington Harbor. Look closely and you will realize that Sunset Beach looks a lot funkier than Huntington Harbor. The pretty, condo-filled marina of the latter is for one kind of taste and, well, Sunset Beach is for the other.

There's no mail service in Sunset Beach, just a small post office. And there's no fire department except a volunteer one. The shops and bars lack that coordinated look of some resorts further south. And that's the way the locals like it. This 26-block stretch of PCH is much more like the beach communities of the past.

You know you're leaving Sunset Beach when you spot the 89-foot-tall wooden water tower. It's been standing here since World War II. In the mid-1980s, some visionary person bought the thing outright and converted it into a home—a multi-million dollar mansion on peg legs with an outrageous view of the Pacific Ocean.

Since Sunset Beach is often overlooked by those seeking the sun, turn off PCH anywhere between Anderson Street and Warner Avenue and enjoy this quiet bit of sand. Sunset Beach (310-723-4511) has volleyball nets, surfing, fishing, showers, playground equipment and a bike path.

Seal Beach

The most interesting portion of this small beach community is located down Main Street between Pacific Coast Highway and the shore. If you drive up and down the streets that parallel Main, you can get a taste of the cottage-style living that attracted residents 50 years ago. Seal Beach and its pier are often overlooked by tourists set on spending time at the better-known beaches at Huntington and Laguna. If you zip right by, you won't realize what a nice beach you're missing. That's good for those who stop, however, because Seal Beach is a pleasant place.

If you're staying on the beach for the day, plan to have lunch or an early dinner at Ruby's at the end of the pier (310-431-RUBY; Ruby's is a popular OC-based chain). There's a terrific view here, and you'll love having some old-fashioned burgers and malts served to you 1940s style. Swing music plays continuously in the background. If you time it right you can get a table at sunset. If you come here on a weekday afternoon you probably won't even have to wait for a table. They're also open at 7 a.m. for breakfast. A bait and tackle shop is next door to Ruby's if you plan on catching your own meal.

Main Street Seal Beach is pleasant and not fancy. The reason is that most of the stores here serve the local residents. That means you will see fewer tourist shops full of beachwear and coffee mugs. You know you're in the heart of town when you reach the drugstore and the post office. You can probably walk both sides of Main Street in an hour or two, depending upon your browsing speed and whether or not you're hungry.

Don't overlook the Seal Beach Courtyard Nursery (225 Main Street). The entrance is a green copper archway that says "Old Towne Gardens."

Attractions and Special Events

Pacific Electric Red Car Museum

Address: Electric Avenue and Main Street
Hours: Open from 1 to 4 p.m. on the second and fourth
Saturdays of each month.

After you've walked the two blocks of Main Street, make sure you walk by the Pacific Electric Red Car Museum—an actual Red Car from the middle of this century from what used to be the finest public transportation system in Southern California. It was also the only public transportation system in Southern California. The Red Cars took beach visitors to Balboa Peninsula and north to Long Beach and even downtown Los Angeles.

The car is located in a tiny park between Electric Avenue and Main Street, and houses memorabilia from the Red Car era.

Selected Restaurants

Cafe Lafayette

330 Main Street
Information: (562) 598-9566
Hours: Monday through Saturday, 8 a.m. to 2:30 p.m.
(breakfast/lunch);, 5 p.m. to 9 p.m. (dinner); Sundays 8 a.m.
to 2:30 p.m. Serving: Breakfast, lunch, dinner

The Times Orange County recommends Cafe Lafayette for their outrageous Dutch pancakes (served until mid-afternoon). It is a charming eatery at one end of this two-block stretch of seaside calm.

Other good eateries: Don Juan's Taco Shop (est. 1961) 131-1/2 Main Street; Grandma's Ice Cream Candies & Coffee at the corner of Main & Pier; and Walt's Wharf, at the corner of Main and Central, for seafood, oysters, and California wines.

Lodging

Seal Beach Inn and Gardens

212 5th Street
Reservations: (562) 493-2416

This nice bed & breakfast is at the corner of 5th and Central Avenue, just a few blocks from Main Street and the beach. It's a restored inn with an Old World theme, and each room is decorated differently. The location is quiet, almost disguised amid this old town neighborhood. Not a bad way to spend a private night or two near the beach.

Belmont Shore

Technically, this little community of ten blocks of shops and restaurants is across the border in Los Angeles County. This spit of land links Seal Beach in Orange County to the city of Long Beach. If you're going to be driving to points north (perhaps to visit San Pedro, or two distinctive Long Beach attractions, the luxury ocean liner HMSQueen Mary and the wonderful Aquarium of the Pacific), skip the freeway and try driving north up Pacific Coast Highway past the U.S. Naval Weapons Station, then turn left on 2nd Street and cross over two bridges. This single street is where all the action is, inviting strollers to get out of their cars on a sunny afternoon (or balmy evening) to window shop and stop for an espresso. The numerous clubs and bars located here serve the local beach cottage neighborhood.

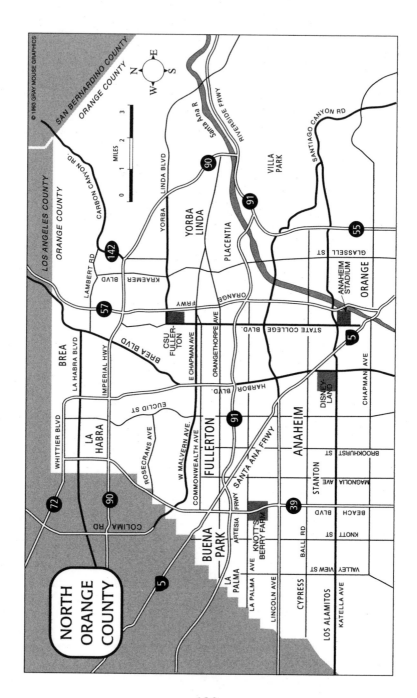

North Orange County

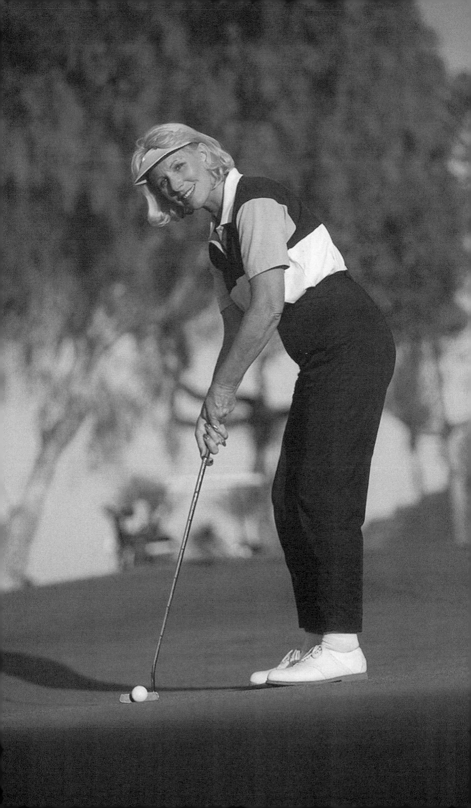

This chapter covers those cities that are geographically closest to Los Angeles and San Bernardino counties. This portion of Orange County also includes the communities of La Palma, Los Alamitos and Stanton, which are primarily residential neighborhoods.

On a map, the northern portion of Orange County looks merely like a paved extension of Los Angeles County. In some places this is true, for the boundary between the counties is pretty arbitrary. The mixture of light industry and suburbs appears identical on both sides of the county line, particularly near the Santa Ana Freeway (I-5). La Palma seems like La Mirada, which seems like Cerritos or Santa Fe Springs (all communities immediately to the north in Los Angeles county). But geographic features such as the Puente Hills, the foothills from La Habra Heights to northern Fullerton, and large parklands such as Cerritos Regional and Ralph B. Clark Regional, give northern Orange County its own distinct character.

Orange County offers many excellent golfing opportunities

Anaheim

This city was founded in 1857 by German immigrants who were primarily interested in cultivating the area for vineyards. They bought the surrounding property for $2 an acre, and named their new land *Anaheim* ("home by the river"). Until the late 19th century, Anaheim was the wine capital of California; however, in 1885 a terrible blight attacked the vines and permanently destroyed the grape-growing industry in Orange County. The farmers turned to Valencia oranges, and the subsequent boom in the cultivation of this citrus gave Orange County its lasting identity.

Walt Disney changed the face of Anaheim forever. After the successful launch of his movie studio in Hollywood, Disney dreamed of creating an amusement park. Disneyland opened in 1955, originally on 160 acres. It attracted one million visitors in the first six months. The rest is history, and Anaheim is now the most populated city in the county.

Outdoors

Anaheim Hills Golf Course
6501 Nohl Ranch Road
Information: (714) 998-3041

The pro shop says you will want a golf cart, because this is truly a hilly course. For around $40, you can expect a short but challenging set of holes with four par fives. Give them seven days advance notice for registration.

H.G. "Dad" Miller Golf Course
430 N. Gilbert Street
Information: (714) 765-3481

This course was designed by the renowned "Dad" Miller, hence the name. It's one course that you'll have no trouble walking, and the greens fee is just $18 on weekends. The course is well maintained.

Santa Ana River Lakes

4060 E. La Palma Avenue
Information: (714) 632-7830
Hours: Daily 6 a.m. to 4 p.m.; 5 p.m. to 11 p.m. night
fishing
Fees: $12 adults, $10 children under 12

It may seem strange, but there's actually a fishing hole near one of Orange County's busiest freeways. This county park consists of three lakes — 135 acres in all — where you can angle for bass, catfish, crappie and trout. Boats, rods and reels are available for rent, or you may bring your own. There is no swimming, sailing or camping. There are two picnic areas and a concession stand for food and bait.

Directions: Take the Riverside Freeway (Highway 91) to Tustin Avenue, turn north one block to La Palma, then right to the lakes entrance at Richfield Road.

Yorba Regional Park

7600 E. La Palma
Information: (714) 970-1460
Hours: Daily from sunrise to sunset

The lake here is not open for boating or swimming, but it does contain bass, bluegill and catfish. You must have a state fishing license to use this facility unless you're under age 16. If your family hates fishing, they can leave you by the lake and take advantage of the picnic tables and barbecues, biking, hiking and equestrian trails.

Directions: Take the Riverside Freeway (Highway 91) east to Imperial Highway, turn left to La Palma and then right one mile to the park.

Attractions and Special Events

The Arrowhead Pond of Anaheim

2695 E. Katella Avenue (at Douglass Road)
Information: (714) 704-2500

This 19,000-seat arena is the home of the Mighty Ducks, the National Hockey League team. The Ducks became the first tenants of this stadium. Called the Pond, for short, the venue opened in 1993 within a stone's throw of Edison International Field (formerly Anaheim Stadium, home of the Anaheim Angels major league baseball team). Some basketball games as well as musical concerts are also staged in the Pond, making this one of the few places in Orange County where the larger arena-sized pop/rock tours come to perform.

Anaheim Convention Center

800 W. Katella Avenue
Information: (714) 765-8950
Hours: Call for information about current events

The Anaheim Convention Center has five huge exhibit halls which are the venue for many shows of interest to consumers. Some are held annually and are very popular. The themes run from cat breeds to saunas and spas and motorcycles. Shows open to the public are widely advertised in both the Orange County Register and the Times Orange County newspapers.

The convention center is located on the south side of Katella Avenue (across the street from the Disneyland parking lot) between Harbor Boulevard and West Street.

Camelot Golfland

3200 E. Carpenter
Information: (714) 630-3340
Hours: Sunday through Thursday, 10 a.m. to 11 p.m.;
Friday and Saturday, 10 a.m. to midnight

Admission: None; arcade and golfing games are reasonably priced

Not one, not two, but five 18-hole miniature golf courses give visitors an incredible variety of challenging putting pleasure. The courses range from easy to hard. There's also a giant arcade with more than 350 different games. There's a pizza parlor if you happen to get the munchies, and during the summer you can enjoy Camelot's own water slide, a popular, zig-zagging maze of pipe-shaped runs.

Camelot is not near the theme parks or any of the many motels in Anaheim. To find it, take Orange Freeway (Highway 57) north to the Riverside Freeway (Highway 91) east, then west one exit to Kraemer and follow the signs.

Disneyland
1313 Harbor Boulevard
Information: (714) 999-4565

See Theme Parks section for complete information.

Family Fun Center
1041 N. Shepard
Information: (714) 630-7212
Hours: Monday through Thursday, 11 a.m. to 9 p.m.;
Friday through Sunday, 9 a.m. to 10 p.m. (go-cart racing
opens at 2 p.m.)

The name of this place describes it perfectly—a mini-park of games and activities where you can take your children and work off some energy having good, clean fun. They have bumper boats (like bumper cars, only in water), an arcade, a maze, batting cages (you know, for batting practice), go-carts, rollerskating and "battle boats" (remote control ships). The price is per attraction.

The Family Fun Center is visible from the north side of the Riverside Freeway (Highway 91) between Kraemer and Tustin Avenue.

Tours

Edison International Field of Anaheim

*2000 Gene Autry Way, near Katella Ave. & State College
Boulevard*
Information: (714) 634-2000
*Hours: Daily 11 a.m to 2 p.m. (when no sporting events are
scheduled)*

This ballpark—once known affectionately as "The Big
A" (for Anaheim)—is home to the Anaheim Angels baseball
team. The stadium received a much-needed remodeling during 1997, and is now state-of-the-art in outdoor amenities,
new seating, and a broader range of concessions available to
keep anyone happy during that seventh-inning stretch. On
days when there is no live sporting event scheduled, you can
tour the stadium. If you've always wondered what the inside
of a professional sports team's locker room is like, here's your
chance to visit the Angel's dugout. You'll see the bullpens,
the press box and the playing field up close.

If you're in town during baseball season, call 714-254-
3100 for ticket information. Edison Field (often called "The
Big Ed" by local sportscasters) is located on State College
Boulevard between Katella and Orangewood Avenues just
off the Orange Freeway (Highway 57).

Attractions and Special Events

Disney ICE

300 W. Lincoln Ave.
Information: (714) 535-RINK; (www.disneyice.com)
Hours: Call for open skating times
Admission: Varies with the program

This wonderful ice skating facility is the official training
spot of the Mighty Ducks NHL hockey team. It features two
rinks: one Olympic size, the other regulation NHL size (Olympic rinks are slightly larger). Opened in 1995, the rinks fea-

ture a second floor viewing area, snack bar, locker room and spectator seating for 1,000. The Mighty Ducks Pro Shop has great skating gear for purchase, and many different skating classes are available to adults and children in both figure skating and hockey. Parents can arrange for birthday parties here for a cool celebration.

Admission is free during Mighty Ducks practice sessions. Disney ICE is located between Harbor Boulevard and the 57 Freeway, just north of the I-5 Freeway.

Historic

Anaheim, perhaps more than any other community in Orange County, boasts a small district near the heart of town where several historic houses from the turn of the century are restored and open for tours. These houses are another reminder that Orange County isn't as young and prefabricated as much of Southern California seems to be at first glance.

Anaheim Museum

241 S. Anaheim Boulevard
Information: (714) 778-3301
Hours: Wednesday through Friday 10 a.m. to 4 p.m.;
Saturday noon to 4 p.m.
Donation: $2

The Anaheim Historical Society maintains this building that once served as the town's public library. Built in 1907, it is listed in the National Register of Historic Places. The building was originally a gift from Andrew Carnegie, and was restored and reopened in 1987. A horse-drawn carriage and horse-drawn fire truck dating from the late 1800s are on exhibit.

The Anaheim Museum also maintains a children's gallery with exhibits geared toward young people, including costumes the kids can dress up in. The museum is located at Anaheim and Broadway just across from the civic center.

Anaheim Historical Society

The Anaheim Historical Society schedules an annual house tour of nearby historic homes. These homes are fine examples of modern restoration techniques. The house tour is usually scheduled in late spring, so try calling in March if you'd like more information about visiting Anaheim's restored Victorian-era homes. Most are located around the neighborhood of Pearson Park (Harbor Boulevard & Sycamore Street), within a square boundary that is formed by North, East, South and West streets.

One example is the appropriately-named **Anaheim House** at 418 N. West Street (714-835-5381), which has tours by appointment only. This three-story structure in the Victorian Queen Anne style is now owned by the American Red Cross, which maintains an historic exhibit inside on the famous relief organization. The house itself dates from 1894.

The Mother Colony House, located at 414 N. West Street, pays homage to a group of German immigrants that came from San Francisco to create a grape-growing community. The house was built with redwood shipped from Northern California, and contains numerous authentic pioneer artifacts. It is a California state historical landmark (#201 in California Historical Landmarks) and Anaheim's first house, built in 1857. That also makes it one of the oldest post-rancho-era houses in all of Orange County.

The Ramon Peralta Adobe (Fairmont Boulevard & Santa Ana Canyon Road, Anaheim Hills) was built around 1871. It contains artifacts that have been collected on the grounds around the adobe. Peralta is one of the oldest family names in the county's history. Gabriel Peralta was a member of an early Spanish expedition through California (in 1776). Juan Pablo Peralta, along with his uncle, Antonio Yorba, shared title to Rancho Santiago de Santa Ana. This 62,000-plus acre ranch was the only Spanish land grant in what is now Orange County; the title dates back to 1810.

Other historic homes in Anaheim include the present home of **The White House Restaurant** (887 S. Anaheim

Boulevard, 714-772-1381), listed in the National Register of Historic Places, and the **Kuchel-Melrose House** (226 E. Adele Street), built around 1860.

Shopping

Anaheim Indoor Marketplace

1440 S. Anaheim Boulevard
Information: 999-0888
Hours: Daily 10 a.m. to 7 p.m. (closed Tuesdays)

Although it is billed as Orange County's "largest indoor swap meet," what you have here are hundreds of small shops in one place hawking every conceivable kind of merchandise, from cameras and T-shirts to sunglasses, embroidery and what-not. There's a play area for young children and a food court. This shopping setup—a single location with food, kiddie diversions and discount merchandise—is becoming quite common around Southern California. Anaheim Marketplace is located north of the Santa Ana Freeway (I-5) near Cerritos.

Book Baron

1236 S. Magnolia Avenue
Information: (714) 527-7022; (www.bookbaron.com)
Hours: Monday through Saturday, 9:30 a.m. to 6 p.m.;
Friday until 7 p.m.; Sunday until 5 p.m.

Located in a supermarket shopping center at the corner of Ball Road and Magnolia, this is one of Orange County's larger used book stores (20,000 square feet, give or take). If you're a book collector, this is one store you must visit. It is neat and well organized, and they have a substantial collection of first editions in the science fiction and horror genres, both paperback and hardcover. Book Baron also has a music department (although it's not nearly as large), and plenty of those old magazines.

Book Baron also has a location at 1310 E. Chapman Ave. in Fullerton (714-526-5913).

Hobby City/Adventure City

10120 S. Beach Boulevard
Information: (714) 527-2323 or 236-9300
Hours: Times and days vary with the season; call for
today's schedule.

These six acres of hobby and collectibles shops that look like a city are aptly named. Hobbyists could easily get lost here for an entire day. There are 24 places to visit in all. Hobby City was the vision of Jay and Bea DeArmond, who bought a three-acre chicken ranch in 1955 and turned it into a hobbyist's paradise. Adjacent to this mini-mall for collectors is a pint-sized amusement parks for tykes called Adventure City, where all the rides are scaled for the small fry, and the admission is just $11.95.

Bea DeArmond's personal collection of rare antique dolls forms the centerpiece of Hobby City. Her collection is housed in a building that is a half-scale-size replica of the White House. Admission to the Doll and Toy Museum at Hobby City (714-527-2323) is nominal. Bea started collecting dolls at age 12. Over the years, the museum has been expanded through donations from others who wanted their rare dolls displayed to the world. There is no admission charge to visit the toy shop inside the White House museum, where they sell old dolls and accessories, toys and doll books and repair antique dolls.

Hobby City's other shops are diverse. Ansdell Piano (714-821-3311) sells new and used pianos of all types, and specializes in restoring older pianos. The Cabbage Patch Shop (714-527-8105) offers collectible soft sculpture dolls by Xavier Roberts, the creator of the phenomenal Cabbage Patch Kids. You'll find an outdoor cabbage patch, lots of clothes and accessories, and about 1,000 babies to choose from.

If antique rifles and pistols are your thing, check out The Flintlock (714-821-6655), carrying all types of old guns, black powder and kits for building your own gun. They also have spinning wheels and weaving looms, recreating a mini-slice of early American craftsmanship. Are you interested in seashells and beads, baseball cards, stamps and coins, rocks and gems, or model trains? If so, there's a separate shop here for any of your hobby interests.

The small-scale amusement rides for little tykes called Adventure City includes a mini-replica of a 1938 steam locomotive, a small ferris wheel, carousel, and two little roller coasters. The main entrance to Hobby City is on Beach Boulevard two miles south of Knott's Berry Farm. If you're coming from Disneyland, head west on Ball Road four miles. There's free parking just before you get to Beach Boulevard.

House of Cactus

10580 Beach Boulevard, Stanton
Information: Call (714) 828-4298 for hours

This nursery is the answer to your search for rare and exotic cacti. The owners of this single-minded botanical bonanza care for some 1,500 varieties of cacti and succulents, from cuttings of common plants to seldom-seen species that cost a few hundred dollars each. Located in the community of Stanton, the House of Cactus is a wonderful place to enjoy these distinctive plants without scouring the desert.

Lincoln Antique Mall

1811 W. Lincoln Avenue
Information: (714) 778-2522
Hours: 10 a.m. to 6 p.m. daily

Many of Orange County's older communities have large storefronts that provide space for many smaller dealers of antique and collectible merchandise, and Anaheim is no exception. The Lincoln Antique Mall has 125 dealers, with antique furnishing, artwork and a special jewelry room. This location is between Brookhurst and Euclid streets.

Magnolia Bird Farm

8990 Cerritos Avenue
Information: (714) 527-3387
Hours: Tuesday through Saturday, 9 a.m. to 5 p.m.

If you want to shop for a bird (as a pet or to breed), you've come to the right place. This pet shop sells only one type of creature: birds. Macaws, parrots, cockatoos, finches, lovebirds and many more species are among the 2,000 (give or take) winged specimens you'll find here, some kept in a 1,000-square-foot aviary. Bird grooming is available, and bird advice is free. This is an amazing emporium for the bird lover.

Dining

La Palma Chicken Pie Shop

928 N. Euclid Street
Information: (714) 533-2021
Hours: Monday through Saturday, 9 a.m. to 8 p.m.; closed Sunday

Thirty-years-young and still going strong, the star of the menu at La Palma Chicken Pie Shop and Bakery is certainly chicken pie. If you want hearty, flavorful chicken pie, you need look no further. Salads, sandwiches, and other home-made specialties—including scrumptious desserts such as strawberry pie and chocolate banana cake—are available everyday. You can eat in or take out. This neighborhood eatery is located in a shopping center at the intersection of La Palma and Euclid. Look for the sign with the chicken on it.

Brea

If you've heard of the La Brea Tar Pits, then it will come as no surprise to learn that brea is Spanish for "tar." No one but rancheros paid much attention to the foothills of Brea until its rich secret—oil—was exploited by Union Oil company beginning in 1895. Actually, the oil wasn't that big a secret: the native Americans used it for medicinal purposes, while Spanish and Mexican settlers used the sticky soil to waterproof roofs. Oil derricks sprouted like mushrooms for a brief period in the early 1900s.

The year 1916 saw the incorporation of Brea as Orange County's eighth city. The oil fields up in Carbon Canyon (surrounding the now defunct town of Olinda) were gradually abandoned, but the town of Brea survived. There are still some oil wells pumping in and around the city limits, but this town has matured into a community of some 50,000 people. Now Brea's best-known attraction is its large shopping mall, one of the busiest in Orange County.

Outdoors

Imperial Golf Course
2200 E. Imperial Highway
Information: (714) 529-3923

This course is extolled for its demanding layout amid rolling hills. Greens fees and cart runs about $50 on weekends, and seven days advance notice is required. The smaller Birch Hills Golf Course, notable for its many palm trees, is located just to the north of Imperial at 2250 E. Birch Street (714-990-0201). Don't get flustered on your approach to the pin if you have to play around an industrial site, a train track, or an oil well—they were here before you.

Shopping

Brea Mall

Imperial Highway and State College Boulevard
Information: (714) 990-2732

This is one of the busiest retail malls in Orange County after South Coast Plaza in Costa Mesa. The majors here include JC Penney, Macy's, Nordstrom and Sears.

Dining

La Vie En Rose

240 S. State College Boulevard
Information: (714) 529-8333

A Tudor-looking structure with an octagonal roof, you can spot this restaurant easily from State College Boulevard (across the street from the Brea Mall) by looking for the American and French flags flying high in front. La Vie En Rose has gourmet French food ("country dining"), a classy, lace-curtain atmosphere, and weekend entertainment.

Buena Park

Buena Park (or Plaza Buena, as it was known in the rancho days) was just another farming community until the Knott Family put it on the map with a berry farm. The community is now a land-locked suburb where three main thoroughfares converge: the Riverside Freeway (Highway 91), the Santa Ana Freeway (I-5) and Beach Boulevard (Highway 39).

If you decide to stay in Buena Park to be near Knott's Berry Farm (see Theme Parks), notice that every motel lobby has displays with hordes of coupons good for discounts on tours and attractions all throughout Southern California. Not all of the attractions are necessarily in the county, but they may be helpful in pointing out other areas of interest if you want to venture farther afield.

Outdoors

Los Coyotes Country Club Golf Course
8888 Los Coyotes Drive
Information: (714) 523-7780

This is a private club with reciprocal play available on weekdays only. Fees are $63 to play Los Coyotes' long, rolling layout. Starting time arrangements can be made the same day.

Ralph B. Clark Regional Park
8800 Rosecrans Avenue
Information: (714) 670-8045
Hours: Daily, sunrise to sunset; Museum: 8:30 to 4:30 p.m. except Mondays
Admission: $2 per car; $4 on weekends

This park may be one of Orange County's best-kept secrets. It rests on a prehistoric fossil site similar to the famous La Brea tar pits of Los Angeles County. Clark has a three-acre lake stocked with bass and catfish, and there are lots of the usual park amenities, such as picnic tables, playgrounds, and ball fields. But not every park has two earthquake faults, too! These faults display 100 feet of vertical displacement—that's seismologist-speak for, "Gets my heart racing!"

The Ralph B. Clark Paleontological Museum has 6,000 square feet of exhibit space, with a full-color mural that depicts life as it existed in this area 400,000 years ago. There are seven full skeletons on display, including a saber toothed cat, mammoth, and ground sloth. Pond turtles and many other land and marine animals that walked, slid and swam over this area have been found in the park's rich fossil beds. The invertebrates discovered here date back 1.4 million years. Here's another fact: this park has produced the largest variety of fossilized salamanders in Southern California, and the first banana slug fossil ever found. What's more: paleontologists estimate that 95 percent of the park's fossils are still underground.

Programs are currently offered to adults and children who want to learn more about paleontology. Every Sunday at 1 p.m., there's a free fossil program at the interpretive center, and special groups can be arranged to work in the fossil beds (but anything you may find has to stay in the park). Every second and fourth Saturday of the month at 2 p.m., there are free nature walks, and there's a summer campfire series for kids. Call for more information.

Attractions

Knott's Berry Farm

8039 Beach Boulevard
Information: (714) 827-1776

See Theme Parks section for complete information.

Soak City U.S.A.

8039 Beach Boulevard
Information: (714) 220-5200

For information on the newest addition to the Knott's theme park experience, see Chapter 3 for complete information

Independence Hall

8039 Beach Boulevard
Information: (714) 827-1776
Hours: Daily 10 a.m. to 5 p.m.

You don't have to pay admission to Knott's Berry Farm to enjoy this remarkable replica of the real Independence Hall in Philadelphia. The Knott family had the structure completed in 1966. Inside, there's a copy of the Liberty Bell (crack and all), historical exhibits, and a large theater that presents a slide show on the signing of the Declaration of Independence. If you can't take your family to Philadelphia anytime soon, this would be a great way to reinforce some of the Revolutionary War history your children are taught in school.

Medieval Times Dinner & Tournament

7662 Beach Boulevard
Information: (714) 521-4740, 800-899-6600

Here's something you won't see every day: a real jousting tournament (held indoors, too). It's A.D. 1093, at least when you step inside Medieval Times, one of the newest dinner theater extravaganzas offered along the tourist strip of Beach Boulevard. While you and yours feast on roast chicken and drink mead (okay, maybe it's just a soft drink), a pageant of gallantry unfolds.

Enjoy horsemanship, swordplay, sorcery, falconry, and a real jousting tournament where knights on horseback charge each other at full gallop. The knights compete to see who will be champion, and a damsel is selected from each audience to be queen.

The price (ranging from $20 to $35 per person) includes dinner, beverages and the show (the bar is extra). Medieval Times is located just south of the Artesia Freeway (Highway 91) on Beach Boulevard near Movieland Wax Museum and Ripley's Believe It Or Not Museum.

Historic

Jaynes Estate Park
7842 Whitaker Avenue
Information: (714) 522-2788
Hours: Thursdays, 10:30 a.m. to 2:30 p.m.; second Sunday of the month, 1 to 4 p.m.; tours by appointment only
Admission: Donation

On this site are two historic homes: the Bacon House and the Whitaker-Jaynes House. Andrew West Whitaker built his house in 1887 upon his arrival from Indiana. His brother James bought 690 acres of land to establish a cattle ranch, but ended up subdividing the property and creating the city of Buena Park. The house was sold to Isaac Jaynes in 1903, and his family resided there until 1965. The city created a park out of the house grounds, and it is now maintained by the Buena Park Historical Society.

The house is wonderfully furnished with authentic period furniture and household items, including the bedroom set of Cordelia Knott (of Knott's Berry Farm).

Next door is the Bacon House, built in 1884 in the "single wall" style of construction. It was moved from its original site and restored at the Estate Park to celebrate America's Bicentennial. Original Bacon family heirlooms may be seen inside this tiny house.

Museums

International Printing Museum & Heritage Theater

8469 Kass Drive
Information: (714) 523-2070
Hours: Tuesday through Saturday 10 a.m. to 5 p.m.
Admission: Adults, $6.50; students and seniors, $4;
children under 12, $2.50

What will you see here? More than 500 years of printing history and 150 working antique printing presses. The guided tour is under an hour. The presses—some of which are demonstrated on the tour—are from many parts of the world and show the various ways the printed word has been set to paper. Type used to be set one letter at a time, and you'll see how that was done in a recreation of a print shop from the 1870s. It's a far cry from today's digital age.

Movieland Wax Museum

7711 Beach Boulevard
Information: (714) 522-1154
Hours: Monday through Friday, 10 a.m. to 6 p.m.;
Saturday and Sunday 9 a.m. to 7 p.m., 365 days a year
Admission: Adults, $12.95; children under 11, $6.95;
seniors, $10.95

This is the wax museum you'll want to see, because the emphasis is on authenticity. This museum is the only one (as far as anyone knows) exclusively devoted to stars of stage, television and movies from the past 70 years. You'll see life-sized celebrities—in wax, of course. There are more than 270:

Marlon Brando, Judy Garland, the crew of Star Trek, Bette Davis, Sylvester Stallone, Michael Jackson and Marilyn Monroe, just to name a few.

This wax museum was opened in 1962, but the tradition of wax sculpture is an ancient one. The Egyptians used a wax process to create deity figures for funeral rites, and the Romans modeled masks and statues made from wax. Movieland likens itself to the famous wax museum in London, England—the one and only Madame Tussaud's.

The figures at Movieland are not just ordinary wax mannequins. The stars are portrayed by duplicating their exact facial and bone structures (taken by measurements from photo sessions with the real person). The hairs are painstakingly implanted strand by strand, and skin tones are matched with uncanny accuracy. If they can't obtain original props, they reproduce them.

The sets where the figures are displayed are recreations from each celebrity's most famous moment, with lighting, animation and sound effects to enhance each scene. Bring your camera, because taking photographs is encouraged.

Movieland Wax Museum is located one block north of Knott's Berry Farm. If you're traveling on either the Santa Ana (I-5) or Riverside (Highway 91) freeways, exit at Beach Boulevard and turn south.

Ripley's Believe It Or Not Museum

7850 Beach Boulevard
Information: (714) 522-7045
Hours: Monday through Friday, 11 a.m. to 5 p.m.;
Saturday and Sunday until 6 p.m.
Admission: Adults, $8.95; seniors, $6.95; children
under 12, $5.95

They call this an "odditorium": a collection of weird and wonderful displays and physical replicas documenting events, people and places from the legendary newspaper serial written and illustrated by Robert L. Ripley (1893-1949). Ripley traveled the world, visiting more than 200 countries in search of the bizarre. He was dubbed the "Modern-day Marco Polo." Whether it was eight-legged pigs or a man with double pupils in each eye, Ripley followed the tale to its source and retold these strange and freakish stories in newspaper cartoons. He entertained millions of readers for decades.

The museum that bears Ripley's name offers a variety of subjects: the "Fiji mermaid," the "Chinese Shrunken Head," a size 36D shoe made for the world's tallest man—and these are the believable ones!

This 10,000-square-foot museum is located across the street from the Movieland Wax Museum, just one block north of Knott's Berry Farm. You can find it easily by taking either the Santa Ana Freeway (Highway 91) or Riverside Freeway (Highway 91) and taking their Beach Boulevard exits south.

Shopping

California Marketplace/Mrs. Knott's Chicken Dinner Restaurant

8039 Beach Boulevard
Information: (714) 827-1776
Restaurant: (714) 220-5080

Across the street from Independence Hall and adjacent to the main gate of Knott's Berry Farm are more than 20 restaurants and shops gathered in the California Marketplace. It's convenient to stroll and shop for gifts because you don't have to pay admission to the park itself. The main attraction of the marketplace is Mrs. Knott's Chicken Dinner Restaurant, an institution in Buena Park since the Great Depression. Mrs. Knott's opens at 7 a.m. for breakfast, but the California Marketplace is open from 10 a.m. to 9 p.m. daily. There is free parking along Grand Avenue off Beach Boulevard.

Dining

In-N-Out Burgers

7926 Valley View (and other Southern California locations)

In-N-Out is a Southern California institution, some 50 years old and still family owned. Burgers, fries and shakes are served up the way they ought to be made. In-N-Out also has the most efficient drive-up of any fast-food chain. The menu is so brief that making up your mind is pretty easy, especially when the aroma of grilled onions provides mouth-watering motivation. Vegetarians, be warned (although they will be happy to make you a burger with no meat — just ask for it "protein style").

All In-N-Outs have walk-up service, but for most customers, the only way to order is from behind the steering wheel. The service is always friendly and they even give you a place mat to put in your lap as you eat your meal in your car. If only they still made "woodies."

Thai Nakorn

8674 Stanton Avenue
Information: (714) 952-4954
Hours: Sunday through Thursday, 10:30 a.m. to 10 p.m.;
Friday and Saturday until 10:30 p.m.

Here is good Northern Thai food—some of it incredibly spicy—at reasonable prices. The recipes are made for Thai palettes, not American ones. I always test a Thai restaurant by ordering pad thai, a wonderful noodle dish with a sweet, tangy flavor; the noodles should melt in your mouth. If you want to do your sinuses a favor, try the hot-and-sour soup with shrimp (seasoned with good stuff like lemon grass, cilantro and chili powder). If this doesn't clear your head, nothing will. People unfamiliar with Thai food should try the Thai iced tea. It's a sweet drink, almost like a milk shake, with a flavor resembling butterscotch. This goes down well after a particularly spicy dish.

Cypress

Cypress is a small community near the border separating Orange County from Los Angeles County. In rancho days, it was grazing land for cattle; in the 1890s, sugar beets were the big crop and a sugar factory was built (first in nearby Los Alamitos and then moving to Cypress) that employed more than 400 people. Dairy farming was also abundant in this region. When the Pacific Electric Line was built from Santa Ana to Watts in Los Angeles in 1906, a stop was put in Cypress (called "Waterville" back then because of the numerous artesian wells in the area).

Eventually, much of the land was subdivided into small ranches, and the lots were popular with oil workers who labored either in Huntington Beach or Brea. The town was originally incorporated in 1956 as Dairy City, a tribute to the number of dairy farms in the area, but the town residents quickly changed it to Cypress for reasons that are now lost to time and distant memory.

Cypress is home to the Orange County bar that gets my vote as best-named establishment: The Honest Lawyer Pub, "est. 1215," according to the sign outside. It is located in Eastgate Plaza at Chapman Avenue and Valley View.

Outdoors

Cypress Nature Park
4201 Ball Road
Information: (714) 229-6780
Hours: Seasonal, call for latest information

The name says it all: this is a refuge in the midst of suburbia, but it's not a landscaped park with playground equipment and baseball diamonds. It's simply a lush, overgrown, roughly-six acres of grassy and wooded fields where you can walk one of five nature trails and smell the flowers.

Birdwatching is particularly good in this park, which is only closed during winter when a flood-control pumping station within the park is usually kept quite busy taking care of rain and runoff water.

Attractions

Los Alamitos Race Course

4961 Katella Avenue
Information: (714) 995-1234
Admission: $2.25 (parking extra)

Although it bears the name of its neighboring Orange County city, this track is a Cerritos anchor, open nearly year-round for both live and simulcast off-track betting (OTB) from Santa Anita, Hollywood Park, Del Mar and Pomona Fairplex race tracks. On days when thoroughbred racing is featured via OTB, the course opens two hours before the first race (about 10:30 a.m.).

Los Alamitos features two types of live racing, four nights a week, during separate meetings: harness and quarterhorse. I personally prefer the quarterhorse racing. If you've only seen thoroughbreds, the quarterhorse race is the equestrian equivalent of a drag race. When the horses make one mad dash for the finish line, your pulse quickens in a hurry. Harness racing resembles a game of chicken; you usually bet on who will break for the finish line at the very last moment.

Harness racing is held from late January through the end of April, and from late August through mid-November. Quarterhorse racing moves in from May to the end of July, and from mid-November through January. Race days are Wednesday through Saturday, with the first post time at 7 p.m. (the gates open at 6 p.m.). There is early-bird wagering available in the Post and Paddock Room from 9 a.m. to 5 p.m. You must be 18 years of age to place bets. Los Alamitos is on the northwest corner of Walker Street and Katella Avenue.

Fullerton

Fullerton was founded in 1887 and named for a Santa Fe railroad employee who was responsible for routing the train through this area. Like some scenario out of a Hollywood movie, two enterprising brothers named George and Edward Amerige bought 430 acres in the area after they heard about plans to build a railway nearby. They convinced George Fullerton, president of the Pacific Land and Improvement Company, to alter his proposed rail route to include their fledgling town. Their shrewd investment turned a mustard field into one of Orange County's largest cities.

Fullerton in those early days had a lot of packing houses for citrus shipping, and the early workers on the railroad were a rough bunch that was not above gunplay. Fullerton was Orange County's answer to the wild west. The rich oil fields to the east (in what is now Brea) brought more settlers, more businesses and more civic pride.

Like several other historic cities in Orange County, the older downtown district is cleverly concealed by the surrounding suburban morass unless you know how to find it. Take the Artesia Freeway (Highway 91) and turn north at the Harbor Boulevard exit. After passing the obligatory strip of chain stores and fast food outlets, you dip below a railroad overpass and come upon old Fullerton (circa 1920). There are a number of antique and collectibles dealers in and around the area bounded by Commonwealth Avenue, Malden Avenue, Chapman Avenue, and Lemon Street. This is an excellent spot to park your car and stroll around.

As you leave this part of Fullerton, take a short drive around the neighborhood north of Commonwealth Avenue and west of Harbor Boulevard. This old neighborhood is unmistakably from the era of World War II. If you ignore the newer automobiles, you will have the illusion of being in the 1940s. The early California bungalows, old-fashioned street lamps and neighborhood markets remind us of an era before the complete suburbanization of this region during the 1960s.

Farther west on Commonwealth between Dale and Gilbert Streets is the Fullerton Municipal Airport, the oldest and still largest general aviation field in Orange County. The site—originally a hog farm—was chosen in 1927.

Shopping

Many quaint shops are within strolling distance around the city center. The British Grocer (305 N. Harbor, 714-738-0229) in the Villa Del Sol plaza stocks authentic British foods, along with other gifts and souvenirs related to Her Majesty's Empire. Amerage Avenue Antiques, Snob Hill, and The Country Rose are just three of the shops you'll find at 122 N. Harbor; they sell collectibles from the Victorian era to '50s Modern.

Fullerton Market

Wilshire Avenue
Information: (714) 738-5332

This free weekly outdoor bazaar is open Thursdays from 4 to 9 p.m. Located along Wilshire Avenue between Pomona Avenue and Harbor Boulevard, it features stalls selling arts and crafts and food, plus entertainment and a farmers market.

Dining

After shopping in historic downtown Fullerton, you can dine at Mulberry Street (114 W. Wilshire Ave., 714-525-1056) or grab a hero sandwich and a brewsky at the Cheers-like Heroes Restaurant (305 N. Harbor, 714-738-4356). Pete & Tony's Downtown Sports Bar & Grill (102 N. Harbor Blvd., 714-879-7570) features monitors that bring in sporting events from around the country.

Angelo & Vinci's Cafe Ristorante

550 N. Harbor Boulevard
Information: (714) 879-4022
Hours: 11 a.m. - 10 p.m. Sunday through Thursday; until
midnight Friday and Saturday

This is truly an unusual setting. Enjoy some hearty Italian food in this converted marketplace dating from the early 1900s. Owner Steven Peck has transformed this structure into a replica of an Italian marketplace. Old wood barrel trusses, terra cotta tiles and brick merge to create different rooms dedicated to various ancestors from the Old Country and the shops they ran as early immigrants to America. Peck, a one-time actor, maintains a gallery of photos of all the famous actors with whom he worked, and various tributes to his favorites highlight the building. The wine cellar is guarded by some famous Hollywood monsters — it helps the wine age better, maybe?

The Cellar

305 N. Harbor Boulevard
Information: (714) 525-5682
Hours: Tuesday through Saturday, from 5:30 p.m.

For really first-class dining, don't overlook the Cellar in the Villa del Sol plaza. This restaurant serves French cuisine and is renowned for its wine selection. The restaurant itself is subterranean; that is, you walk down below street level to enter the restaurant and dine in style. The wine list is mind-boggling. Best of all, this restaurant has that "hideaway" quality that can be refreshing in the midst of such a huge urban sprawl as northern Orange County.

Steamers Cafe

138 W. Commonwealth Avenue
Information: (714) 871-8800
Hours: Call for performances

This nightspot has become the premiere venue for hearing jazz in Orange County in just a few years of existence. It sports a nice room with good acoustics — that's all music lovers need to know in order to give their seal of approval. Both Southern California jazz artists and major label artists visiting from around the U.S. make appearances here. Jazz fans used to have to travel to L.A. to hear any decent jazz music — not any more. Thanks, Steamers!

Outdoors

Coyote Hills Golf Club

1440 E. Bastanchury Road
Reservations: (714) 672-6800

Fullerton's foothills provide graceful slopes for this excellent course, rated one of the top 200 "service courses" in the U.S. by Golf Digest magazine. PGA veteran Payne Stewart had a hand in designing this course with Cal Olson, and there are waterfalls, bridges and 250 acres of charm. Take the Yorba Linda exit west from the 57 Freeway, turn right on State College to Bastenchury.

Fullerton Arboretum

Associated Road and Yorba Linda Boulevard
Information: (714) 278-3579
Hours: Daily 8 a.m. to 4:45 p.m.

Here is an ecological reserve of native birds and plants, with 76 acres divided into distinct climate zones. This arboretum is relatively new, so it will take some time before it is as lush as others in Southern California. It offers a welcome break from the buildings and roadways on the northeast corner of the Cal State Fullerton campus.

In the middle of exotic fruit trees, a cactus garden, and a riparian zone sits a late 19th-century home. Heritage House was built in 1894 by Dr. George Clark, a physician and coroner. The family home is a fine example of Eastlake-style Victorian architecture. The surroundings, such as the garden and the nearby outhouse, are maintained as they would have been during that era. You may tour the house, but it is by appointment only.

One weekend a year in October, the arboretum sponsors an "arborfest." The volunteer staff demonstrates the living skills of Victorian times. Cider is pressed from apples and you can take a hay ride.

The Fullerton Arboretum also sells inexpensive native plants on weekends (Saturdays 10 a.m. to 4 p.m., Sundays 1 to 4 p.m.). The Arboretum is easy to find: take the Orange Freeway (Highway 57) north to Yorba Linda Boulevard, turn left and left again at Associated Road and follow the signs.

Laguna Lake Park & Equestrian Center

Euclid Street between Lakeview and Laguna Road (just north of Rosecrans Avenue)

A well-kept secret in the foothills of Fullerton is a beautiful little park named for the small lake at its heart. Laguna Lake has lily pads and other colorful flora around its modest perimeter, and pleasant bridle trails circle the lake. Don't have a horse? That's okay, the paths are perfect for strolling too. This is a nice getaway, disguised and waiting for you and your picnic basket.

Fullerton Municipal Golf Course

2700 N. Harbor Boulevard
Information: (714) 871-5141

The course is narrow with much water, and the greens are harder than they look. Fees are $12 to $16 (with senior rates available). Seven days advance registration required.

Craig Regional Park

3300 N. State College Boulevard
Information: (714) 990-0271
Hours: Sunrise to sunset

Craig Park is a sports enthusiast's delight: there are base-ball diamonds, tennis and racquetball courts, volleyball, and wide open green fields covering 124 acres in all. The lake offers fishing for bluegill and catfish, and there are ducks for the children to feed.

Directions: Take the Orange Freeway (Highway 57) to Imperial Highway, head west to State College Boulevard and turn left.

Events and Special Attractions

Vanguard Theater

699-A S. State College Boulevard
Information: (714) 526-8007

This local theater group performs both well-known and more obscure plays year-round, usually on Thursday through Saturday evenings. Holiday was a recent production. Call for current production, showtimes and admission (generally less than $20).

Museums and Galleries

Anthropology Museum
California State University, Fullerton
800 N. State College Boulevard, Humanities Bldg. Rm. 313
Information: (714) 278-2844
Hours: Monday through Friday, 1 to 5 p.m. (when school is in session); Sundays 2 to 4 p.m..
Admission: Free

The CSU Fullerton graduate students maintain this exhibit of artifacts that illuminate the department's current archaeological excavations and research. The exhibits change from year to year. Past themes have been on the indigenous native Americans of Southern California (including displays of basketry, tools, and weapons), artifacts from west African kingdoms, and themed exhibits on such areas of research as skeletal biology.

Fullerton Museum Center
301 N. Pomona Avenue
Information: (714) 738-6545
Hours: Wednesday through Sunday, noon to 4 p.m.;
Thursday until 8 p.m.
Admission: Adults, $3; students, $2; children under 12, $1

This small museum features a rotating schedule of exhibitions on science, history and the arts. The focus is largely on Native American culture (such as "Music of the Maya") and the early colonial period of both North and South America. One exhibition featured reproduction of some unique works by a Peruvian author who lived in the Andes in the early 17th century.

The Fullerton Museum Center—a representative of Spanish Colonial "revival" architecture—is located at the corner of Pomona and Wilshire Avenue just east of downtown, and forms one end of the Thursday-night Fullerton Market. Admission on Market nights is free.

Muckenthaler Cultural Center

1201 W. Malvern Avenue
Information: (714) 738-6595
Hours: Tuesday through Friday, 10 a.m. to 4 p.m.;
Saturday and Sunday, 12 to 4 p.m.
Admission: $2; students and seniors, $1; children under
12 free

This home, built circa 1915, features ornate fireplaces, a circular bronze-and-hardwood staircase, and a glass atrium. This Italian Renaissance-style mansion was donated to the city in 1965 to serve as a cultural center. It currently serves as an exhibit space for many rotating art and craft exhibits, from classic to contemporary. In 1993, a 238-seat outdoor amphitheater was completed to present theatrical productions.

La Habra

La Habra is a quiet suburb that borders L.A. County on the north and Fullerton to the south. "La Habra" is probably a corruption of the Spanish word abra, meaning "gorge" or "canyon." One local historian maintains that the city's name means "pass through the hills," and indeed, La Habra does lie between the Puente Hills and the Coyote Hills in the northwest corner of the county. La Habra is one of the oldest remembered usages of Spanish place names in the county, as this tiny valley was once part of the land holdings belonging to the San Gabriel Mission (in present-day Los Angeles County).

The land in both the mission and rancho days was used mostly for cattle grazing and later sheep herding (the arrival of some Basque settlers were responsible for the switch). Later settlers began planting walnut and citrus trees.

The town took official shape in 1896, when its first post office, general store and grammar school were started. Packing houses for the citrus and walnuts sprang up, as did the Pacific Electric and Union Pacific train depots. La Habra citrus became a big name in California during the early 1900s. Farmers found that avocados grew especially well along the northern foothills (in Los Angeles County, known as La Habra Heights) and soon the Hass avocado was thriving in this region.

Outdoors

La Habra Tennis Center

351 S. Euclid Street
Information: (562) 690-5040
Hours: Monday through Friday, 8 a.m. to 9 p.m.; Saturday
and Sunday, 8 a.m. to 6 p.m.

Twelve outdoor, lighted courts make this one of the largest venues in Orange County for the tennis buff. A well-stocked pro shop and several teaching pros on staff will help you sharpen your game. Take the Artesia Freeway (Hwy. 91) west to Euclid Street and turn north.

Museums

Children's Museum at La Habra

301 S. Euclid Street
Information: (562) 905-9793
Hours: Monday through Saturday, 10 a.m. to 5 p.m.;
Sunday 1 p.m. to 5 p.m.
Fees: $4 for adults; children $2.50

This fine children's museum in Portola Park is housed in a Union Pacific train depot dating from 1923. The depot has been restored to its original glory and is listed in the National Register of Historic Places. A railroad ticket window serves as an imaginative entrance.

Inside, there are many things for children to see: a bee observatory (a working beehive, that is), a model train village operating in the depot's baggage room, and a nature walk where children touch "real" animals (they've been stuffed and mounted by a taxidermist).

Relatively new is an elevated model train track in the reception area. Two trains chug around the room suspended 8-1/2 feet off the floor on a 102-foot-long track. Even though it is not mounted on a traditional table display, the trains run past billboards, houses and other small buildings that are painted on the walls beside the tracks, like backdrops in a movie. The train track has regular crossing gates and flashing lights. The miniature railroad was donated by Lionel Corporation of Michigan, the famous scale-model train maker.

There is a playground and picnic area, and authentic railroad cars sitting on tracks outside. There's even a miniature carousel. Take the Orange Freeway (Hwy. 57), exit at Lambert Road and drive west. Turn right on Euclid.

Dining

The Cat & The Custard Cup

800 E. Whittier Boulevard
Information: (562) 992-6496

Homesick for some English cuisine and atmosphere? Try this attractive restaurant where the Continental cuisine is well-prepared using some distinctive California touches, and there are special dinners where select wines are poured to complement the chef's specialties.

Los Alamitos

In 1896 William Clark, an ex-senator from Montana, bought more than 20 square miles of what was once Rancho Los Alamitos. His intention: to raise sugar beets and process them into refined sugar. The Los Alamitos Sugar Company became the center of this new town, providing work and housing for some 400 people. This company town had all the accouterments of frontier living: bars, a pool hall, and even ladies of easy virtue. The town had such an Old West look to it that a silent western, Bond of Blood, was filmed here in 1919 because there was no better Hollywood set at the time than the real Los Alamitos.

The sugar beet business went bust in the mid-1920s due to a pest infestation. The next major economic boost to the area came from the 1,300-acre Armed Forces Reserve Station that borders Seal Beach. During World War II it was a Naval Air Station, where Navy and Marine fliers were trained in aerial combat. Since then, the location has been variously used by all the armed forces and the California National Guard.

The bid to gain a racetrack during the 1950s failed (neighboring Cypress won instead), and with that lure of gambling lost, Los Alamitos shed the last vestiges of its frontier reputation and moved into the suburban 1960s.

Outdoors

Cypress Golf Club
4921 Katella Avenue
Information: (714) 527-1800, 821-1552

Los Alamitos Race Track is located in Cypress, so why shouldn't Cypress Golf Club be found in Los Alamitos? Go figure... Looking for some twists in your golf game? Try this course designed by Perry Dye, filled with lakes and a different wrinkle from hole to hole. Day, evening and weekend rates are all very reasonable (under $100 for the green fee). The club is located just three miles east of the 605 Freeway on Katella Avenue.

Museums

Los Alamitos Museum

11062 Los Alamitos Boulevard
Information: (562) 431-8836
Hours: Tuesday and Sunday, 2 to 4 p.m.; other days by
appointment

Many of Los Alamitos' residents have lived here for five generations. This location—once the site of the town's volunteer fire department—pays homage to those families who put Los Alamitos on Orange County's map.

Placentia

Nothing typifies Southern California as much as the juxtapositions that abound in Placentia. It is one of several communities where agriculture coexists alongside new commercial developments. Migrants work the fields alongside the Placentia civic center. The golf course has oil wells on it. Turn-of-the-century historic homes sit adjacent to corner shopping centers.

Placentia is loosely translated from Latin as "a pleasant place," an apt name at the turn of the century when this community was mostly just orange groves. A wide array of immigrants—German, Italian, French, English, Polish, Basque, Irish, Canadian, and South American—brought a welcome diversity to this area. One pioneer named George Hinde formed a spiritual colony called Societas Fraterna, where the members were vegetarian—even back then this trend was starting in California.

The orange growers got together in the early 1900s to establish a railroad station for shipping out their crop, and soon the town of Placentia began to take shape. Oil changed the character of Placentia, when the largest "gusher" in California was found in 1921. (Union Oil even named one of its tankers La Placentia in recognition of the town's voluminous output.)

Placentia became a city in 1926. Its "Santa Fe Old Town" is a neighborhood shopping district of several square blocks near Bradford, Chapman and Santa Fe Avenues. Many of the buildings are still undergoing restoration and need more merchants, but several authentic carneceria (grocery stores) and cantinas (restaurants) are open serving Placentia's Hispanic community.

Outdoors

Alta Vista Country Club Golf Course

777 E. Alta Vista Street
Information: (714) 528-1103

This is a private club with a reciprocal program for members of other clubs. Green fees are in the $35 to $45 range (cart extra). More than 6,000 yards of rolling grounds are bordered by homes. There are several out-of-bounds holes. Seven days advance registration required.

Tri Cities Park

2301 Kraemer Boulevard
Information: (714) 993-8232
Hours: Daily 5:30 a.m. to 10:30 p.m.

This city park still has the remnants of an orange grove—once Placentia's raison d'etre. Tri Cities has a large, 10-acre lake suitable for boating and fishing (stocked twice a year with catfish). This park has lots of picnic areas and bike paths. During the summer, concerts at sunset are popular.

Historic

Bradford House

136 W. Palm Circle
Information: (714) 993-2470
Hours: Call for times on guided tours
Fee: Donation

Built around 1890, this was the home of citrus grower Albert Bradford. The house is in the National Register of Historic Places, and it is a typical Orange County version of the Queen Anne style of building. The exterior is dominated by a three-sided porch. Inside are many period furnishings and details. The house is available to for special group events, including wedding receptions.

Directions: From the 57 freeway, take Yorba Linda east to Bradford Avenue and turn left. At Palm Circle, turn right and continue one block past Kramer Boulevard. Parking is allowed on the surrounding streets.

George Key Ranch

625 W. Bastanchury Road
Information: (714) 528-4260
Hours: By appointment only

The George Key home was built in 1898 and is listed in the National Register of Historic Places. The botanical garden and orange grove are indicative of the life-style that gave Orange County its name. Sadly, Orange County's famous citrus groves are mostly gone. The remnants of the symmetrical rows of trees that dot the county are one of the few reminders of this colorful industry.

This house, like the Bradford House, is available for special events and receptions. Call for availability.

Yorba Linda

The name for this community is a grafting of Bernardo Yorba, a prominent land owner, with the word linda, Spanish for "pretty." It is similar to the name of the now-defunct mining town of Olinda just to the north. Yorba Linda is also the birthplace of Richard Nixon, certainly the city's most famous son. A substantial number of Quakers from the Midwest, including Nixon's family, migrated to this part of Orange County.

Richard Nixon, the 37th president of the United States, was born in his parents' Yorba Linda home on January 9, 1913. The family stayed in Yorba Linda for a decade and then moved to Whittier. His birthplace has been restored, and the site was chosen for his presidential library.

Ranching, from Spanish colonial times to the early 1900s, was the principal business in Yorba Linda. Besides livestock, growing produce was important, too—mainly avocados, citrus, tomatoes, and cabbage.

Yorba Linda is the eastern terminus of the Imperial Highway, a 45-mile stretch of roadway that reaches all the way to El Segundo, where Los Angeles International Airport meets the Pacific Ocean. The Imperial Highway Association first planned the route back in 1929, but the last leg wasn't completed until the 1960s. This road that traverses two counties makes for an interesting drive through Southern California's wide array of urban, suburban and industrial communities.

Outdoors

Yorba Linda Regional Park
7400-8100 La Palma Avenue
Hours: 7 a.m to 9 p.m. daily

Bike trails, playgrounds, picnic tables — this park has everything you want when you need to daydream or take the children somewhere to play. There are some lovely artificial ponds that are used for breeding catfish and, naturally, there are plenty of ducks to feed.

Attractions

The Richard M. Nixon Library and Birthplace
18001 Yorba Linda Boulevard
Information: (714) 993-3393
Hours: Monday through Saturday, 10 a.m. to 5 p.m.;
Sunday 11 a.m. to 5 p.m.; open daily except Thanksgiving
and Christmas
Admission: Adults, $5.95; children 8 to 11, $2; children
7 and under, free; seniors and students, $3.95.

Despite the controversial nature of his presidency, there's no denying that this is a beautifully designed museum dedicated to the life of one of America's most famous politicians. Unlike the other presidential museums, this one was built without taxpayer money. The Richard M. Nixon Library showcases the career of Nixon from law school to his days as a congressman, his vice presidential years with President Dwight D. Eisenhower, and later his own two-term presidency. The memorabilia from the campaigns of the 1950s is quite interesting, as is the display of unusual gifts that a president receives (such as a pistol from Elvis Presley). The most fascinating room is a marble hall atrium full of life-size statues of the famous leaders Nixon met. Chairman Mao, Chou En Lai and other world leaders sit or stand, chatting with Charles de Gaulle and Nikita Kruschev in lifelike poses. A high-tech console before the assembled group allows visitors to select one of the subjects by button to hear Nixon's comments about that personality.

The other room you won't want to miss is the one dedicated to the Watergate scandal that toppled Nixon's presidency. The room is a display of photos, documents, and video monitors about the affair, with several stations where you can put on headphones and listen to actual excerpts from one of the infamous tapes. Monitors scroll and highlight the text because the voices on the tapes are so difficult to understand.

The museum also contains a fine replica of the Lincoln Sitting Room, Nixon's favorite room in the White House. After visiting the First Lady's Garden, you may step inside the house Nixon's father built and hear the former president's own voice describe what life was like during his boyhood.

A short film highlighting Nixon's life runs continuously at the library, and a small gift shop sells replicas of political campaign buttons, the usual assortment of knickknacks, and copies of Nixon's many published books and memoirs. Young children might get restless, but if you're interested in American politics in any way, this is a museum and a half.

To find the Richard M. Nixon Library, take Highway 57 north and exit at Yorba Linda Boulevard. Turn east and look for the museum on your left.

Historic

Yorba Cemetery
6749 Parkwood Court (at Woodgate)

When Bernardo Yorba died in 1858, he left instructions in his will for a chapel to be built south of his hacienda, and a cemetery to the north. His home and chapel are gone, but the cemetery survived as the oldest privately established burial ground in Orange County. This also makes it one of the oldest in California. It is located on the lands granted to Yorba in 1834 by the new government of Mexico. It is difficult to find, however, and there's no access to the burial ground; it's locked behind a wrought-iron fence. If you're particularly curious about early California history, you can at least visit this hilltop site by taking the Riverside Freeway (Hwy. 91) east to Imperial Highway. Turn north and then make a right on Esperanza Road. Turn left on Fairlynn Boulevard and then right on Woodgate. The cemetery will be on your left in the midst of a housing tract.

Dining

Main Street Mexican & Italian Restaurant

4902 Main Street
Information: 777-9427
Hours: Monday through Thursday, 11 a.m. to 10 p.m.;
Friday and Sunday, 11 a.m. to 11 p.m.

This simple, family restaurant on the town's original Main Street is also located a few blocks east of the Nixon Library. Notice the Yorba Linda Hardware Store across the street, established in 1927. Yes, they feature both Mexican and Italian food, including their outrageous four-foot burrito. Don't be surprised if you see many folks sitting on benches outside this small eatery; they're waiting for a table.

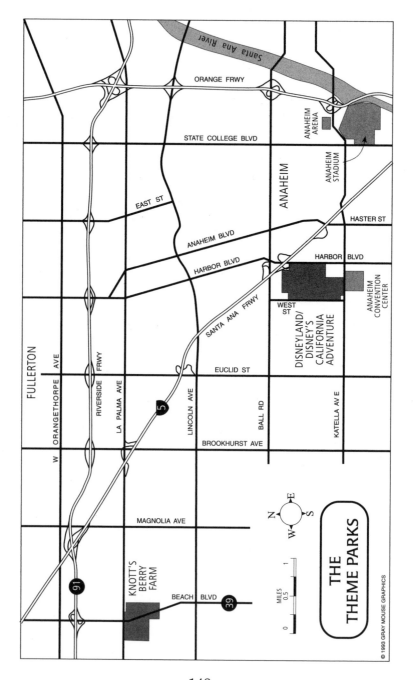

THE THEME PARKS

© 1993 GRAY MOUSE GRAPHICS

148

The Theme Parks

O range County can point with pride to this singular fact: two of the most popular tourist attractions in all of the United States—Disneyland and Knott's Berry Farm—are located right here. Their combined presence attracts several million visitors each year to Southern California. Both parks are more than 30 years old, yet with their unique landscapes, rides and shops, are still bright and lively places to bring the family.

The latest addition to this theme park haven is Disney's California Adventure, opened in February 2001, that features rides and attractions that celebrate the Golden State. California Adventure is adjacent to Disneyland, with the two entrances facing each other.

Disneyland, Knott's Berry Farm and Disney's California Adventures are located in the northern portion of Orange County, in Buena Park and Anaheim. Traffic can get congested on the surface streets bordering these attractions, but there are multiple ways to get to both parks. Years of experience on the part of the parks' owners makes your getting in and out of the parking lots fairly simple.

At each park visitors will find just about everything needed to have a good time. If you plan to stay all day and the sun is shining, those in your group who are sensitive to the sun should keep sunscreen handy and wear a hat, because there are often long lines for the major rides. Wear comfortable shoes, because you'll do a lot of walking.

Knott's Berry Farm, Bigfoot Rapids

Disneyland

Located off the Santa Ana Freeway (I-5) at 1313 Harbor
Boulevard
Hours: Vary with the season; call ahead for the schedule.
During off-season, usually open from 10 a.m. to 6 p.m.
on weekdays, and 9 a.m. to midnight on weekends.
During the peak summer season, open from 9 a.m. to
midnight daily; Main Street opens at 8 a.m., but the rest
of the park is roped off until 9 a.m. Special events can
affect these hours. It's wise to call for hours so you
won't be disappointed if the park is closing at dusk.
Admission: Disneyland sells one-, two- and three-day
passports. A two-day passport is a good deal if you're
staying nearby and are afraid you won't be able to see it
all in one day. Call the park for the current prices; the
passports include unrestricted use of all the rides, but
don't include purchasing gifts and food or the price of
playing arcade games.
Information: (714) 999-4565

Disneyland is not only the world's most famous theme
park; it was also the first and, in my opinion, it's still the
best. Walt Disney had a heckuva' idea when he imagined his
playground for people of all ages amid the orange groves of
Orange County. Disney thought it would be fun to recreate
the worlds and characters of his and others' imaginations,
and the timing was perfect. However, he wasn't ahead of his
time; he was right on time. But with the advent of other
Disney parks (especially Disney World in Orlando, Florida,
and those in Tokyo and France) and the proliferation of the
thrill-ride orientation of the Six Flags chain (such as Magic
Mountain north of L.A.), Disneyland may have lost a bit of
its exclusive feeling. Theme parks are no longer a novelty.

Just try to tell that to the children you see fidgeting (or
being pushed in strollers) at the front gate. They don't call

this The Magic Kingdom for nothing. Step inside Disneyland and you can forget normal space and time. The continuum of fun and sights in the park is unmatched.

One of the many fun things about strolling around Disneyland is the number of live musicians and singers performing throughout the park. A barbershop quartet often sings near the Carnation Ice Cream Parlor. Dixieland can be heard around New Orleans Square. Swing music—the big band sounds from the '40s—is played most every night in the center of the park, where the more mature folks like to dance. Cajun and country can catch you off guard in Critter Country or Frontierland. And just about any hour, you can rock out in Tomorrowland as local bands crank up the volume on a stage that emerges from the ground in front of a dance floor and burger stop.

If you're wondering what rides are a "must see," don't worry—your kids will be way ahead of you. In the early days there were a few rides that became obsolete as time and technology passed them by (the now retired Mission to the Moon comes to mind), yet some rides still linger—usually tie-ins to the Disney film and television legacy that is enjoying a revival on Disney's own cable channel and on videocassette. For example, kids enjoy cavorting on Tom Sawyer's Island, but will probably never connect it with the Disneyfied version of Mark Twain. A few rides are extremely simple and refreshing in this high-tech age, such as Storyland Boats, but that's the great thing about Disneyland: childhood is timeless, and the Disney magic will work again and again on each new generation. Try taking your tyke on It's a Small World and the Casey Jr. Circus Train and you'll see what I mean. Carnivals and county fairs might have the occasional kiddie train ride, but none of them are inside a Magic Kingdom, where Goofy and Minnie Mouse stroll among the crowds giving kisses, hugs and posing for pictures.

There's almost no excuse not to enjoy yourself at Disneyland. The staff works hard to make your stay easier.

There are baby changing rooms, a lost and found area if your parents get lost, a first aid center, stroller and wheelchair rentals, lockers, ATM machines, and every imaginable kind of food concession — today's theme parks now serve bottled water and fresh fruit along with the usual fast food fare.

There are two ways to approach the park, both off the Santa Ana Freeway (I-5). If you take the Harbor Boulevard exit, turn south and the entrance is on the right. If you exit at Katella Avenue, head west for several blocks to Harbor, then turn right (north). The entrance will be on your left.

When you enter the pay parking lot, you'll be directed to a space by attendants. You can then hop one of the colorful trams that whisk arriving and departing guests to the front gate; otherwise, it's quite a long hike. Tram stops are clearly marked. Parking rows are also marked by various Disney characters (so you can remember if you parked in the Timon or Simba lot).

Main Street USA

Once inside the gates, you encounter Main Street USA, Walt Disney's meticulous recreation of a typical American town circa turn of the century. You can proceed directly ahead into the park, or look over your shoulder and board the Disneyland Train that circles the park. If you've been to Disneyland before, this is a quick way to get to New Orleans Square, Fantasyland, or Tomorrowland without wading through the crowds. By the way, there are storage lockers, wheelchair and stroller rentals, and a bank located in the entrance plaza, so take advantage of them. You can always return, via the train, to retrieve items or deposit things in your locker that you've bought.

The storefronts on Main Street are quaint and look old-fashioned (even if the paint jobs are fresh); the sidewalks and street are swept constantly, and the wares and food that you'll find as you stroll down Main Street are enough to keep many adults busy all day. Children like to hop on the fire truck or horse-drawn buggy that run continuously up and down the street toward the center of the park (especially handy when your feet get tired—and they will get tired). If you arrive early enough before the crowds, or linger in some of the alleys adjacent to Main Street, listen closely and you'll hear various sounds and old-time music emanating from the recreated businesses located upstairs above the real gift shops.

Unless you are among the first to arrive at the park in the morning, don't bother to make a headlong rush to the most popular attractions like the Matterhorn or Splash Mountain—too many folks are there already. There will be plenty of time to stand in those lines. Relax, take your time, and let yourself browse down this street and slip into the Disneyland mood. The one exception is to make reservations at the Golden Horseshoe Jamboree, where you'll see an excellent old-time revue. Only the first show is first-come, first-served. This is also the venue for a new show featuring Woody and Jessica from *Toy Story 2*.

In general, the east side of Main Street (on your right as you head into the park) has the pricier boutiques and collector's merchandise, while the large Emporium in the first shop on the left has the T-shirt and stuffed animal action. The portrait studio, about halfway down Main Street, is a nice place to get a silhouette of yourself (hand cut while you wait and suitable for framing). Several times a day, a parade rolls along Main Street USA. When you see some of Disneyland's many minions putting up the ropes along the curb, it's time to pick your viewing spot. There will be a large crowd, so don't wait too long. The parades vary in theme depending upon the time of year or the timing of a special Disney anniversary or new movie.

Baby services with places to change your infant or prepare a formula are located at the end of Main Street just shy of the entrance to Tomorrowland. Diapers are available in case you run out. There's a first aid center at the end of E. Plaza Street, right off Main Street.

Tomorrowland

The future always fascinated Walt Disney, and he hired a lot of creative folks to help bring futuristic visions into reality. In the 1950s, when Disneyland was built, the future looked a whole lot different than it does now. Shrinking to the size of an atom or traveling to the moon (both were premises of popular attractions) are almost naive notions these days compared to new concepts like "virtual reality" that are changing technology every day. Disney's interest in the future was allowed even greater expression at Disney World's Epcot Center in Orlando, Florida. But here, in the original Tomorrowland, before it received its multimillion dollar facelift, the future had become considerably less exotic. Ironically, it had aged.

In 1998, Tomorrowland experienced the largest single renovation in the park's history. The theme of the area now reflects ways that the future has been *imagined* in the past, with motifs inspired in part by the visions of Jules Verne and H.G. Wells. The concept is not 100% successful, but it is a definite improvement over the quaint version of tomorrow as originally conceived.

The entrance to this section of the park is now dominated by huge, copper globes known as the **Astro Orbitor**, an updated version of the old rocker jets. Riders go round and round, up and down, in two-seaters, controlling the height of their vehicle with a joystick. I like it for the view you get of the park. This is great fun if you're pretending to "dogfight" with your friend directly ahead of you.

Star Tours, the Disneyland collaboration with George Lucas (creator of the *Star Wars* films), is a must. To know how this ride works would spoil the fun for first-timers. It's deceptively simple, and never fails to get people laughing and whooping. You are taken on a passenger shuttle to the moon of Endor (where the Ewoks live). This ride is supposed to be a simple tour, but, well, things sort of happen . . . . Waiting for this ride is made easier because you zigzag through the docking terminal, where R2-D2 and C-3PO are repairing a Star Tours shuttle, bickering the whole time. Scenes of other Star Tours that are available are flashed on a large projection screen. And boarding information is given in several Star Wars languages.

Space Mountain is a terrific roller coaster in the dark, a feature that I suspect is part of its continuing popularity. The only thing you can see while inside the mountain are swirling galaxies, comets and stars, and the space car you ride in sort of glows in the dark as if lit by black light. The drops inside Space Mountain are not big, but watch out for those hairpin spirals. The ride has been improved with amusing TV programs from the future broadcast over monitors in the waiting area, and an outrageous soundtrack provided by Orange County surf music legend Dick Dale that accompanies you on your journey.

Captain Eo, the 3-D space/dance video that starred Michael Jackson, has been retired to make way for *Honey, We Shrunk the Audience,* a 3-D takeoff on the popular series of Disney movies featuring comic actor Rick Moranis. Ex-Monty Python Eric Idle is also featured as host of a *faux* inventors awards ceremony where the guest of honor is the tardy-but-well-meaning Moranis. It would spoil the special effects to tell more of the story, but let's just say that before you exit the theatre you will have experienced what it's like to be reduced to the size of a bug. Don't worry, the perils are all very humorous (unless you have a phobia about mice—you've been warned).

The Tomorrowland **Autopia** is a popular pretzel-turning course for small motor vehicles that kids and adults can drive safely because they're restricted to a winding track with a raised center divider that keeps the cars from straying too far. Kids can control the speed of the car. Sometimes these simpler rides that recreate the adult world give kids the biggest charge. It has been upgraded by combining it with the old Fantasyland Autopia, lengthening the ride. The roadside has also been spruced up with novel traffic billboards, and brand-new cars have the distinctive personalities and fluorescent colors of those talking cars seen in the popular Chevron gasoline commercials.

Innoventions, a multimedia museum of sorts where live demonstrations and interactive exhibits show off innovative technological advances, is fine for young people who might benefit from its educational theme.

One way to exit Tomorrowland without backtracking to Main Street is to board the **Disneyland Railroad** on its way to the **Primeval World** — a place where dinosaurs still roam unhindered by modern man (neat trick, that). Your train manages to leave the world of 65 million years ago without a problem, and soon you'll find yourself back at the Main Street station.

Adventureland

This section of the park gives visitors the feeling that they're in a strange marketplace in some exotic foreign country. The concept has been kept fresh by adding hipper merchandise, a great steel drum band that entertains visitors from the rooftop of one shop, and the addition of the **Indiana Jones Adventure.** You accompany the intrepid archaeologist in a runaway jeep that is headed for decidedly dangerous places. Thrills and chills are abundant in this indoor ride — watch out for those poison darts! The wait for this ride is enhanced by great set pieces from Jones' archaeological dig uncovering a vanished civilization of ambiguous origins, including cryptic pictographs carved into rock and temple walls. A vintage 1930s newsreel describes the mysterious temple that you will visit.

The **Jungle Cruise** is one of the first and undeniably the corniest ride in all of Disneyland, yet it still packs them in. Why? Because the lame jokes told by the jungle boat guides have taken on a life of their own, refined over time by the young men and women who pilot you down these dangerous waters. Their pun-laden patter is the real star of this adventure. Your boat glides through a lush, tropical jungle where head-hunting natives, ferocious wild animals and water-spouting hippos constantly remind you of the wisdom of keeping "your hands and arms inside the boat." The clueless visitors to this harsh, unforgiving rainforest — depicted by animatronic figures onshore — are silly stereotypes from a simpler time when Americans' knowledge of the jungle world was limited to old Tarzan movies. But everything is so good-natured that it isn't offensive. Beware: your boat's pilot may need to shoot a hippo that gets too close, so be prepared. Best part of all, this may be the only theme park ride in the United States that shows visitors the "back side of water."

Other attractions in Adventureland: the **Enchanted Tiki Room**, with its comical show of singing birds (robot birds, that is) and winking totems, and **Alladin's Storytime**. I just enjoy touring the shops while listening to the live steel-drum band that cooks up some great Jamaican melodies.

The former Swiss Family Robinson Treehouse is now the revamped home of **Tarzan,** the one depicted in the Disney megahit motion picture. Ever wonder how the King of the Jungle lived? This little self-guided tour should answer all your questions, and it shows you glimpses of scenes from the movie as well.

New Orleans Square

In New Orleans Square you will find one of the most popular rides in Disneyland: **The Pirates of the Caribbean.**
Pirates is a "have to" ride: every time you come to Disneyland,
you have to ride it. You are sure to spot something you missed
the last time. Its charm comes from its glamorous depiction
of pirate life, created via the animatronic technology Disney's
engineers pioneered and perfected in the 1960s. Life-size
mannequins stuffed with electronic and hydraulic wizardry
wink, talk and sing. Pirates is not designed to get you wet,
although, as you take off into the bayou evening on your boat,
beware of that first drop—if you're in the front of your boat,
people have been known to get wet (and brag about it later).
Pirates of the Caribbean has some magnificent set pieces that
look terrific: a burning New Orleans, a ship laying siege to a
fortress (with cannonballs whizzing past and just missing
your boat), and a carousing crew of shipmates turned loose
in town.

When you first cruise into the attraction, you'll gently
slip past the Blue Bayou, one of the fancier restaurants in
Disneyland. The ambiance is provided by the chirping crick-
ets and dancing fireflies that are part of the Pirates ride. The
illusion is of dining outside on a bayou evening. (Alas, they
don't take reservations, so expect to wait for a table.)

The other significant attraction in New Orleans Square
is the **Haunted Mansion**, which, if you've seen it before,
lacks the element of surprise after all these years. However,
if you've never been inside, the stunts are clever even by
today's jaded standards—and little kids still get scared at
the beginning when the House exit conveniently disappears.
The ghost host tour guide offers visitors his own exit, but no
one has taken him up on it yet. After walking the first hall-
way, everyone piles into a "doom buggy" for the rest of the
Haunted House tour. I can never decide which effect I like

best: the talking head in the crystal ball, or the ghosts that suddenly decide to hitchhike with you.

Don't stroll through New Orleans Square too quickly, for the shops in the French Quarter are a nice break from the hectic pace that is often the result of a day at Disneyland. Take a moment to browse. While the kids are on **Tom Sawyer's Island** in Frontierland, check out the Disneyland Art Gallery above the Pirates of the Caribbean. It's an interesting exhibit and easy to miss — look for the curved staircases on either side of Pirates and you'll see a sign and landing indicating its location. The exhibits inside vary with time. (For example, during the Tomorrowland renovation, visitors could view architectural renderings and concepts of how the future would be reinterpreted by the Disney brain trust.)

Need more time to relax? Sit down with a mint julep and listen to a Dixieland band. Better still, hop onto the **Mark Twain** paddlewheel boat as it travels the "Rivers of America" and see if you can spot your youngster bouncing across the pontoon bridge on Tom Sawyer's Island.

Frontierland

Frontierland and New Orleans Square are hard to separate; they somewhat blend together. The Rivers of America opposite New Orleans Square is an unofficial marker of sorts. Here you can see the sailing ship *Columbia*, the *Mark Twain* paddlewheeler, or walk back toward the park's central square. Frontierland has a **Shootin' Arcade** and the **Golden Horseshoe** saloon.

This area of the park becomes packed after dark in anticipation of Disneyland's after dark triumph called **Fantasmic!** This live multimedia show features an amazing combination of lights, music, special effects and performers who pass before your eyes on the Rivers of America. Huge Disney characters are projected onto a wall of water, producing some amazing effects. Mickey Mouse, in his guise as the

Sorcerer's Apprentice (from *Fantasia*), delivers these visions of his imagination from Tom Sawyer's Island. He is interrupted by the forces of evil, with whom he must do battle. In the finale, Mickey faces off with the huge dragon from *Sleeping Beauty*. The show is scheduled twice daily during the summer, and on weekends only during off season. There's no extra charge for Fantasmic!, but getting a good spot can be difficult if you don't pick one early.

Before we leave Frontierland, let's mention its only thrill ride: **Big Thunder Mountain.** This is a "runaway" train ride that flies through a mountain being mined for precious ore. This ride is not terrifying, just fun, but do this one before you eat!

Critter Country

One of the more popular rides, **Splash Mountain** is an unusual hybrid. It's a flume ride through a mostly bucolic setting dominated by characters from Uncle Remus' *Song of the South,* who serenade you until your flume approaches the moment everyone stands in line for: the five-story drop. If you think this looks vertical from outside the attraction, wait until you ride it. It is vertical! It's a quick but effective rush. Note: You will get wet on this ride. Really wet. Of course, for a lot of people that's part of the fun, especially on a hot Southern California summer day.

Critter Country is also home to those fun-loving Country Bears and their **Country Bear Playhouse,** featuring more animatronic characters performing an old-fashioned music hall show featuring singalong songs. The wait between shows is not long, and this is a nice way to rest the feet between standing in lines for the big rides.

This area of the park is also where you can usually see and be seen with Pooh, Tigger and Eyeore, the beloved characters from the classic A.A. Milne *Pooh* stories.

Fantasyland

King Arthur's Carousel, the centerpiece of Fantasyland, is a lavish merry-go-round that everyone enjoys. The fairy tale rides in Fantasyland seem to be favorites with young and old alike. I still like to go on **Peter Pan**, flying high above London to Never-neverland. And notice the always-busy **Mr. Toad's Wild Ride** (watch out for that train!). **Snow White and the Seven Dwarfs** shortcuts the story quite a bit, but the little ones won't know the difference, and **Alice in Wonderland** does have those caterpillars for cars. Alice seems like the longest ride, and it includes everything from Lewis Carroll's classic, from the Queen of Hearts to the Cheshire Cat.

These "fairy tales come-to-life" are the rides that parents take with their young ones on their laps, pretending that the ride is strictly for kids. Bringing these famous fairy tales to life via rides-in-the-dark was a stroke of commercial genius 40 years ago, and it's still working.

The shops in Fantasyland are particularly charming, considering that they have Cinderella's castle as a lovely backdrop. You can cross the moat directly in front of the castle, or enter Fantasyland from side entrances connected to Tomorrowland and Frontierland. If you walk across the moat, this is one of the best picture spots in the park. Notice the live birds that take advantage of the water here. (By the way, you can walk through a portion of the castle on an unguided tour of sorts; just look for the entrance to your right as you pass through the castle gate.)

The main attractions in Fantasyland are the aforementioned **Storybook Land Boats, Casey Jr. Circus Train**, and **Dumbo**, where you ride inside a flying elephant. There's also the **Mad Hatter's Tea Party**, which is great if you love being dizzy. You climb into giant tea cups that spin around as fast as you can make them go by using a wheel in the middle of the cart while the whole platter of teacups revolves as well.

It's a Small World is certainly a must-see attraction, especially if you have young ones. Its charm is in its universal brotherhood theme that always bears repeating. The ride features hundreds of children from around the world, in traditional costumes, singing the famous theme song while riders glide past in small boats. Don't miss viewing the amazing clock outside this attraction, that sounds the time every quarter hour; it marks the hour with a special parade of animated characters. Holiday note: Disneyland began a tradition of jazzing up this attraction during the month of December with Christmas decorations, and a change in the soundtrack to include "Jingle Bells."

The **Matterhorn,** located between Fantasyland and Tomorrowland, is the granddaddy of Disneyland rides. One of the original thrill rides, the Matterhorn is still a major favorite. Riders "bobsled" down the mountain, darting in and out of its caverns for brief glimpses of the park before whipping into another hair-raising turn. This ride is downright spooky at night. And what's making that ominous growl you hear as you ascend the mountain's interior? Could it be the Abominable Snowman, Mr. Yeti himself?

Toon Town

Disney's association with W*ho Framed Roger Rabbit?* and various other cartoons throughout the decades provided the inspiration for this park-within-the-park: Toon Town. This small-scale town recreates the elastic world inside cartoons, with lots of fun things for young children to see and do. One of them is **Gadget's Go-Coaster,** a fast ride scaled down for smaller riders. Toon Town also has a trolley, talking manhole covers and other delightful sights. Toon Town is behind It's A Small World.

The wackiest fun is on **Roger Rabbit's Cart-Toon Spin**, a boisterous updating of Mr. Toad's Wild Ride, where your out-of-control toon taxi careens around various explosive hazards and toonish pranks. Smaller children are liable to be frightened on this one, because it's quite jerky and the volume is loud — leave this for the older kids who will enjoy the noise, and spinning the car around to their heart's content.

Toon Town is also the home of Mickey and Minnie Mouse, and you can line up to meet and greet the famous pair at their own separate houses. Have your photo taken with them, and see the type of decor each favors. Minnie's kitchen is particularly fun, with its interactive kitchen appliances, while Mickey's house is fashioned as a living museum to his cinematic legend.

Special Events

Disneyland always has a parade of some kind, both during the day and after dark. If you're anywhere near Main Street, you can't miss them. To get a choice spot, however, I recommend standing next to It's A Small World. This is at the north end of the parade route away from Main Street. There are fewer people mulling about so you can usually get right up front for a good view. The parades usually pump up the latest animated movie from Disney Studios, but they are always charming, produced with the same polish of a Broadway musical. Performers dance and sing from high atop the floats, and right in the street where they often approach the littlest spectators for some Disney interaction.

If you're at Disneyland after dark (and I highly recommend it), you'll enjoy one of the best fireworks displays in Orange County, always held around 9 p.m. Disnleyland recently upgraded the entire show with new state-of-the-art fireworks, and it is breathtaking. The nightly descent of Tinkerbell from the Matterhorn to Cinderella's castle just prior to the fireworks show is the kickoff, and it's a spectacular stunt in itself.

Back on Main Street near the park's entrance, be sure to take your kids to see **Great Moments With Mr. Lincoln**, located to your right just inside the main entrance. The park almost retired Honest Abe a few times, but veteran fans of this attraction were so outraged at the prospect of losing the Great Emancipator that their protests convinced the folks at Disneyland to reconsider. Don't miss this inspiring exhibit, where you will see and hear Lincoln move while he speaks the Gettysburg Address (without using any cue cards).

Lodging

The Disneyland Hotel

Location: 1150 W. Cerritos Avenue
Information: Call (714) 956-MICKEY

Many folks like to stay at the Disneyland Hotel, just five minutes away from the park entrance via the Disneyland Monorail. (This is one Disneyland ride that should have been adopted by cities long ago as a means of public transportation.) The hotel is loaded with amenities, including its own 60 acres of shops, restaurants, and a new super aquatic play area called "Never Land," modeled after the lagoon from the movie "Peter Pan." Amid the Misty Mountains is a 100-foot-long water slide that plunges into the lush lagoon pool. Palm trees and the ever-popular Hangman's Tree accent this tropical playground. Food is available from the Goofy's Kitchen restaurant or Hook's Pointe & Wine Cellar.

It goes without saying, but I'll say it anyway: avoid Disneyland during the height of the summer (too hot, too crowded) and during any major holiday. Visit on a weekday, and the lines will be shorter and you'll be able to see more of the attractions without waiting in lengthy lines.

Disney's California Adventure

Hours: Varies with seasons and holidays; call ahead for operating hours
Admission: Adults: $43, $33 for children
Information: (714) 781-4565, or www.disneyland.com

Visitors to the Disneyland Resort now have a choice: they can visit the grand old matron of theme parks, Disneyland, or they can visit Disney's California Adventure, a brand new park with the Golden State as its theme. This was an unprecedented expansion in Disney's long history in Southern California, and I was prepared to be skeptical of the results. But I admit that within minutes I was charmed by this tribute to my home state.

One conspicuous feature is that at various points inside the park there are California-based food companies highlighting how they make their products, as well as providing a great way for visitors to sample their finished products. Plaques and exhibits dot the park throughout, revealing small tidbits of California history and tradition. Many of the buildings are scale replicas of famous structures from San Francisco and Los Angeles, or homages to legendary places such as Monterey's Cannery Row.

You enter the park by walking between the letters CALIFORNIA, a simple alphabet sculpture standing 12-feet tall. Just inside the turnstiles are a pair of beautiful murals depicting some of the most familiar landmarks, wildlife, and natural wonders of the state. This motif is a foreshadowing of what you will see inside, and the designers readily admit they wanted to achieve the effect of two giant postcards. The Golden Gate stretching between them is, in this case, a literal entry way to the main portion of the park.

California Adventure is divided into three main theme areas: Paradise Pier, a model of the great seaside amusement

parks that dotted Southern California's coastline during the
first-half of the 20th century; the Hollywood Pictures Backlot,
a recreation of the movie mecca's golden age; and Grizzly
Peak Recreation Area, aptly named for the numerous outdoor adventures found in California. There is also an area
called Condor Flats, with shops and exhibits inspired by one
of the state's other great industries: aerospace.

Just inside the main entrance — past the first gift shops
— a giant disk of the sun that reflects the light from its larger
namesake in striking ways throughout the day sits atop a
wonderful wave fountain. It's an elegant landmark — and
provides an obvious rendezvous spot that visitors often need
when friends or family members decide to wander off in different directions for a few hours.

Paradise Pier

Straight ahead is Paradise Pier, dominated by the profile
of the California Screamin' roller coaster, situated next to a
boardwalk-lined lake. Midway games, ice cream, and corn dogs
are part of the ambiance. Even more fun is the roller coaster
track built directly overhead, so you can't help but hear the
screams of delight as riders enjoy the view from above. The
sound of California-themed music (remember the Beach
Boys?) plays throughout the area.

The state-of-the-art coaster called California Screamin'
is one smooth ride. The variety of steep plunges, sharp-angled
turns, and plenty of track should keep any coaster aficionado
happy. The cars dive into terrific banked turns and a 360-
degree loop around the silhouetted face of Mickey Mouse (at
night, a circle of lights race along the same silhouette as each
series of cars flips through). At several points the train passes
through partially-enclosed tunnels to accentuate the aural
effects of this ride. At over a mile in length, the ride is more
than three minutes long. A soundtrack of special music is on
board to enhance the experience. I'd give this coaster an "A"
rating.

The pretty Jumpin' Jellyfish ride is actually parachutes that gently raise and lower you up and down for a nice view of Paradise Pier. It's a fun ride for smaller tykes, or those who like slower, milder ascents. Mulholland Madness is in the tradition of Mr. Toad's Wild Ride. This crazy ride traverses L.A. freeways during a "sig alert" — a traffic jam.

Another ride that dominates the skyline is the Maliboomer, a 180-foot-tall ride that goes straight up. Riders are buckled into seats with their backs to a girder tower before being sent aloft in a matter of seconds. The view of the surrounding community of Anaheim and the Disneyland Resort is spectacular, but this ride is not for those with queasy stomachs. Once the chairs reach the zenith of the tower, they bounce up and down for a few times before finally coming to rest on the loading platform.

A truly old-fashioned carnival ride, the Golden Zephyr takes riders on a spin round and round. The vehicles are gleaming silver rockets and twirl in a circle. The centrifugal force drives your rocket farther away from the center of the ride and out over the lake.

Walk inside Orange Stinger (a hollow orange nearly three stories tall) and seat yourself in an old-fashioned swing. Hang on while the ride lifts and twirls. The hum of a beehive accompanies your quick spin around this giant sphere. The ride is simple and harmless, like the ultimate playground swing with a great view. Suitable for all ages.

King Triton's Carousel is a merry-go-round that complements King Arthur's Carousel in the original Disneyland park. Triton, of course, is the patriarch of that plucky Ariel, the heroine of *The Little Mermaid*. The "horses" are various undersea creatures, and it's a lovely feature along this boardwalk.

An assortment of classic carnival midway games line the boardwalk, and there are plenty of food options. A playground area for smaller children called the S.S. Rustworthy is a nice way to let off steam.

Last but not least, the Sun Wheel is a classic Ferris wheel that is 150-feet tall. The riders' gondolas slide back-and forth along the spokes. At night, the wheel is highlighted with a dazzling light display.

Of all the eateries in Paradise Pier, the Pacific Wharf Cafe, featuring the cuisine of Wolfgang Puck, is the nicest. There's casual dining with a full bar upstairs — that features a great panoramic view of the roller coaster and other rides across the lake. A more elaborate sitdown menu is located downstairs. Upstairs, sample the sushi and Cobb salad. The Pacific Wharf Cafe is one of three restaurants within the park that serve alcohol — a first at Disneyland in Anaheim. Sipping a nice pinot grigio is a pleasant way to pass the time while watching the festivities all around you.

Hollywood Pictures Backlot

Just east of the Sun Plaza lies the world of movie magic, presented as a Hollywood street substituting for Disneyland's Main Street USA. It's a wonderful deception, with palm trees and replicas of real Hollywood buildings, right down to the art deco touches. There are Frank Lloyd Wright block-style edifices, and sly references to the familiar icons of the movies' Golden Age. I was accompanied by someone who was born and raised in Hollywood, and Disney's recreation passed the test of authenticity. At any moment, it looks as if real moviemaking will break out, with swooping camera and sound booms and bright lights wheeled into place for that long shot or intimate close-up.

The Disney Animation Studio is one of the largest attractions of the new park, featuring interactive demonstrations about the art of animation. There is also the Hyperion Theater, a 2,000-seat venue featuring the live stage show "Steps in Time." It's one of the largest buildings in the park and will surely have many uses in years to come.

Another attraction on this backlot is Superstar Limo. It's a tongue-in-cheek drive from Los Angeles International Airport to your very own Hollywood premiere. Celebrities and hangers-on vie for your attention as you pass an assortment of Tinsel Town landmarks. The joke goes further, with a sycophantic agent who smothers you with praise from your limousine's own personal videophone. We all know it's exaggeration, but it's fun nonetheless. If the line is long, you may want to spend your time elsewhere.

MuppetVision in 3-D is an attraction that originally debuted at Walt Disney World in Orlando, so undoubtedly there will be some first-time visitors to California Adventure who have seen it. I had not, but as a fan of the old Muppet Show (Jim Henson's great British-made television show from the mid-1970s), I was hooked right away.

During the show, Statler and Waldorf are in their usual places in an opera box high above stage right, heckling as vociferously as ever. The plot of this movie, a tour through the experimental 3-D research facilities of Muppet Labs, features a cast of crazies: the demented Gonzo; the truly awful vaudeville comic Fozzie Bear; the patriotic and severely proper Sam the Eagle; and of course, Kermit the Frog, who tries in vain to keep the mayhem down to a dull roar. Miss Piggy is the chanteuse of this show, and seeing her in 3-D is certainly a revelation. I never knew that this porcine superstar could water ski.

Places you can eat at the Hollywood Pictures Backlot include the ABC Soap Opera Bistro, where every waiter really wants to act, and a food court called Hollywood & Dine.

Grizzly Peak Recreation Area

The third major theme within California Adventure is the Grizzly Peak Recreation Area, dedicated to the pursuit of fun and wonder in this state's great outdoors. California offers a wealth of gorgeous mountain ranges and redwood forests, starkly beautiful deserts, and sunny beaches. The extremes of snow, surf, and sun are one of California's greatest tourist assets, and Disney has captured the essence of what makes it great to live in or visit our state.

Immediately behind the Sun Court disk at the Park's entrance is the 3-D movie, *It's Tough to be a Bug*, another attraction borrowed from Walt Disney World. Visitors to this attraction will get a bug's eye view of the world.

The Grizzly River Run is a long water-rafting ride, with riders spinning semi-helplessly down a series of rapids and underneath and down waterfalls in the shadow of a large mountain. The mountain is sculpted in the shape of a grizzly bear. It's a ride that appeals to water lovers, which is another way of saying that you will get wet, but you'll have fun in the process.

Bountiful Valley Farm is a real farm and farmer's market. One acre of crops produces products that hold special significance to California agriculture. Date palms, avocado and citrus trees, poppies, and other plants function like a year-round county fair. No wonder California is sometimes called the breadbasket of the U.S.

Another tribute to California agriculture is the Golden Vine Winery. This working wine-making facility displays those precious grapes on the vines and includes a multimedia presentation. A Robert Mondavi-sponsored establishment offers a nice place to relax with a meal that features the local wine varietals.

Your youngsters will love the Redwood Creek Challenge Trail, a place where children dash and climb and skip among lots of cool outdoor structures. While they are busy, you can take in the 20-minute film *Golden Dreams,* a 70mm movie narrated by Whoopi Goldberg. The movie is an historical travelogue about the many people who came to California over the centuries. Just outside the theater is a striking replica of San Francisco's Palace of Fine Arts.

Condor Flats

My favorite ride in the Condor Flats section of the park is Soarin' Over California. The simulated hang gliding ride is a virtual airborne tour of California's wonders. The illusion is cast while you sit in a chair that is hoisted aloft into a curved projection arena. It's impossible to tell how high you are, or where the boundaries of the theater were when you first walked in. The wonders that pass below, above, and around you are accentuated with sound and even the sensation of wind. Yosemite's El Capitan, the Golden Gate Bridge, the Anza-Borrego Desert, and Napa Valley are just some of the beautiful places you'll visit from your aerial perspective. It's a wonderful four-minute experience that is sure to be as popular as the Star Tours or Indiana Jones rides in Disneyland.

Downtown Disney

This new pedestrian mall that connects the two theme parks with the Disneyland Hotel provides an attractive outdoor experience for those who really like shopping. There is a 12-screen theater complex as well as many specialty shops such as the Lego Imagination Center. There are also several nice restaurants and nightclubs: the Rainforest Cafe, the ESPN Zone, the House of Blues, Ralph Brennan's Jazz Kitchen, Y'Arriba Y'Arriba, and Naples Ristorante. While the park's hours will vary with the time of year and holiday season, when I visited Downtown Disney for the first time, the nightclubs were open until 2 a.m.

One of the biggest Disney stores on the planet is located here, conveniently next to the tram stop. The World of Disney is a block-long store at the east end of Downtown Disney. It's like being transported into a Disney catalog. Clothing, eyeglass cases, china, collectible animation cells, and scented candles are just some of the items you can find in this huge store.

Adjacent to Downtown Disney is the new, 750-room Grand Californian Hotel, designed in the Arts and Crafts school of architecture. This new hotel is within the boundaries of the new park, so guests will certainly feel like they have special privileges. Also within walking distance is the Paradise Pier Hotel (formerly the Pan Pacific Hotel), overlooking the park and an ideal place to view the scene at night.

Parking & Directions

To handle the increased traffic and parking needs of two resorts where once there was but one, Disney built the largest parking structure in North America. It's a 10,000-space, six-story edifice on Disneyland Drive near the Ball Road offramp of the I-5 freeway. If you are driving south on I-5, the transition from freeway to a parking space is swift and relatively easy. Walking the length of the structure itself is a bit daunting at first glance, but escalators take you straight to the familiar Disneyland trams, and the trams will have you at the entrance to both parks in less than five minutes. If you're driving north on I-5, the Disney Way transition is not so simple, and you have to make many turns and watch the signs carefully to end up at the same place. My advice is to go straight to Ball Road instead of exiting at Disney Way, so you won't be confused by too many changes in direction.

Knott's Berry Farm

Located at the corner of Beach Boulevard and
Las Palmas Avenue
Hours: open weekdays from 10 a.m. to 6 p.m., and 10 a.m.
to 10 p.m. on weekends.
Information: (714) 220-5200
Admission: $36 for adults, $26 for children and seniors

Knott's Berry Farm was once just that—a berry farm owned by Walter and Cordelia Knott, who moved to Buena Park in 1920. Their reputation for growing the tastiest berries in Orange County brought folks from miles around to patronize their little roadside food stand. Soon Cordelia Knott began selling freshly cooked chicken and pies, and that venture was equally successful. The Knotts had a thriving business in what became known as Buena Park. By the 1940s, Cordelia's kitchen was a popular restaurant.

Walter Knott, who had a fascination with the Old West, had the inspiration one day that people who visited the berry farm might like to see a bit of history recreated. He began with a few buildings made to look like an authentic frontier town. As more buildings were added (some of them were actual old structures brought from other towns), the replica of the Old West became a fixture on Beach Boulevard. Today, it is one of the most visited tourist attractions in America.

The newest addition to Knott's is a 13-acre water park called Soak City U.S.A., located directly across the street from the main Knott's entrance. It's nearly 2 million gallons of fun water slides and tubes will keep the summer heat away all day long (see below).

When you get to Knott's, lockers are conveniently located at the main gate, inside the Ghost Town (just to the left of its main gate), and near the Wild Water Wilderness. Baby stations are outside the main gate next to the first-aid center (behind the Chicken Dinner Restaurant), next to the Wild Water Wilderness schoolhouse and in Camp Snoopy; stroller and wheelchair rentals are available to the right of the main entrance. The lost and found is at the Information Center outside the main gate.

Overall, Knott's Berry Farm has a milder pace and feel than most other amusement parks, making it a nice change for family vacationers. Knott's tributes to Native Americans and Southern California's Hispanic heritage are welcome features of this park, as is Camp Snoopy, the park-within-a-park that caters to younger children. One more important thing distinguishes Knott's from other parks: the preserves. Knott's really does have the best fruit jams and jellies in Orange County, if not in all of California, and that's why visitors buy gift packs to ship to friends and relatives around the world. All in all, Knott's is a landmark well worth the visit.

California Marketplace

The selection of food and kitchen items is plentiful in the Farm Market, located in the California Marketplace. This shopping area is conveniently situated just outside the main gates where visitors can shop without paying admission to the park. There are clothing stores, a candy parlor, a Snoopy shop, and an international gift shop as well. Knott's Chicken Dinner Restaurant has been a fixture here since 1934 when Mrs. Knott herself was doing the cooking.

Ghost Town

Knott's Berry Farm has always appealed to our nostalgia for simpler times. That charm lingers today in the part of the park called the Ghost Town. You can stroll (or push a stroller) down streets with shops and historic displays that pay homage to the West as it really was. You can take a lesson in panning for gold after walking through a dark mine shaft. You can walk into the **Calico Saloon** and watch an old-fashioned dance hall revue featuring such "legends" as Judge Roy Bean and Lillie Langtry. And there's plenty of fun in the outdoor, wild west **Stunt Show** held at scheduled times throughout the day. Look for the times posted at the entrance to the amphitheater.

The big star of Ghost Town is now **GhostRider,** an enormous wooden roller coaster with a mine-shaft-car motif. At its highest point, it is 118-feet high, offering a 108-foot drop that is just the beginning of this two-minute ride through noisy peril. If you like banked curves (a wooden coaster with banked curves, are you kidding me?), sudden plunges, and speeds in excess of 50 miles per hour — hey, knock yourself out. I was fascinated to learn that because the coaster is wooden, it actually offers a smoother ride than steel-based coasters (which are stiffer), but of course, it is a lot noisier. If you like speed, ride later in the day when the sun has had a chance to warm up the entire structure.

Kids will enjoy the **Butterfield Stagecoach** and the **Calico Mine Ride.** For train buffs, there's a beautiful 110-year-old train called the Calico Railway that looks the same today as during its glory years of service in Colorado. The woodwork inside the handsome passenger cars is all original. One word of caution: watch out for the outlaws who occasionally board the train in search of your valuables! The **Timber Mountain Log Ride** is pretty tame by today's thrill ride standards, but it's a pleasing—although not relaxing—way to ride in water, with one nice drop at ride's end where you can enjoy a splash. Cameras trained on each log as it emerges from a mountain cave automatically record your picture in case you want to buy a souvenir at the end of the ride.

Inbetween the rides and the dance hall shows, you'll find many shops featuring Western crafts (great gifts), fashion (something for you) and toys (for the kids). Virtually all the buildings have nooks and crannies with displays about Western life and times, some with authentic Western artifacts. A small school house and church are the real McCoy, both dating back to the 19th century. Elsewhere, a blacksmith demonstrates the skills that were needed to maintain the equipment of the Old West. A weaver works a loom. Cowboys and ruffians saunter about. Knott's Ghost Town is a living museum. You can even talk to an old geezer in the town jail. He knows everybody. Lastly, there's the **Haunted Shack**, one of those weird places where gravity is defied and strange things occur. Young ones can still be wowed with this one.

Indian Trails

Adjacent to the Ghost Town is Indian Trails, a two-acre section of the park opened in 1992 devoted to the art, folklore and lifestyle of the Native American cultures from three regions: the Northwest coast, the Great Plains and the Southwest. Tipis, hogans and other structures depict Indian daily life. It's a nice counterpoint to the old Ghost Town. The landscaping was carefully planned, incorporating a hundred varieties of trees, shrubs and cactus that are indigenous to the three geographic regions represented here.

Notice the 27-foot-high totem pole of incense cedar wood at the Indian Trails entrance. It took two years to carve. The Pacific Northwest tribes are represented by a "big house"; the Southwestern section has two Navajo hogans and some adobe dwellings; the Great Plains area contains real canvas tipis with authentic paintings representing various tribes.

Storytellers and dancers appear periodically to teach and entertain visitors in the ways of our Native American ancestors. Fine Indian crafts (real, not imitations) are on sale in the Bottle Shop, a fascinating building that was made with thousands of bottles stuck through its walls.

You shouldn't leave Indian Trails or Ghost Town without having your picture taken, wearing suitable Western garb and posing with your dance hall sweetheart. The tintype look of these photos make them a popular souvenir.

Wildwater Wilderness

Ghost Town has always been the centerpiece of Knott's, and it really is a convenient way to travel back in time to America's 19th century. But both Ghost Town and Indian Trails were designed during a simpler era, before video games and ultra fast roller coasters. If your offspring haven't grown up with Lone Ranger reruns and other Western favorites, you might find the older kids need a little modern excitement.

Bigfoot Rapids is designed to give visitors the thrill of riding white water rapids without the danger. Take my word for it, you get wet, really wet. On a hot summer day, kids can't wait to get on this ride.

Riders sit inside large, round, free floating rafts (no underwater tracks here). It's a bit like riding a giant inner tube. The rafts drift, spin and shoot through the large water course, bouncing up and down. It's a ride that provides a modest thrill for those people who shun roller coasters because they're afraid of heights. But beware those waterfalls! As the rafts drift beneath certain rock overhangs, buckets of water cascade down on the helpless rafters. The wet factor of this ride is so high that Knott's does a bang-up business just outside the ride's exit, selling underwear, socks and sweat pants to those silly enough to go on the ride unprepared. (You can store a change of clothes in one of the handy park lockers.)

Before leaving this part of the park, be sure to check out the **Wilderness Nature Center.** Park rangers show off some fascinating creepy crawly creatures and will explain many things about the natural world.

The Roaring '20s

Northwest of the Wild Water Wilderness and Ghost Town is the Roaring '20s, a part of the park that is more like a traditional carnival midway. You'll have ample opportunity to try to win that stuffed animal playing games of skill. The smaller rides have names like **Soapbox Racers, XK-1** and **Whirlpool**. There's an arcade full of all the latest games (they should call this the Roaring '90s arcade) and, yes, there are bumper cars.

The most unusual ride in the Roaring '20s is probably **Boomerang**. The premise is clever: riders board a roller coaster with harnesses that hold you in place while you are taken *backwards* up a vertical incline and then released. The train shoots through two 180-degree loops and a couple of maddening spirals before zooming up another incline . . . and then you have to repeat the experience in reverse! The ride is definitely not for the faint-hearted. During the day it is scary enough, but at night the line grows appreciably longer as riders seek the total disorientation of flying upside down with few points of reference.

The **Skyjump Parachutes** are just a few steps away from the Boomerang, if you want a chance to feel like you've jumped out of a plane with a parachute. One or two people step inside a cage (a metal basket, that is, with no top) and are pulled straight up to the top of a tower that offers a spectacular view of Orange County. You pause for perhaps a second, and then the cage is released and riders plummet down rapidly, the parachute above the cage opening in a colorful but entirely fake attempt to slow your descent (the parachutes are pretty to look at though). Your cage is brought to a safe halt every time, thankfully, many feet from the ground. The ride is brief, and is like riding a glass elevator without the glass, or even a building. If you are afraid of heights, skip this one.

Still not fast or high enough? Well now you can put your heart to the ultimate test: a plunge on the aptly-named **Supreme Scream**. Riders are strapped into open seats that are then raised up the outside of a 30-story tower (or 252 feet, to be exact). After an agonizing pause to "enjoy" the view, riders are flung straight down (G force: 4.0 maximum) until just before hitting bottom, where the chairs bounce up again and the experience is repeated a couple of times, bouncing with diminishing height. The best way to describe it is this way: imagine you're a window-washer outside a skyscraper, and your platform suddenly plunges earthward. If you are afraid of heights, this will either cure you or send you packing to the funny farm.

For those with milder tastes, **Kingdom of the Dinosaurs** is a ride that carries visitors into a crazy scientist's time machine ("by accident," of course) and suddenly you're 65 million years younger in the era of dinosaurs. It's slightly campy, in keeping with the Roaring '20s theme. The dinosaurs move, growl, hiss and glower in the dark, and visitors avoid predators and molten lava long enough to travel back to our time and into the adjacent gift shop, featuring real fossils on display and replicas of famous dinosaur finds.

Across from the Bumper Cars and next to the Hollywood Beanery (try the fish 'n chips) is **Knott's Good Time Theater.** This is an indoor venue that features seasonal entertainment, from rock 'n roll oldies shows in summer to ice follies in winter. The Theatre is not used year-round, so check at the park entrance to find out what is on tap.

Lastly, the **Magic and Sports Shop** has some fun gifts. Sports memorabilia and trading cards have become a big business these days, and Knott's has wisely chosen not to ignore this trend. The Roaring '20s theme makes it fitting that Babe Ruth and other early baseball greats should be found in this shop.

Fiesta Village

Walking east from the Roaring '20s, visitors arrive at Fiesta Village, a celebration of Southern California's Hispanic heritage. The buildings pay homage to the architecture that is so closely associated with this area, and the food is Mexican, naturally. Entertainment is regularly showcased in Fiesta Plaza, where you might hear everything from mariachis to distinctly un-Hispanic gospel music. There are more fun rides such as the **Tampico Tumbler**—short and simple vertigo inducers that might help work off some of those calories you're bound to take in after grazing through the many food stops in the park.

Jaguar is a nice roller coaster, more modest in scale than GhostRider but a swift and twisting ride nonetheless, gliding along a steel track that meanders around portions of the park and the Toltec-style temple from which riders depart. This is a good break-in roller coaster for those who aren't certain if speed is their favorite thing.

Camp Snoopy

Emerging from Fiesta Village you come to Camp Snoopy, a mini-amusement park for the youngest family members. The **Grand Sierra Railroad** choo-choos around Reflection Lake and over a draw bridge that is pulled up every time a Paddle Boat goes by. You can catch the **Paddle Boat** at the dock in Camp Snoopy. For kids who want to "fly" a vintage WWI Sopwith Camel like Snoopy, there's the **Red Baron** ride. There is also a balloon ride, a pontoon bridge, a tiny tot roller coaster called **Twister**, the Rocking Horse toy shop, the **Bear-y Tales Playhouse**, and a petting zoo. Snoopy has an "Animal Friends" show featuring wild animal education. There's also the **Inventor's Workshop** with a rare collection of inventions by Thomas Edison and hands-on displays of scientific principles such as electromagnetism.

Knott's Soak City U.S.A.

Hours: 10 a.m. - 8 p.m. daily; noon - 8 p.m. weekends;
June through September
Admission: $21.00 adults, $14.95 ages 3-11;
($12.95 pre-season, April 13-May 13: adults and kids);
season passes available
Two locations:
8039 Beach Blvd., Buena Park, (714) 220-5200
(Right Next to Knott's Berry Farm), and
2052 Entertainment Circle, Chula Vista, (619) 661-7373
(www.soakcityusa.com)

The newest water park attraction in Orange County is here, a park devoted to the California beach experience of the '50s and '60s. Changing rooms, a surf shop and food stands have decor and names like Muscle Beach that conjure up the idyllic surfing life of the Southland's past. **Old Man Falls and Malibu Run** is a monstrous tower with three separate speed slides, and 4 tube (enclosed) slides. The **Sunset River** is a lazy tubing waterway that provides a relaxing glide around the park at 3 m.p.h. (This is where you'll find the parents.) A kid's play area called **Gremmie Lagoon** has a small octopus slide for the smaller fry. You probably have the picture — this is a water-filled fun park that will keep you and your kids splashing and laughing all day.

Of particular interest is **Tidal Wave Bay**, 750,000 gallons of body-surfing or boogie—boarding pleasure (complete with lifeguards on duty). This is an excellent place for budding young surfers (or former surfers) to keep honing those skills. The **Beach House** is a three-story monument to water guns and other interactive squirty things that kids will enjoy unleashing again and again — on each other. And for the truly adventurous, how about trying **Banzai Falls**, the steep high-speed slide for racing side-by-side.

I'd say this is a sound birthday party investment: Knott's provides the water, you provide the youngsters.

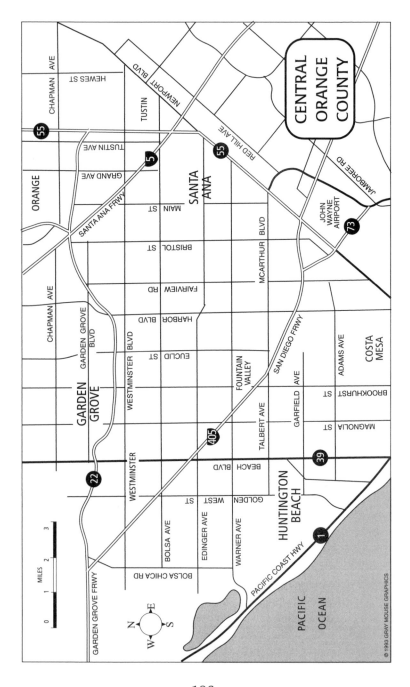

Central Orange County

Costa Mesa

Throughout the late 1800s this area consisted of a few farms, some apple orchards, and a trio of tiny hamlets— Fairview, Paularino, and Harper—that never quite coalesced into a single community. The city of Costa Mesa was eventually named in 1920 as a real estate subdivision. The name means "coast tableland" in Spanish, which is fairly descriptive of the area. During World War II, Costa Mesa was the site of the Santa Ana Army Air Base, a military installation that existed only from 1942 to 1946. Today, there's no trace of the base; the Orange County Fairgrounds and Orange Coast College occupy the land.

Outdoors

Costa Mesa Public Golf and Country Club
1701 Golf Course Drive
Information: (714) 754-5267

There are actually two 18-hole courses here, Mesa Linda and Los Lagos. Green fees and cart runs about $40 on weekends, with seven-day advance reservations required. Los Lagos has three lakes and lots of trees; the Mesa Linda course has many bunkers. The longest hole is the Los Lagos 14th at 526 yards and a par 5.

Succulent Strawberry Fields Abound in Orange County

Mesa Verde Country Club Golf Course
3000 Club House Road
Information: (714) 549-0522

A private club with a limited reciprocal program, this course has been the site of several PGA/LPGA and Senior tournaments. Weekdays are less expensive at $65 (weekends are $85). There are three par 5 holes here.

Attractions & Special Events

Goat Hill Junction
Fairview Park
Placentia Avenue and Swan Drive
Information: (949) 54-TRAIN

Fairview Park is the home of "Goat Hill Junction," a train that pays homage to the iron horse, run by the Orange County Model Engineers. Club members offer free train rides every third Saturday and Sunday of the month from 10 a.m. to 3:30 p.m. Children ride on a one-eighth scale railroad, pulled around three miles of 7.5-inch gauge tracks, by diesel, steam, electric and gasoline-powered locomotives.

Few model train clubs in America have as much track. In fact, the Orange County Model Engineers Club has one of the largest model train systems in the world, with many switches and side rails, a depot and two trestles.

To get to Goat Hill Junction, use Harbor Boulevard. Turn west on Wilson Street and then right on Placentia Avenue. If you approach from Brookhurst Street, go east on Hamilton/Victoria and turn left on Placentia. Goat Hill Junction is on the right about one-half mile, bordering the Mesa Verda Golf Course.

Robert Mondavi Wine and Food Center

1570 Scenic Avenue
Information and schedule: (714) 979-4510

Robert Mondavi—a noted Napa Valley winery—opened this site in 1989 to sponsor programs in wine appreciation. The facility presents wine tastings, cooking demonstrations, concerts and other special programs for groups as small as eight or as large as 175.

The 10,000-square-foot building has several dining areas, both indoor and out, plus a one-acre sculpture park and rose garden terrace. Local businesses, consumers and restaurateurs can select from a changing schedule of culinary events that are modeled after similar educational programs offered at the Robert Mondavi Winery in Napa.

The center may be booked for private catered events ranging from casual receptions to fancy, black-tie gatherings. The wines and cuisine are specifically matched to complement the occasion. If you're interested in learning about the center's regular schedule of public events, call the information line.

Orange County Fair

Orange County Fairgrounds, Fair Drive and Fairview Road
Information: (714) 751-3247
Hours: Daily until midnight; second and third
weeks in July
Admission: $2 to $6; children under 5 free; parking is $4

Now celebrating its second century, the annual county fair is a huge exhibition by any measure. Since agriculture is one of California's largest industries, it's no surprise that this county fair includes the same general traditions of any American county fair, but the California aspects are unique. The gardening/flower pavilion is just one example. Quite literally, Orange County could hold its county fair any season of the year because there is always something blooming in Southern California year-round.

There are a number of historical displays that trace the growth of the citrus industry which gives the county its name. During the 1940s, the citrus industry accounted for 75,000 acres of trees throughout the county; sadly, there are precious few acres left today.

Besides the expected—livestock shows and rodeos, carnival rides, tons of food and drink, contests for arts, crafts and cooking, agricultural exhibits and live music—the Orange County Fair also features unusual events such as ostrich races, dog acts, acrobats and speedway racing. The equestrian exhibits and shows are especially good, because Californians raise more horses than citizens of any other state.

There is a kiddie carnival section for tykes who aren't ready for the spin-and-scream variety rides, and plenty of petting opportunities with prize-winning hogs, goats, and other assorted barnyard friends. The Flower and Garden Show and the Fine Arts and Photography Hall are well-attended. The photography contest awards prizes in both amateur and photojournalism categories. Musical entertainment on the Arlington Stage is free with admission. You'll see and hear some well-known oldies, country, and rhythm 'n blues acts.

If you're in Orange County during the second and third weeks in July, this fair is definitely recommended. If you miss the fair, you can still introduce your young children to farming basics. On Fridays, Centennial Farm, located on the fairgrounds (714-751-3247), offers one-hour tours that teach youngsters the basics of planting and sowing crops. These tot seminars are held near the stables, and include some animal petting, too.

Orange County Performing Arts Center

600 Town Center Drive
Ticket information, programs: (714) 556-ARTS

This gorgeous venue features two performance halls, the larger Segerstrom Hall, and the more intimate Founders' Hall. The Performing Arts Center is home to the Opera Pacific and Orange County Philharmonic Society. Segerstrom Hall also hosts guest orchestras, classical soloists, Broadway musicals and touring dance companies. The acoustics are splendid, but the third tier balcony may give you vertigo if you don't like heights, so double-check at the box office. Pop and jazz performers are also booked at the Center, often in the smaller Founders' Hall in the same building.

You may tour the facility on Monday, Wednesday and Saturday at 10:30 a.m. The half-hour tour is free, but you'll have to pay for parking in the adjacent parking structure.

South Coast Repertory

655 Town Center Drive
Information: (714) 708-5500, 708-5555, (www.scr.org)

SCR is one of the finer stage venues in the United States. If you attend any production of SCR, expect to see both new works and classics of the stage, well-staged and featuring the cream of local and national acting talent in an intimate setting. Critically acclaimed from coast-to-coast, South Coast Repertory has given many new playwrights their first big break. Chekov, G.B. Shaw, Tennessee Williams — all are given first-rate treatment here. The auditorium has excellent sight lines. SCR also has a "Second Stage," a smaller theatre in the same facility that offers more experimental and newer, lesser-known works.

December at SCR's Main Stage features A Christmas Carol, and this particular production of the Charles Dicken's classic is so popular that SCR had no choice but to stage it annually. If you're visiting Orange County during the holidays, make the extra effort to add this high point to your trip and you won't be sorry.

Historical

Diego Sepulveda Adobe
1900 Adams Avenue
Information: (949) 631-5918
Hours: First and third Saturdays, noon to 4 p.m.

Built in the early 1800s, this abode building was used by vaqueros—the Spanish term for cowboy—as a way station. Vaqueros herded cattle for Mission San Juan Capistrano and later for Ranchero Diego Sepulveda. The adobe now functions as a museum depicting early life in Orange County. It is #227 in the book California Historical Landmarks.

Directions: Take the Harbor Boulevard exit south from the San Diego Freeway (I-405), turn right and proceed to Estancia Park. Look for the "State Historic Landmark" signs.

Museums

Costa Mesa Historical Society Museum
1870 Anaheim Avenue
Information: (714) 631-5918
Hours: Thursday and Friday, 10 a.m to 3 p.m.
Admission: Donation

This former bank building has been converted into the local repository of Costa Mesa history, including collections of memorabilia and photographs dating in particular from the Santa Ana Army Air Base during World War II. The local historical society has thousands of documents and artifacts on hand. A one-room showroom for a repository of historical documents, genealogy and photographs about life in Costa Mesa from the turn of the century.

Shopping

Orange County Marketplace

88 Fair Drive
Information: (949) 723-6660
Hours: Weekends, 7 a.m. to 4 p.m.
Admission: $1 (children under 12 free); parking is free

Located on the Orange County Fairgrounds, this is Orange County's largest regularly scheduled swap meet. Imagine 1,500 booths and you can guess the rest. If you're a bargain hunter, how can you resist? Swap meets are particularly fun in the Southern California climate, making it easier to browse.

South Coast Plaza/Crystal Court

South Coast Plaza Village/Metro Pointe
San Diego Freeway (I-405) between Bristol and Bear Street

This complex of four distinct shopping centers is Disneyland for Adults. South Coast Plaza is one of the highest-grossing retail centers in America. Provided you love to shop, this place will supply many hours, even days, of fulfillment.

The mother center, South Coast Plaza, is shaped like a giant "H" and has six department stores: Sears, Nordstrom, Macy's, Macy's Men's Store, Saks Fifth Avenue and Robinsons-May. Some of the biggest names in retail chic are in the boutique line-up: Gucci, Tiffany, Chanel, Armani, Ralph Lauren. The Metropolitan Museum and the Orange County Art Museum both have stores here; the latter maintains a gallery with revolving art exhibits that shoppers are free to enjoy. South Coast Plaza alone houses 200 shops and restaurants. There's absolutely no reason to go hungry here, because you can find both fast food and haute cuisine. Coffee emporiums, chocolatiers, and sidewalk cafes (admittedly, indoor sidewalks) can be found down every concourse in the mall.

A special treat for young visitors to South Coast Plaza is the Carousel Court (the eastern courtyard between Sears and Robinsons-May). The large carousel is in use year-round, but it's especially busy when Santa Claus is camped out next door. The surrounding shops in this section of the mall are all popular with children: FAO Schwarz, The Disney Store, and several kiddie clothing boutiques.

Directly west of South Coast Plaza, across Bear Street, are Crystal Court and Metro Pointe. While South Coast Plaza

Coffeehouses

Orange County is fast becoming a mecca for coffeehouses. Casual places serving cappuccino and cheesecake have multiplied everywhere. There are several in Costa Mesa alone.

The Blue Marble Coffeehouse

1907 Harbor Boulevard
Information: 646-5776
Hours: Sunday through Thursday, 6:30 a.m. to 11 p.m.;
Friday and Saturday until midnight

This shop features a reading library and board games for the customers. Every Tuesday night is comedy night, and there's a talent show in the last Monday of the month. You can enjoy live music on Friday and Saturday.

The Coffee Bean & Tea Leaf

3333 Bristol Street (in South Coast Plaza)
Information: 549-1766
Hours: Monday through Friday 10 a.m. to 9 p.m.;
Saturday 9:30 a.m. to 6 p.m.; Sunday 10:30 a.m. to 6 p.m.

Expect standing-room-only around the Coffee Bean, because South Coast Plaza patrons are in dire need of some java to keep up their waling and shopping stamina.

emphasizes clothing and traditional gift stores, Crystal Court retailers are primarily the type devoted to home furnishings. During the holiday season, a magnificent Christmas tree with a dazzling array of decorations soars three stories to the roof of Crystal Court. A miniature train chugs in and out of the tree, while a larger scale train carrying young shoppers circles the court at this time of year.

An excellent restaurant inside Crystal Court is Bangkok Four, located on the third floor. On a clear day, the view east-

Diedrich's Coffeehouse

474 E. 17th Street
Information: 646-0323
Hours: Sunday through Thursday, 6 a.m. to 11 p.m.;
Friday and Saturday, open until midnight

Diedrich's has several outlets in Orange County, and their blends are first-rate. Why? Because Carol Diedrich, the founder, was raised on a coffee plantation in Guatemala. You might say that he knows his beans. He was the first Orange County coffee merchant to roast beans on a large-scale, commercial basis (other coffeehouses sell his blends). For his four shops in the county, Diedrich's roasts up to 500 pounds of beans daily. At this location, there's a large patio, a reading library, and gift items for sale.

Rock N Java

1749 Newport Boulevard
Information: 650-4430
Hours: Sunday through Thursday until midnight;
Friday through Saturday until 2 a.m.

Rock N Java is aimed at a young clientele. The decor is "comfy, broken-in" and there are outdoor tables around a makeshift area for live music. The background music is alternative rock. The fare ranges from sandwiches and pasta salad to bagels and eggs for breakfast.

ward toward Saddleback Mountain is quite appealing. The Thai food here is excellent, and the black-and-white decor is striking.

In contrast to both South Coast Plaza and Crystal Court, Metro Pointe is an outdoor complex, featuring electronics, bedding and kitchen shops, a two-story Barnes & Noble, and movie theaters.

Across Sunflower Street (north of the main mall) is South Coast Plaza Village, another outdoor mall with an assortment of one-of-a-kind boutiques, gift and antique shops, and a number of notable restaurants, featuring Indian, vegetarian, Japanese, Chinese, Italian and Mexican cuisine — how's that for cultural variety? This village is a soothing retreat from the giant bustle of South Coast's main mall.

For a unique ending to your day at the South Coast Plaza shopping complex, how about taking in a murder mystery? The restaurants at South Coast Plaza Village play host to a theatrical group that stages comic murder mysteries every Saturday at 7 p.m. The cost is $55 per person for dinner and the mystery. Call 714-675-9726 for reservations.

Not far from South Coast Plaza is a beautiful sculpture garden designed by Isamu Noguchi at the behest of big-time Orange County developer C.J. Segerstrom. A small stream surrounds a cactus island, and granite, marble and stone sculptures dot the landscape. This is a delightful place to take time out, either before or after shopping. The park, officially known as California Scenario, is located at 611 Anton Boulevard and Park Center Drive near the Westin-South Coast Plaza hotel and next to the Comerica Bank building. Call (714) 435-2100 for more information. Open daily until midnight.

Dining

Henry & Harry's Goat Hill Tavern

1830 Newport Boulevard
Information: (949) 548-8428
Hours: Noon to 2 a.m.; Sunday opens 10 a.m.

If you are a connoisseur of beer, you will think you've died and gone to heaven when you step inside the Goat Hill Tavern. They have 127 different kinds of beer on tap. Bottled beers hail from all over the globe. If it isn't here, you probably won't find it anywhere else in Orange County—or even the West.

Scampi

1576 Newport Boulevard
Information: (949) 645-8560
Hours: Monday through Friday 11:30 a.m. to 3 p.m.
(lunch); 5:30 to 10 p.m. (dinner), until 11 p.m. weekends

Linda and Fernando Navaratta own this excellent Italian restaurant that won a Five Star Diamond Award from the American Academy of Restaurant Sciences. Traditional Italian specialties—pasta, chicken, veal and seafood—are prepared by chef Fernando, who was trained in Europe.

Located on Costa Mesa's busy Newport Boulevard, you can spot this restaurant on the east side of the street by looking for the bright orange awning and little Italian flags flying over its simple exterior. Once inside, if you can't make up your mind, try the pasta tri colore, a sampler of three pastas.

Fountain Valley

The farmers who settled in this area called it Fountain Valley because they could dig virtually anywhere and find a source of artesian water. The land was so swampy, in fact, that the only significant agriculture in the rancho days was the raising of a few cattle. During the mid-1800s, according to historian Jim Dick, so many evangelistic meetings were held in tents that the area was nicknamed "Gospel Swamp." A drought in the late 1870s helped drain the land sufficiently that it became more productive for growing crops.

The farm land has been gradually replaced since the 1960s by houses and industrial parks, with the exception of one large uninterrupted stretch of land known as Mile Square Park. Quiet middle-class neighborhoods are the rule in Fountain Valley, with no obvious downtown core or historic "Main Street."

Outdoors

Mile Square Park
16801 Euclid
Information: (714) 962-5549, 839-8611
Hours: Daily, sunrise to sunset

Mile Square Park is an oasis of parkland in a sea of suburban housing. The park is honeycombed with asphalt paths that allow cyclists and hikers access to all of its mile-square area. Near the park's center is a special field used by model vehicle enthusiasts to launch and land remote-control aircraft or maneuver remote-control automobiles.

An annual civic highlight is the five-day fiesta that concludes on the Fourth of July with a fireworks spectacular. The fiesta includes carnival games and rides, live concerts and plenty of food.

Two lakes within the park are stocked with bass, bluegill, carp and catfish. Picnic tables and barbecues abound.

There are also not one, but two, golf courses with lots of shady trees.

Mile Square Golf Course

10401 Warner Avenue
Information: (714) 545-7106, 968-4556
David L. Baker Memorial Golf Course
10410 Edinger Avenue
Information: (714) 418-2152

Mile Square Golf Course is an inexpensive course that is wide, flat and easy to walk. It's a good place to practice driving without worrying about severe obstacles. Be sure to reserve seven days in advance. Nearby is the David L. Baker Memorial Golf Course, a full 18-hole course with eight par 4s.

Attractions

Fountain Valley Golf & Recreation Center

16800 Magnolia Avenue
Information: (714) 842-1111, 842-1011
Hours: Daily 9 a.m. to 8 p.m.; Saturday until 11 p.m.
Admission: Varies with the games you want to play

The main features at this family amusement center are a go-cart track, two 18-hole miniature golf courses, a kiddie big top (children's ride area), and a large video arcade. The hours and prices vary with each attraction, so call ahead. This recreation center is located near the intersection of Warner and Magnolia.

Fountain Valley Skating Center

9170 Recreation Circle
Information: (714) 847-6300, 847-0022
Hours: Evenings
Admission: $4.50 days; $5.50 evenings; $1.50 for skate rental

Roller skating on a good old-fashioned wooden rink is back in style. It's good clean fun and exercise for adults and young people, and it's easier to master than ice skating. There are special adult nights on Tuesdays, Thursdays and Sundays. There's also a skate club that specializes in dance skating—a version of ballroom dancing on wheels. This skate center is located next door to the Fountain Valley Golf & Recreation Center, just south of the San Diego Freeway (I-405) near Warner and Magnolia Avenues.

Casa de Tortuga ("House of Tortoises")

Information: (714) 962-0612 (for directions)
Hours: By appointment only

If you or someone in your family has an interest in reptiles—specifically, tortoises and turtles—then Casa de Tortuga is the place to go. This is the private residence of Walter Allen, where more than 500 turtles and tortoises roam in his yard or live inside aquariums. Allen has a network of pools and waterfalls using 5,000 gallons of water that forms part of the tiny ecosystem for his collection. For the land species, Allen maintains pens that resemble horse barns.

Allen's tortugas include some very rare specimens, including the Galapagos variety that can exceed 300 pounds. He has a license from the California Department of Fish and Game to keep endangered species.

Visitors can view these animals (but not touch) for 30 or 40 minutes, provided you arrange an appointment. Donations are welcome.

Garden Grove

Garden Grove was once a sea of citrus groves and an active agricultural community, but the post-World War II baby boom converted this community into wide swaths of tract housing. Architectural imagination was sacrificed in the rush to fill the demand for housing. In this flat part of the county, there is little to relieve the neighborhood tedium, but Garden Grove can proudly point to having one of the country's most famous houses of worship.

One of Garden Grove's local legends is the Reverend Robert Schuller. Schuller began preaching his Sunday morning services atop the roof of a drive-in movie snack bar. His parish drove up and used the drive-in's grounds as its parish center. The congregation grew, and Schuller eventually housed his pulpit in the towering complex known as the Crystal Cathedral.

Outdoors

Atlantis Play Center

9301 Westminster Avenue; Information: (714) 892-6015
Hours: Tuesday through Friday, 10 a.m. to 2 p.m.;
Saturday, 10 a.m. to 4 p.m.; Sunday, 12 to 4 p.m.
Admission: $1 person (under 2 free); adults must be
accompanied by a child

This is a four-acre park for small children with the legendary Atlantis as its theme. There are sea serpents, whales, dragons and other aquatic creatures transformed into playground equipment. The surrounding fence and lush landscaping offer a feeling of serenity and lots of shade. There's a snack stand open on the weekends, but you may also bring a picnic lunch. Children under seven must be accompanied by an adult. Birthday parties can be scheduled here.

To reach Atlantis, take the Garden Grove Freeway (Hwy. 22) to the Magnolia exit. Head south to Westminster Avenue, then east one block and follow the signs.

Attractions and Special Events

Crystal Cathedral

12141 Lewis Street
Information: (714) 971-4000

The polished, gleaming fantasy of glass known as the Crystal Cathedral is the famous home base for Reverend Robert Schuller and his Hour of Power television show. This worship service is broadcast around the world every Sunday from the cathedral. Regardless of your religious persuasion, the twelve-story glass cathedral is an unusual landmark to see if you're in the area. Massive glass doors open during Sunday services to permit those who still use the parking lot for churchgoing to enjoy the view. It was, and still is, the quintessential Southern California religious experience.

Directions: Take the Chapman Avenue exit off the Santa Ana Freeway (I-5) and head west for a few blocks to Lewis Street. It's on the left and you can't miss it. Tours are offered daily between the hours of 9 a.m. and 3:30 p.m. (Sundays from 12:30 to 3:30).

The Crystal Cathedral stages two extremely popular Biblical spectacles during the year, one at Easter and the other at Christmas.

Glory of Christmas

At the Crystal Cathedral
Information: (714) 971-4017
Hours: November 30 through December 30; call for exact performance times
Tickets: Adults, $20-$30 (discounts for children under 13)

The Crystal Cathedral's gigantic nativity pageant is an annual must-do for thousands of Southern California residents and visitors. The stage is the cathedral itself (nine stories high), and features angels soaring overhead, live animals—the works. People of many denominations enjoy coming to see this live epic.

Crystal Cathedral

Glory of Easter

At the Crystal Cathedral
Information: (714) 544-5679
Hours: Two weeks before Easter; call for exact
performance times
Tickets: Adults, $20 - $30 (discounts for children under 13)

This pageant recreates the crucifixion and resurrection of Christ, complete with angels, animals and a huge cast. As with the Crystal Cathedral's Glory of Christmas, this is a sort of nondenominational representation of one of the Bible's great stories, and it is played to the hilt for appreciative audiences every year.

Strawberry Festival

Main Street and Acacia Parkway / "Village Green"
Information: (714) 638-0981
Hours: Memorial Day weekend
Admission: Free

This four-day festival is more than 30 years old, and harks back to this community's fame as a strawberry-growing mecca. Most of the strawberry patches are gone now, but the festival in honor of the ruby fruit continues to produce bushels of enjoyable family activities on Memorial Day weekend.

Look for the world's largest strawberry shortcake on hand in the "Village Green" area near Main Street and Acacia Parkway. There's also a parade held on the Saturday of that weekend, beginning at 9th Street and Chapman Avenue and proceeding to Euclid Street and Stanford Avenue.

Plenty of booths offer food, carnival games, arts and crafts and other wares. The festival helps raise money for local charities.

Historical

Historic Main Street

Between Garden Grove Boulevard and Acacia Parkway

Like the older cities of Fullerton and Orange, Garden Grove has retained its own remnant of yesteryear—a short quarter-mile of antique shops and other boutiques along a brick street lined with old-fashioned lamp posts. You can park for free at the corner of Main Street and Acacia Parkway, then stroll down Main toward Garden Grove Boulevard. The shops carry both swap meet-style collectibles as well as legitimate antiques for the discerning gift shopper. A gourmet grocer, Zlaket's Market, is the oldest family-owned business in the city (founded 1927), and offers exotic foodstuffs and a good bottle of wine. Model train hobbyists shouldn't miss Barry's Trains, where the owner has just about anything you might need for your hobby. The Sleepy Hollow Antique Mall on the corner of Garden Grove Boulevard and Main is a recent addition, featuring 6,000-square-feet of collectibles, from antique furniture and Depression glass to the Beatles.

The Stanley Ranch Museum (formerly "Heritage Park")

12174 Euclid Street
Information: (714) 530-8871
Hours: Sunday, 1:30 to 4 p.m. Call for tour information.
Admission: Free

This old house, built in 1891, is now a museum for displays on early life in Garden Grove. A "general store" doubles as the docent headquarters. The house is a two-story, blue-and-yellow gingerbread affair surrounded by a white picket fence. Walt Disney's original studio (a garage dating from 1923) is also located on the grounds of this historic park, as is an old barber shop and a shoe shop.

Dining

Azteca Restaurant

12911 Main Street
Information: (714) 638-3790; Hours: Daily 11 a.m. to 10 p.m.

From the outside this restaurant looks like an old two-story adobe, fitting in nicely with the surroundings of Garden Grove's historic downtown Main Street. Locals like to stop in here for a good dinner in the dark, warm interior.

Huntington Beach

The inland portion of Huntington Beach is situated on high ground, and became an important growing region in Orange County, as well as one of the richest oil fields in California. While Standard Oil pumped the black gold out of the ground during the 1920s, farmers harvested celery, asparagus, peppers, potatoes and corn.

Ambitious real estate developers, hoping to start a new resort, christened the bluffs above the ocean "Pacific City," and eventually a Pacific Electric railway track connected this new area with Long Beach, in Los Angeles County. The rich resources of white sands, oil-rich fields and fertile farmland quickly brought prosperity to what is now Huntington Beach.

The big oil fields are largely gone now, but traces still remain in the form of those unique seahorse-like pumps that bob up and down day and night. They can be seen almost anywhere, and usually where you least expect it. Huntington Beach is also discussed in Chapter 1, The Coast, page 84.

Outdoors

Meadowlark Golf Course
16782 Graham Street
Information: (714) 846-1364

Meadowlark is one of the less expensive courses in Orange County; a weekday tee time costs around $40 (reservations 10 days in advance). The greens are small, the course is narrow, and there are several water hazards. Four par 5 holes make this a challenging course.

Huntington Central Park
Talbert Avenue and Golden West Street
Information: (714) 960-8847, 536-5281

This 350-acre park in the center of Huntington Beach has six miles of cycling and strolling trails and two lakes. It plays host to more than 200 bird species, and its location makes it a popular spot with migrating flocks during winter. Some of the birds you might spy include tricolored blackbirds, vireos and Townsend's warblers.

The Shipley Nature Center (714-960-8867) is an 18-acre preserve in the midst of Huntington Central Park, with nearly a mile of self-guided nature trails. Signposts point out the flora of the woods and marsh. There is a park naturalist available for group tours. The visitor's center has a small nature museum with live snakes, turtles and other local species. The hours at Shipley vary with the season.

The Huntington Beach Central Library is located within the park. It boasts the largest children's library in California. It currently has the largest genealogical collection in Southern California.

One of the unique features of this park is its 18-hole Frisbee golf course (with a basket representing each "hole"). There is also a 1.25-mile jogging course with eighteen exercise stations.

Huntington Central Park also has a 25-acre equestrian center with a full-time riding school (714-842-7656). A variety of equestrian events are often held on Sunday afternoons, including polo matches.

To find Central Park from the northbound San Diego Freeway (I-405), exit at Warner Avenue and head west; turn left at Golden West Street. The park is on both sides of Golden West. From the southbound San Diego Freeway, exit at Golden West Street and turn south.

Historical

Newland House Museum

19820 Beach Boulevard
Information: (714) 962-5777
Hours: Open for self-guided tours Wednesday through
Thursday, 2 to 4:30 p.m.; Saturday and Sunday, noon to
4 p.m.

This Victorian farmhouse, built in 1898, is the oldest home still standing in Huntington Beach. It was built on a bluff once inhabited by Native Americans. The home served as the centerpiece of the Newland Ranch (which remained in operation until the mid-1940s). It has been restored and preserved as a museum reflective of the times, with authentic period antiques and a gift shop.

When it was first built, the local newspaper described it as a nine-room, two-story "cottage." The Newland family raised ten children here. Perhaps most indicative of this turn-of-the-century house is the dining room: its fireplace provided the only heat in the house.

The sun porch of this home sheltered Mrs. Newland's collection of more than 150 Indian baskets. The Newland's discovered that their house was built on the site of an ancient Indian village, and they allowed archaeologists to dig for artifacts dating back more than 7,000 years.

The Newland House Museum is listed in the National Register of Historic Places.

Shopping

Old World Village

7561 Center Avenue
Information: 898-3033

Tucked away in the middle of Huntington Beach is a gathering of Bavarian-style shops with cobbled lanes. Old World Village, a self-styled "shopping, dining and entertainment center," is unique in Southern California in that many of the proprietors live above their establishments, European-style. The stores feature imports from Europe, South America and Asia: jewelry, timepieces, porcelain, crystal, linens and other giftware.

There are several restaurants: The Old World German Restaurant (714-895-8020) holds an annual Oktoberfest; Stefano's (714-373-5399) is an Italian cafe; Einbecker Inn (714-892-9997) is a sidewalk cafe with German fare; Old World Bakery (714-891-1362) serves pastries and gourmet coffee drinks; Randy's Weinstube (714-894-8937) has live European entertainment; and the Rathskeller (714-894-6612) is a Bavarian pub.

Dining

Alice's Breakfast Cafe

Central Park West
Information: (714) 848-0690
Hours: 7 a.m. to 1:30 p.m.

This cafe is nestled inside the western half of Huntington's Central Park. Alice's home cooking can be eaten on the premises or taken out for a picnic in Huntington Beach's Central Park. Homemade cinnamon rolls and other tasty treats make this a popular spot for breakfast or lunch.

Orange

Downtown Orange doesn't immediately come to mind when visitors to Orange County think of places to explore. But Orange's historic city center will surprise you if you're expecting a modernized, suburban world. A quaint, old-fashioned traffic circle marks the center of town. There's an old bank building on the corner. This is a real Main Street U.S.A., not the idealized one at Disneyland.

In 1869, two lawyers named Alfred Beck Chapman and Andrew Glassell accepted 1,385 acres of land from the Rancho Santiago de Santa Ana in lieu of their legal fees. The partners laid out a one-square-mile town, and platted the area surrounding the future town circle into 10-acre lots that sold originally for six dollars an acre! They named their new town Richland, but the postal authorities said there was another California town with that name, so they chose "Orange" instead. The name was appropriate, because the city became a busy place for the fruit packing and shipping business. The old part of town is now recorded in the National Archives as a historic site.

This section of Orange (pun intended) has something more to offer than just a charming glimpse of the city's architectural history. You can virtually wallow in the past by visiting the more than 100 antique dealers clustered together in Old Towne. Orange has positively the best collection of antique shops in the county.

Historic downtown is located just northeast of where the Garden Grove Freeway (Hwy. 22) and the Santa Ana Freeway (I-5) intersect. If you're traveling on I-5 either north or south, take the Chapman Avenue exit and head east. If you're on the Garden Grove Freeway heading in either direction, take the Glassell Street exit and head north. Either way, you'll know when you hit the traffic circle. Park anywhere and prepare to shop and explore the area.

In and around Old Towne are a number of residences that were constructed between 1889 and 1929, and are regarded as significant examples of varied architectural styles. Bungalows, Mediterranean, a carriage house and others are all within walking distance. Once a year in October you can take A Walk In Time tour of these homes. Call the Old Town Preservation Association at 714-639-6840 for the exact date and time of this year's tour.

Further north on Glassell are many charming old homes that have been adapted to businesses ranging from vintage clothing shops to cafes — worth a little more time to explore completely.

To the northeast of the traffic circle, the city stretches out toward the Anaheim Hills into beautiful residential neighborhoods with lots of horse property. If you're interested in seeing what the equestrian-suburban life looks like, drive along any street east of Orange Park Boulevard and north of Chapman Avenue and you will see lots of beautiful horse country. In just a few minutes it becomes hard to believe you're just a few miles from the motel-ridden corridors of Harbor and Beach Boulevards further west, a sign that much of Orange County's rural charm is still intact if you know where to look.

Shopping

Old Towne Orange
Chapman Avenue and Glassell Street

The merchants here boast that this historic crossroads is the "antique capital of California," and they may be right. Walk up or down Chapman Avenue (north and south of the traffic circle) and you will encounter door after door of antique shops, roughly 36 in all (but some of these are megashops where individual collectors maintain stalls within the larger establishments). You can find just about anything: jewelry, furniture, paintings, dolls, porcelain, art glass and country furnishings. Since all these shops are competing for your attention, the variety is astounding and the prices range from the sublime to the outrageous. There's bound to be a treasure here that you won't want to pass up. I went by this area one Saturday to browse and found that the entire day was gone by the time I'd seen every shop.

It's difficult to single out any one store along this quaint street. Just For Fun Antiques (140 S. Glassell, 714-633-7405) has coin-operated goodies and old display advertising; the Orange Circle Antique Mall (118 S. Glassell, 714-538-8160) has 100 dealers in one place; Vignale Antique Gallery (109 W. Chapman) displays fine Oriental art; Muffs (135 S. Glassell, 714-997-0243) is into home restoration hardware; the list goes on and on. You really have to walk this area to believe the number and variety.

The Old Towne antique shops also carry some fab '50s and '60s memorabilia. Mr. C's Rare Records (148 N. Glassell, 714-532-3835) stocks classic albums with their sleeves in mint condition. Trini Lopez? Joanie Sommers? Vanilla Fudge? Stan Kenton? You name it, they probably have it.

Before you leave this charming town circle, stop in at the Watson Drug Store and Coffee Shop (116 E. Chapman, 714-532-6315) where you can still sit at an honest-to-goodness lunch counter (or if you prefer, the sidewalk patio). The menu features grilled cheese and fries, handmade shakes and malts (made with real ice cream) and other homemade favorites such as meatloaf with mashed potatoes and gravy. This is the real thing, not a 1990s recreation of an American tradition. Hours: Monday through Saturday, 6:30 a.m. to 9 p.m.; Sundays, 8 a.m. to 6 p.m.

Another good place to dine in between antique shopping is Felix (36 Plaza Square, 714-633-5842), a sidewalk cafe featuring Cuban cuisine.

One more site to check out: The Moreton Bay Fig Tree, in front of the Holly Family Cathedral (566 S. Glassell St.). It's big, it's tall, it's a tree. How many trees are designated historical landmarks? It was originally planted in 1875, and now it's 80-feet tall and 150-feet in circumference. You can't miss it, literally.

The Block at Orange

Providing a stark contrast to the old-fashioned hometown flavor of downtown Orange is this glitzy open-air mall that blends the latest retail styles with restaurants and other entertainments into one 21st-century extravaganza. The centerpiece is a 30-screen AMC "Film City" theatre complex, featuring love seats and all the latest digital sound systems.

The most outrageous venue here is Vans Skate Park, an indoor/outdoor paradise for roller skaters and skateboarders. All the ramps, bowls, half-pipes and other obstacle course standards are supplied in abundance. There's a retail store attached where you can make sure you're outfitted in the latest sidewalk surfing gear, but the world's largest skateboard park is the real attraction and two-hour sessions go by quickly. There's also plenty of space for spectators. Protective gear is required, and you can rent it all if you don't bring your own.

My favorite retailer here is probably Hilo Hattie's, the famous Hawaiian mercantile business making its first appearance on the mainland. Here's where you can get the real island duds, and some Kona coffee too. Check out the enormous hibiscus blossoms outside the entrance.

Other big retailers here include Virgin Megastore, Borders Books & Music, Ron Jon Surf Shop, Old Navy, and "Off 5th" Saks Fifth Avenue. This is only a sample of the more than 100 stores.

Hungry? Besides the usual food court, there's a Restaurant Row offering truly diverse cuisine, a Dave & Buster's restaurant and video arcade, and a nightclub center called Graham Central Station.

To find the Block at Orange, take the Garden Grove Freeway (I-22) to the City Drive exit and follow the signs.

The Bookman

840 N. Tustin Avenue
Information: (714) 538-0166
Hours: Monday through Friday, 10 a.m. to 8 p.m.;
Saturday, 10 to 6 p.m.; Sunday, 12 to 5 p.m.

The Bookman is one of Orange County's largest and best-stocked used book stores. Here you'll find out-of-print and collectible titles, from children's books and fiction to metaphysical and military books. You can browse through its 8,000 square feet of well lit shelves stocked with who-knows-what treasures for your personal library. The Bookman is located just south of Collins in the Toy City Shopping Center.

Doll City U.S.A.

2040 N. Tustin Avenue
Information: (714) 750-3585
Hours: Monday through Saturday, 10 a.m. to 6 p.m.; closed Sundays

This 7,700-square-foot shop boasts the largest selection of dolls and accessories under one roof in the country. They carry dolls from manufacturers all around the world. You'll find expensive collectors items as well as everyday dolls.

To get to Doll City, take the Newport Freeway (Hwy. 55) north to the Katella exit, go west and turn right on Tustin Avenue. If southbound on the 55, exit at Lincoln, go west and turn left on Tustin Avenue. It is just south of the Mall of Orange next to an Alpha Beta supermarket.

Outdoors

Eisenhower Park

2894 N. Tustin Avenue
Information: (714) 744-7272
Hours: Daily sunrise to sunset

This charming little park is a great oasis for a picnic. It is located near Olive, an old part of Orange County that has vanished into history. The sloping grounds near the Santa Ana River was chosen by Padre Junipero Serra to be the site for another mission (in addition to the one at San Juan Capistrano that he founded originally), but the mission was ultimately built farther north in San Gabriel. Olive remains an unincorporated part of the county, with no adobes left to distinguish this old community.

Eisenhower Park has an animal farm with goats, sheep, chickens and ducks for children to see and pet. A small lake is stocked with trout.

Historical

Pitcher Park/Fire Museum

Corner of Cambridge Street and Almond Avenue
Museum hours: First Sunday of the month, noon to 3 p.m.

Pitcher Park is a short walk away from the Orange traffic circle. This small piece of property was once part of a family farm. When the Pitchers moved from Kansas in 1912, Mr. Pitcher worked in the downtown plaza as a real estate broker, but the family grew walnuts and apricots. Their barn and "honey house" have been restored and are open to the public. Pitcher Park gives you a quiet picture of what it was like to live in Orange County in the early part of this century, when farm fields and orange groves dominated the landscape. The property has been renovated and landscaped with 33 different types of vegetation, including an herb garden.

Another added attraction at Pitcher Park is Orange's new fire museum; the displays include a man-pulled fire wagon dating from 1907. The museum is housed in the Pitcher barn.

Dining

Orange Hill Restaurant

6410 E. Chapman Avenue
Information: (714) 997-2910

Heading east on Chapman past Canyon View Road, you will come to Orange Hill Restaurant, a prominent structure on the hillside in front of you. Chapman curves to the left and begins to go uphill. Look carefully and you will see the sign marking the steep driveway leading up to the restaurant. This hilltop perch provides an amazing view of northern Orange County, and on a clear day you can see the Pacific. The cuisine is continental, oriented toward surf-and-turf, tastily prepared; the service is top drawer. There really isn't a bad table for enjoying the view, although getting a window table is iffy without reservations.

P.J.'s Abbey Restaurant

182 S. Orange Street
(714) 771-8556
Hours: Daily from 9 a.m. to 8 p.m.; open 7 a.m. on
weekends.

This lovely restaurant is inside a restored church, beautifully appointed with wonderful stained glass windows and old-fashioned decor. The 1890s structure was restored a few years ago through painstaking care, including stripping off decades of paint to reveal beautiful redwood construction. The windows were imported from Belgium by the original Baptist congregation, and are now set off by the restaurant's ingenious decor — including some pews now used in the waiting area. This establishment offers good food in what you can probably imagine is a family atmosphere.

Taco Mesa

3533 E. Chapman Boulevard
Information: (714) 633-3922
Hours: Daily from 10 a.m. to 10 p.m.

This may be the best Mexican fast food in Orange County. Thankfully, there are three in the county (the others are in Costa Mesa and Mission Viejo). The storefront setting belies the excellent cuisine inside, which you order from a counter and then help yourself to the wonderful condiments laid out at the salsas bar. Co-founded by chef Marco Calderon, your palette will enjoy a marvelous variety: huevos rancheros for breakfast, tortas for lunch, green corn tamales or prawns for dinner. Tacos? Yes, they have them too. But the ingredients are unlike any you'll find at a drive-through food restaurant, and the soups (sopas) and çoffees and sweet fruit beverages will continually delight you. In Costa Mesa, visit Taco Mesa at 647 W. 19th Street.

Santa Ana

Santa Ana is the county seat. It experienced the same explosive post-World War II growth as its neighbors in north Orange County. Today, the predominance of Hispanic residents and culture in this city is readily apparent. The shops, restaurants and businesses along Main Street, in the heart of downtown, cater to the Spanish-speaking community. Most of the signs offer information and advertising only in Spanish. Some believe that metropolitan Santa Ana shows a glimpse of Southern California's future: a place where English is primarily a second language, and Mexican traditions reclaim what was once a Spanish-speaking colony.

Downtown Santa Ana between 2nd, Civic Center Drive, French and Broadway streets is on the National Register of Historic Places, and has been undergoing extensive redevelopment to encourage the return of business to this aging district.

Outdoors

Centennial Regional Park
3000 Centennial Road
Information: (714) 571-4200
Hours: 5 a.m. to 10 p.m.

At 87 acres, Centennial is one of the smaller regional parks in Orange County, but it has great playground equipment, soccer and softball fields, and a ten-acre lake stocked with fish. The flat terrain is also good for remote control aircraft flying. It is located at the corner of Edinger and Fairview.

Cycling tip: Centennial is near one of the longest uninterrupted cycling paths in Orange County: the Santa Ana River Bikeway. It stretches 29 miles from the Anaheim Hills to the shore at Huntington Beach. This two-lane path follows the historic bed of the Santa Ana River (now paved with concrete for better flood control). It is marked by a broken white line; area streets are bypassed through the use of "on ramps" and "off ramps." There are rest stops along this bikeway where you can freshen up and fill your water bottle. From the Anaheim Wetlands Preserve near Weir Canyon Road and the Talbert Nature Preserve (more wetlands) in Costa Mesa to the mouth of the river in Newport Beach, this trail literally bisects the county. This is a full-day's ride, easy.

River View Golf Course

1800 W. 22nd Street
Information: (714) 543-1115
Willowick Municipal Golf Course
3017 W. Fifth Street
Information: (714) 554-0672

Here is a pair of good public courses within the city of Santa Ana. River View runs along the Santa Ana River (its concrete-paved channel, that is). The fees are modest and the course is kept in good condition. Willowick is flat and narrow, and is definitely walkable. It is slightly more expensive than River View ($20 on weekends). Both courses require seven days advance reservation.

Attractions and Special Events

Discovery Science Center

2500 N. Main Street
Information: (714) 542-CUBE; (www.discovery cube.org)
Hours: Daily 10 a.m. to 5 p.m. (excluding holidays)
Admission: $6 for youths; $8 for adults

The Taco Bell Discovery Science Center is a place where young people can get interactive with the physical sciences. Because it's a great place that is just the right size, you and your youngster can easily see all the exhibits and programs here in just a couple of hours. Kids enjoy eight thematic areas: human perception, quake zone, dynamic earth, space exploration, principles of flight, exploration, human performance and a special kid station.

I enjoyed stretching out on the bed of nails myself, but if that seems too scary for you, try measuring your vertical jump against the best athletes in the world. Or observe a tornado up-close. This is really an imaginative center, and it includes a 3-D laser light theater and a convenient food court (a Taco Bell and a Pizza Hut, of course) when your caloric intake is low.

Take the Main Street exit from either direction on the I-5 (Santa Ana) Freeway and you can't miss it: look for the enormous cube poised on one point next to the freeway overpass.

Santa Ana Zoo (Prentice Park)

1801 E. Chestnut Avenue
Information: (714) 836-4000
Hours: Daily 10 a.m. to 5 p.m.
Fees: Adults, $4; children, $2

This tiny zoo is very old, very clean, and a real bargain. But don't expect acres of wildlife habitats and animals shows. Although it is easily overlooked and eclipsed by the famous San Diego Zoo to the south, the Santa Ana Zoo serves an excellent purpose. It provides an uncrowded, quiet place to take the kids for a close-up look at some extremely rare and endangered species.

The zoo has a number of exotic animals that you won't necessarily find at the larger metropolitan zoos. For example, there's a hyrax, a rare animal related to elephants that is no bigger than a rabbit. There are rare birds such as the black currasow. But most impressive is the amazing collection of primates, including ring-tailed lemurs, colobus monkeys, guenons, langurs, capuchins, macaques, gibbons, sakis and golden lion tamarins from South America that are smaller than a house cat.

The zoo recently opened a great new aviary named Colors of the Amazon, featuring species such as Roseate Spoonbill and Emerald Toucanet.

The zoo is also home to African servals (similar to North American bobcats) and a pair of mountain lions from Southern California's own wilderness backyard. There is a barn-yard petting zoo where docents are available to answer questions. There are elephant rides and a small play area if your toddler needs exercise.

The zoo is located in a nondescript part of Santa Ana adjacent to the Santa Ana Freeway. It is currently undergoing a slow renovation, which will update its various habitats to improve the welfare and display of the animals. In keeping with the zoo's size, there is one small snack stand and gift shop. The whole zoo is tidy (you can tell by the cleanliness of the animal exhibits that the people here are excellent caretakers), and—wonder of wonders—even the restrooms are clean.

Historical

Orange County Historical Society
P.O. Box 10984, Santa Ana, CA 92711
Information: (714) 543-8282

Founded in 1919, the Orange County Historical Society is dedicated to preserving public interest in the history of both Southern California and Orange County itself. The society offers many lecture series throughout the year, and announces periodic tours of historical sites in Orange County. These tours are often the best (and only) way to learn about Orange County's early heritage. Call or write the Society for more information about upcoming local events and membership.

Santa Ana City Library
26 Civic Center Plaza
Information: (714) 647-5250

For local history buffs and scholars, this library is a treasure trove of Orange County history. The library itself is a beautiful marble building. A History Room on the main floor is filled with a remarkable collection of books, newspapers, personal journals and other memorabilia. The History Room is open on Monday and Saturday from 2 to 6 p.m. I confess I have a soft spot for this library; this is where I checked out my first copy of Dr. Seuss' And To Think That I Saw It On Mulberry Street.

Old Orange County Courthouse

211 W. Santa Ana Boulevard
Information: (714) 834-3703
Hours: Monday through Friday, 9 a.m. to 5 p.m., by appointment
Admission: Free

Restored in 1992, this courthouse has a museum on the third floor depicting Orange County's history during the late 19th and early 20th century. The beautiful structure, with an exterior of Arizona red sandstone, was used as a courthouse from 1901 to 1969. You can see a judge's chambers, jury room and even a court reporter's office on the tour. It is #837 in the book California Historical Landmarks.

Historic Homes

Santa Ana has several historic homes worth viewing in a section of town once nicknamed the "Nob Hill" of Orange County. The Harmon-McNeil House at 322 E. Chestnut Street is listed in the National Register of Historic Places. The Howe-Waffle House at 120 Civic Center Drive W. (714-547-9645) was the home of the first woman physician in Orange County, Dr. Willella Waffle. The Queen Anne-style home was built in 1889 by the second mayor of Santa Ana, Alvin Howe (also a doctor and the husband of Dr. Waffle). There is a small medical museum inside that distinguishes this turn-of-the-century home tour from many others. The house is located at the corner of Sycamore and Civic Center Drive, and is open every third Saturday of the month from 10 a.m. to 2 p.m. There is a donation for the self-guided tour.

Museums

The Bowers Museum of Cultural Art

2002 N. Main Street
Information: (714) 567-3600
Hours: Tuesday through Sunday, 10 a.m. to 4 p.m.
Admission: Adults, $8; seniors and students, $6; children
under 12, $4

Once an obscure, overlooked museum in the middle of Orange County, the Bowers Museum has been reborn. Now known as the Bowers Museum of Cultural Art, this local landmark recently underwent a four-year, $12-million renovation, doubling its exhibit space and providing a superb showcase for its permanent collection of historic Californian and pre-Columbian artifacts.

Before the 60-year-old Bowers Museum closed for renovation, it was recognized primarily by its bell-tower facade. Fortunately, the architects of the museum's expansion remained faithful to the original design, thus continuing its homage to mission era architecture. In addition to the bell-tower entrance, there is an attractive courtyard and balcony that lend charm to this setting.

The Bowers' permanent collection reflects the predominant cultures that helped shape early California: the local Native American Indian tribes and the Spanish and Mexican influences from the 1700s until 1850, when California became a state. But the Bowers is also concerned with the collection, preservation and display of artifacts from many Pacific Rim cultures. Much of the art, therefore, represents the lives of people as far away in space and time as Australia and Melanesia of 40,000 years ago. Exhibitions on Colombian gold jewelry, classic Chinese pottery, and even African ceremonial masks, mix with the regular displays of California Indian culture.

In the permanent exhibit "Vision of the Shaman: Song of the Priest," the museum presents an outstanding collection of Mesoamerican artifacts from the classic and post-classic periods (from 1200 B.C. to the time of the Spanish conquest). Among the pieces are sculptures, vases, incense burners and other items. The Native American Arts gallery contains the crafts of North American tribes, including baskets, pots, clothing and carvings.

The Bowers Museum also has galleries devoted to the rancho period of California history and the early agricultural days of Orange County. In one upstairs gallery the film California Legacies: The Story of Orange County runs continuously in a small alcove called the Heritage Theater. Exhibits display the photographs, papers and personal effects of some of Orange County's earliest citizens.

There's no need to visit this museum and walk away hungry. Topaz Cafe is a pleasant eatery on the premises that features southwestern cuisine (call 714-835-2002).

Getting to the Bowers is easy. Take the Santa Ana Freeway (I-5) to 17th Street, turn right and then make another right at Main Street.

Discovery Museum of Orange County

3101 W. Harvard Street
Information: (714) 540-0404
Hours: Wednesday to Friday; 1 p.m. to 5 p.m.; Saturday and Sunday, 11 a.m. to 3 p.m.
Donation: $5

Not to be confused with the Discovery Science Center, the Discovery Museum of Orange County is heaven-sent to teachers all over Southern California. It's an eleven-acre site containing four historic buildings, and is landscaped with gardens and orchards reminiscent of early county life. Collectively, these sites are the "museum" of Orange County's cultural heritage. A number of school and after school programs are available for students in Orange, Los Angeles, Riverside and San Bernardino counties. The public may tour the facility on weekends.

The centerpiece of the Discovery Museum is the H. Clay Kellogg House, a restored Victorian home. Such a place makes a perfect spot for a Victorian Cottage Tour, where the volunteer docents give young visitors a glimpse of Victorian life through artifacts, crafts, costumes, and special activities. Scheduled tours offer what is called the basic "petticoats, butterchurns and jacks" package—introductions to the inventions, skills and customs of 19th century life. Other tours, offered to youth and scouting troops, give overviews of Orange County history, Victorian "gadgets and gizmos," and "seed to stem" programs about herbs, roses and the citrus industry. These programs are designed to increase the scientific appreciation of students as well as convey historical awareness of Orange County's past. Your child may celebrate a Victorian-style birthday here, and weddings are catered as well. Call for details.

Directions: Take the Haster Street exit off the Garden Grove Freeway (Hwy. 22). Turn left on Garden Grove Boulevard, right on Fairview Road, then right on Harvard. Parking is free. The Discovery Museum may also be reached by traveling 2.25 miles north of the San Diego Freeway (I-405) on Fairview and turning left on Harvard.

Shopping

Libreria Martinez Books and Art Gallery

1110 N. Main Street
Information: (714) 973-7900
Hours: Monday through Saturday, 10 a.m. to 8 p.m.;
Sunday from 11 a.m. to 7 p.m.

Proprietor Rueben Martinez originally began selling books out of his barber shop in the early '90s because of his intense interest in promoting literacy. He paid particular attention to books focusing on Latino culture, and made sure he had many volumes written in Spanish. He soon ran out of room in his barber shop, and this storefront is the result: 3,000 square feet of book space on the main downtown thoroughfare through Santa Ana. This is a truly unique store in Orange County, and worth a visit. And Martinez still cuts hair by appointment.

MainPlace Mall

2800 N. Main Street
Information: (714) 547-7000

This is an enclosed atrium mall with 190 shops and department stores, plus six movie theaters. Skylights, fountains and neon relieve some of the tedium of ordinary indoor malls. MainPlace's concierge has a "language bank" to guide you to multilingual merchants. There is also shuttle service to nearby hotels, and an American Express Travel Service for foreign currency exchanges.

MainPlace is in a good location right where the Santa Ana Freeway (I-5) and Garden Grove Freeway (Hwy. 22) intersect. Take the Main Street exit from either freeway and you'll have no trouble finding it. The only drawback is the limited parking area.

Dining

Orange County Mining Company

10000 Crawford Canyon Road
Information: (714) 997-7411
Hours: Sunday through Thursday, 5 p.m. to 10 p.m.;
Friday and Saturday until 11 p.m.

This restaurant features American cuisine in a nice, woody atmosphere atop a hill overlooking Orange County. On weekends they feature an "oldies" dance session. You'll find this restaurant at the corner of Chapman Avenue and Crawford Canyon.

Tustin

Columbus Tustin and Nelson O. Stafford purchased the first acreage in the city of Tustin in 1868. The original town was mostly flat, and dotted with sycamore trees and yellow mustard. The exception was a hill to the east that was called Katuktu ("hill of prominence") by the Gabrielino Indians. The Spanish named it Cerrito de las Ranas ("Hill of the Frogs"), while American settlers chose the descriptive "Red Hill" because of the color of the cinnabar mined here.

Tustin began subdividing his land, thus creating Tustin City. But because neighboring Santa Ana won the last Southern Pacific Railroad stop, Tustin had trouble competing for business and new residents. Perhaps the largest single construction project in Tustin's history was the U.S. Navy "lighter than air" dirigible base built in 1942. The tall hangars built for the blimps that patrolled our Western shores in wartime are still standing, and are visible for many miles.

Outdoors

Peters Canyon Regional Park

Jamboree Road and Canyon View Avenue
Information: (714) 538-4400
Admission: $2 per vehicle

One of Orange County's newest regional parks is 350 acres in size, with five miles of trails suitable for hiking, horseback riding and mountain cycling. There's a large lake (Peters Canyon Reservoir) that's terrific for birdwatching, but fishing is not permitted because it's designated a wildlife preservation area, much like Santiago Oaks Regional Park in Orange. Ironically, this park used to be nicknamed "Golf Canyon" because there was actually a nine-hole course here, the first one in Orange County. Another historical footnote: one end of the park was used as a mock battlefield for training World War II troops.

To reach the park, take the Costa Mesa Freeway (Hwy. 55) north to the Chapman Avenue exit, turn east and then turn right on Jamboree. The park will be on your right when you reach Canyon View Avenue.

Tustin Ranch Golf Club

12442 Tustin Ranch Road
Information: (714) 730-1611

A championship-class course that's 6,700 yards: narrow, desert-like, with a lot of water hazards. The course was designed by Ted Robinson. If you want to hone your accuracy, this is an unforgiving test ground—highly rated by the pros. The back nine is particularly beautiful. Green fees are between $55 and $90 (cart included).

Attractions

Marconi Automotive Museum

1302 Industrial Drive
Information: (714) 258-3001
Hours: By appointment only
Admission: Adults: $5, children: under 12 free

Located in an inconspicuous business park is a museum of wonderful racing cars, owned by Dick Marconi and his son John. These racing buffs have collected more than 70 amazing automobiles, from Ferraris to Lamborghinis and other exotic formula 1 cars. They also have lots of racing memorabilia on display. The Marconis book this museum for groups so they can donate proceeds to children's charities. If you want to see some amazing cars, give them a call and make an appointment.

Tustin Marine Corps Air Station

Red Hill and Barranca

While this base has been officially closed, you can see its amazing hangars from these streets. The twin hangars are among the tallest, unsupported wooden structures on the West Coast, and are listed in the National Register of Historic Places. The giant hangars were originally built to house blimps that watched our coastline during World War II, but in recent years before the base's closure, they were used to house Marine helicopters. Their fate as historic landmarks is still uncertain.

Shopping

The Market Place
Santa Ana Freeway (I-5) at Jamboree Road

This appears to be the new wave in shopping centers: assembling "superstore-style" stores in one open-air location. From the Santa Ana Freeway, you can't miss the dark, brick-red color scheme, or the large neon signs that advertise the Market Place at night.

Home furnishings stores form one half of this outdoor center, with more traditional consumer goods stores (books, children's toys and clothing, discount shoes, electronics and music) comprising the other half. The center occupies all four corners at the intersection of El Camino Real and Jamboree. A number of eateries within this complex offer everything from gourmet coffee and tea to pizza and hamburgers. You won't go hungry while you spend the day shopping here.

Directions: Take the Santa Ana Freeway (I-5) north or south to Jamboree Road; the Tustin Market Place is on the east side of the freeway.

Dining

Elizabeth Howard's Curtain Call Dinner Theater

690 El Camino Real
Information: (714) 838-1540
Showtimes: Tuesday through Saturday, seating at
6:15 p.m.; Sunday, 11:15 a.m. matinee and 5:25 p.m.
evenings

Broadway and prime rib anyone? The King and I, Anything Goes—only big, classic Broadway musicals are on the theatrical bill of fare at the Curtain Call, a 300-seat venue now well into its third decade as a Tustin dinner theatre institution.

Directions: Located one block north of Newport Avenue in El Camino Plaza, right off the Santa Ana Freeway (I-5).

The Barn

14982 Red Hill
Information: (714) 259-0115
Hours: Sunday through Thursday, 11 a.m. to 2 p.m.
(lunch), 5 to 9 p.m. (dinner); Friday and Saturday, open
until 10 p.m.

This building dates back to 1914, and you can't miss it because it truly is a barn. American food—steaks, seafood, salad bar—is the fare here. There's also live entertainment, dancing and satellite-broadcast sports events.

McCharles House

335 S. C Street
Information: (714) 731-4063
Hours: Tuesday through Saturday, 11:30 a.m. to 4 p.m.
(lunch, tea); Thursday through Saturday, 5:30 to 8:30 p.m.
(dinner)

Tea and English cuisine the way it was meant to be are offered here, with scones, cucumber sandwiches, curry, curd and trifle. The ambiance inside and out is provided by this old Victorian home, where diners are served in four quaint rooms.

Zov's Bistro and Bakery Cafe

17440 E. 17th Street
Information: (714) 838-8855
Hours: Monday through Saturday, 11 a.m. - 2:30 p.m.
(lunch); Tuesday - Thursday, 5 p.m. to 9 p.m. (dinner),
Friday and Saturday until 10 p.m. The bakery opens at 7
a.m. for continental breakfasts.

A touch of Armenia flavors the menu at this popular eatery, recommended by Orange Coast magazine as one of the most popular neighborhood eateries in Orange County. Delicious breads and creative desserts bookend such treats as roast rack of lamb. Corner of Yorba and 17th Streets.

Villa Park

If you are not familiar with Southern California, San Marino in Los Angeles County is a beautiful and wealthy community near Pasadena that is often overlooked by those concerned with seeing (or living in) Beverly Hills or Bel-Air. Villa Park is Orange County's answer to San Marino. Smaller, to be sure, and more subdued than the showy wealth of Newport Beach, Villa Park's low profile belies the status and income of its residents.

Villa Park, which was once entirely citrus groves, was nicknamed the "banana belt" because temperatures never seemed to drop below freezing (the bane of citrus growers). Incorporated in 1962, its three square miles make it Orange County's smallest city.

There are no particularly exotic shops or bold attractions to speak of here, but if you want to drive around and check out the elegant homes with their immaculate landscaping, leave the Costa Mesa Freeway (Hwy. 55) at Katella Avenue and head east. Katella becomes Villa Park Road; the majority of the community lies north of this road between Wanda Road and Loma.

Westminster

Westminster was founded by a Presbyterian minister as a colony for like-minded farmers. Dairy farming became its principal business, as its residents were determined not to grow wine-making grapes, like their neighbors in Anaheim. Although the citizens were strong supporters of the temperance movement, time and economics eventually forced local farmers to grow grapes as well, along with celery, sugar beets and—naturally—oranges.

Westminster was incorporated in 1957, and with the influx of Southeast Asian immigrants, has grown to a large, thriving core of commerce in the heart of Orange County.

Shopping/Dining

Little Saigon

This is a multi-block district that has been transformed during the past 25 years by the influence of thousands of refugees from Southeast Asia. This portion of Westminster has become a truly international shopping and dining district. Park anywhere in and around the streets bordered by Brookhurst Street on the east, Magnolia Street on the west, between Bolsa Avenue and Bishop Place. You can't miss the assortment of two-story mini-malls with signs in both Vietnamese and English.

Little Saigon is a nice break from the more predictable shopping attractions of the county, and is an adventure for non-Asians. The bill of fare in all the eateries is either Vietnamese or Chinese, and the clothing stores offer fabrics you probably won't find anyplace else. Imported goods, jewelry, toys—all are offered for sale in shops with a marketplace feel. You may not understand what folks around you are saying, but that's part of its amazing appeal: you can leave the country without leaving the county.

In particular, be sure to visit the Asian Garden Mall (9200 Bolsa Avenue). Here the various indoor shops offer a variety of wares in a spacious, modern mall. All of Little Saigon is a busy spot on weekends, and shoppers come from many miles to browse, buy and enjoy the cuisine. Traffic and parking are less of a hassle on weekdays.

Events

Tet Festivals
First weekend in February

Celebrate the Vietnamese new year with the lively celebrations held throughout Little Saigon in February. This rich, multicultural experience includes parades with music, dancing, exotic costumes, and firecrackers.

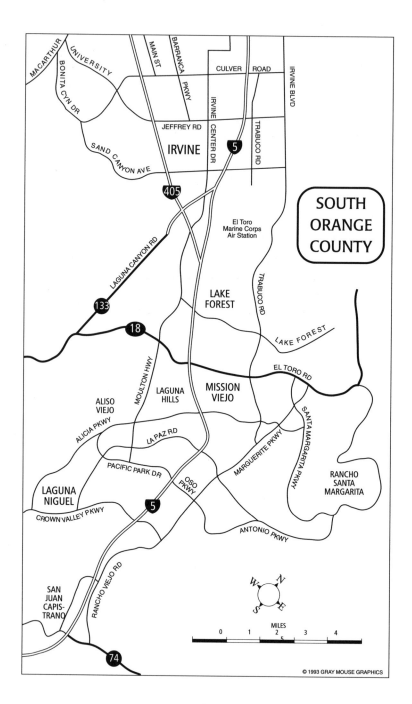

SOUTH ORANGE COUNTY

© 1993 GRAY MOUSE GRAPHICS

South Orange County

The southern portion of Orange County is dominated by one geological feature: the V-shaped Saddleback Valley, which is bounded along the coast by the San Joaquin Hills, and on the east by the Santa Ana Mountains. The "V" narrows at San Juan Capistrano, leaving only two means to head south: the San Diego Freeway (I-5) and Pacific Coast Highway. These routes parallel each other until they reach San Onofre and Camp Pendleton, where motorists on Pacific Coast Highway must merge onto the freeway to continue farther south, because Camp Pendleton is a restricted military area.

The Saddleback Valley was once the province of four Mexican families and their ranchos: Rancho Trabuco, Rancho Mission Vieja, Rancho Canada de Los Alisos and Rancho Niguel. The largest of these was Mission Vieja—literally old mission—named for Mission San Juan Capistrano, which lies within the boundaries of the old rancho. The rancho also encompassed the southern portion of what is now the city of Mission Viejo.

Much of the sheer newness of south Orange County, with the exception of the older San Juan Capistrano, makes it appealing to residents who are tired of urban blight and graffiti. But when every neighborhood is brand new, there is a certain charm—seasoning, if you will—that's still needed before these communities blossom fully.

Mission San Juan Capistrano,

Aliso Viejo

Not yet an incorporated city in its own right, Aliso Viejo is nestled along the western side of the Saddleback Valley, opposite Mission Viejo and Laguna Hills, with Laguna Canyon just behind its foothills. Aliso Viejo has one notable attraction as of this writing, a new golf club.

Aliso Viejo Golf Club
25191 Golf Drive
Information: (949) 252-1070

This is the first course in Orange County designed by Jack and Jackie Nicklaus, featuring three, 9-hole courses designed to challenge your swing while you enjoy a nice view of Saddleback Mountain. Twilight golfing is available. Close to the new San Joaquin toll road (Highway 73), exit at Aliso Creek Road and head north a few lights to Glenwood Drive. There's no clubhoue here (yet), just nice weather and good views.

Irvine

Placing Irvine in this chapter is an arbitrary decision; it stretches from Newport Beach and the San Joaquin Hills all the way across the plain that forms the northern portion of the Saddleback Valley. Since it is farther south than the majority of Orange County cities, I've decided to include it with the South County. Ask an Irvine resident what part of the county they live in, and they're likely to tell you the housing "village" they live in rather than say "Irvine," so this whole geographic question is probably moot anyway.

Irvine is the ultimate master-planned community—the largest of its kind in the United States when it was incorporated in 1971. It remains a model for other planned suburban communities. It was literally designed, the same way Paris and Washington, D.C., were. Although Irvine will never rival these cities as architectural and political hot spots, it has drawn thousands of people to its boundaries, seeking a carefully landscaped world where they can shut out many of life's nastier realities. This is not to say that Irvine is problem-free, but if you want to see a city where every park, every signpost, and every shopping center follows a prescribed pattern of land use and display, this is the prototype. It's often imitated, but there's only one Irvine.

Irvine is divided into many villages—separate housing tracts with distinct appearances and densities. Every type of housing—condos, apartments, townhouses, duplexes and "detached" homes—is seen here. All were carefully planned and mixed throughout the vast holdings of the Irvine Company. This was a company town in the modern 20th century sense: people here didn't work for the company, but they sure owed their lifestyle to it.

The Irvine Company was named for James Irvine (1827-86), a Scotch-Irish settler who bought many of the old ranchos that stretched from the Santa Ana Mountains to the sea. Ranchos Lomas, Santiago de Santa Ana, and San Joaquin comprised 93,000 acres, including nearly one-fifth of Orange County (no Southern plantation ever rivaled a California rancho for size).

Here is the University of California, Irvine. When it was built in the mid-1960s, it was an ultra-modern campus sitting alone in the midst of strawberry fields. The entire campus was once visible from MacArthur Boulevard and even from Newport Avenue farther to the northeast. However, the campus is now shrouded by the buildings and mature trees that have sprung up as the population grew.

Irvine is recognizable from the air by its cluster of shiny and (relatively) new office towers clustered near John Wayne Airport. Irvine and its neighbor Newport Beach have become centers of multi-million-dollar commerce, prospering in nearly perpetual sunshine. The airport and nearby hotels are more evidence of the importance of this bustling county crossroads, where once there was nothing but citrus groves and strawberry patches. Many fine restaurants have sprung up to cater to Irvine's upscale lifestyle.

Outdoors

The Greens at Park Place
3301 Michelson
Information: (949) 250-7888

Here is an 18-hole golf course exclusively devoted to putting. The greens, ranging from 53 feet to 127 feet, are immaculately groomed and were conceived by popular course architect Ted Robinson (who was also behind the Tijeras Creek and Tustin Ranch golf courses in Orange County). Groundskeepers constantly reposition the pin locations so that players won't become bored with the layout. What better way to work on your putting than on a course like this one, which you can complete while your kids are having fun down the street at the Palace Park *(see below, under "Attractions")*. Located at Michelson and Carlson, just east of Jamboree.

UCI Arboretum

Campus Drive and Jamboree Road
Information: (949) 824-5833
Hours: Monday through Saturday, 9 a.m. to 3 p.m.
Admission: Donation

This campus arboretum, dedicated to preserving endangered flora, contains plants from nearly every part of the globe, arranged together by continent. To find this wildlife preserve (part of San Joaquin Marsh) in the midst of Irvine, look for a small service road off Campus Drive, just south of the Campus-Jamboree intersection (watch for the big banner that says "UCI Arboretum"). A bird sanctuary is also part of this unspoiled area, and can be found at 3512 Michelson Drive. Call (949) 453-5500 for information about birdwatching tours.

Oak Creek Golf Club

One Golf Club Drive
Information: (949) 653-5303, 653-7300

This is another gem of an 18-hole course designed by Tom Fazio, the same person responsible for the twin courses at Pelican Hill. The rancho-style clubhouse is in the center of a course filled with eucalyptus trees. Located near the I-5 Freeway, exit at Jeffrey Road and then turn left on Irvine Center Drive.

Rancho San Joaquin Golf Course

One Sandburg Way
Information: (949) 451-0840, 786-5522

Large, undulating greens and a hilly course give you plenty to work with here, and it's only five minutes from John Wayne Airport. The green fee is modest on weekends (includes cart); it's half that on weekdays if you forego the cart. Seven-day advance reservations are recommended. There is also a practice area and a driving range.

Strawberry Farms Golf Club

11 Strawberry Farms
Information: (949) 551-1811

This course is planned around a 35-acre reservoir, with waterfalls that enhance the experience. Think of it as the wildlife course of Orange County, just a few minutes from the I-405 Freeway and UC Irvine. Weekday course fees are modest, but weekends and holidays are more expensive.

Turtle Rock Nature Center

1 Sunnyhill
Information: (949) 854-8151
Hours: Monday and Wednesday, 2 to 4 p.m.; Saturday,
11 a.m. to 2 p.m.
Admission: Donation welcome

You may see some wild animals as you stroll along the paths of this little park. If you visit inside the nature center, snakes, raccoons, and turtles are on display at eye level for young visitors. Exhibits are informative, and illustrate how we can all protect the environment.

William R. Mason Regional Park

18712 University Drive
Information: (949) 854-2491
Hours: Open daily until sunset
Fees: Nominal parking fee

A day-use park near the UC Irvine campus, Mason Regional Park has a nice lake with ducks. Barbecue fire rings and playground equipment make this a good picnic stop. There are bicycle trails, a fitness/parcourse (the kind where you interrupt your jog to work out at certain exercise stations), a Frisbee golf course, horseshoe pits and volleyball courts. Hobbyists use the lake to sail their model sailboats. There's also a nature trail and interpretive programs.

Attractions and Special Events

The Mezzanine
19800 MacArthur Boulevard
Information: (949) 724-1066

They call it "Whodunit dinner theater." The intrepid Mystery Cafe presents their comical mystery productions at the Mezzanine Restaurant on Fridays and Saturdays at 8 p.m. You will sink into the recreated world of film noir, brought to you live by actors, waiters and musicians. "Noir Suspicions," "Murder at Cafe Noir" and "Mumm's the Word" are some of the productions the Mystery Cafe cast has staged in the last few years.

The production is enacted among the diners before, during and after your meal. The audience is encouraged to participate, actively trying to solve the mystery. Or you can just sit back and enjoy. Orange Coast Magazine gave Mystery Cafe its vote for "Best Dinner Theater" in the county.

The price is $48 per person on Saturdays, $38 per person on Fridays (which includes a three-course meal, show and tax). Private shows can be scheduled Sunday through Thursday. The Mezzanine Restaurant is located at the Brinderson Towers, south of the John Wayne Airport.

Irvine Barclay Theater
4242 Campus Drive
Information: (949) 854-4646

This performance hall is located on the UC Irvine campus, presenting a variety of classical and pop concerts featuring name artists as well as student productions and local community groups. Dramatic presentations, classical and modern dance, and symphonic concerts featuring both the UC Irvine Fine Arts Department and traveling companies hold limited engagements in this intimate hall. Call the box office for current programs.

Palace Park

3405 Michelson Drive
Information: (949) 559-8336
Hours: Monday through Thursday, 11 a.m. to 10 p.m.;
Friday, 11 a.m. to 3 a.m.; Saturday, 10 a.m. to 1 a.m.;
Sunday, 10 a.m. to 11 p.m.

This very large playground for kids and adults is located adjacent to the San Diego Freeway (I-405). A miniature golf course is just the beginning. There is a go-cart track, bumper boats, batting cages, an indoor "laser runner" battle game, an arcade, and a McDonald's. Special birthday party packages are available. Your kids will not be bored here, I guarantee it.

Wayne Gretzky's Roller Hockey Center

3150 Barranca Parkway
Information: (949) 653-0900
Hours: Call for public skating times

The name literally says it all: this facility is devoted solely to roller hockey, the kind you play on in-line skates and using hockey sticks just like the Great One himself, Wayne Gretzky. The former NHL superstar lent his name to this distinctly non-ice version of a hockey venue. There are three rinks here, two covered, one uncovered. Devoted mainly to amateur leagues for all ages, public skating is open every day and on Saturday nights ($6, $4 for children under 12). There are also classes on the art of stopping and starting on in-line roller skates.

You can rent skates and sticks, of course, and shop in the store for hockey merchandise, including some Gretzky memorabilia. There are also some items on permanent display from Gretzky's storied career.

Historical

Old Town Irvine Hotel
14972 Sand Canyon Avenue
Information: 551-0909

This long block of restored buildings, including a blacksmith shop and general store, dates from Irvine's first century. All of these buildings have been converted into restaurants and a working hotel. The tenants weren't permitted to alter the basic structure of the buildings, so you can still enjoy their appearance by driving by or dining here. Old Town Irvine is right next to the western edge of the Santa Ana Freeway (I-5). You can reach it by taking the Sand Canyon exit.

Galleries and Museums

Irvine Museum
18881 Von Karman Avenue (Tower 17, Douglas Plaza)
Information: (949) 476-0294
Hours: Tuesday through Saturday, 11 a.m. to 5 p.m.
Admission and parking: Free

This is a "first" among California museums. The subject matter and artists belong to the school known as the California Impressionists. The paintings are from the collection of Joan Irvine Smith (of the same Irvine family), who has acquired more than 2,000 such paintings. Most of these works, which date between 1890 and 1930, depict California-inspired land and seascapes. The exhibit includes paintings by such notable artists as Granville Redmond, Guy Rose and William Wendt.

California impressionist paintings are highly environmental in theme and mood. Smith wants her collection to foster a greater understanding between those people who are devoted to land development and those who are concerned with the environmental toll of more development in Orange County. It's a tug-of-war that finds unusual expression in this gallery.

The museum is on the twelfth floor of an Irvine office building, so you may want to call for precise directions.

Irvine Historical Museum

5 San Joaquin
Information: (949) 786-4112
Hours: Tuesday and Sunday, 1 to 5 p.m.
Admission: $1 donation suggested

Built in 1877, this building is the city's oldest standing structure. Its original function was as the cookhouse for the Irvine Ranch cattle camp. It now houses a one-room museum featuring exhibits on the history of Irvine Ranch. Antique farm equipment is on display, and there is a "dress up" area for children.

Take the San Diego Freeway (I-405) to the Culver Drive offramp and turn south. The museum is next to the San Joaquin Golf Course.

Shopping

Irvine Spectrum

Intersection of I-5 Freeway at Alton Parkway exit / I-405
Freeway at Irvine Center Drive exit

Here is one of the brightest, wildest shopping, dining and movie theatre destinations in south Orange County. The Spectrum has a huge, 21-screen mega cinemaplex (including an IMAX theatre), and is surrounded by some excellent restaurants and shops. The amount of neon put into this center makes it hard to miss if you're traveling on either the I-5 or I-405 freeways.

For dining combined with entertainment, David & Busters is an enormous choice, featuring all manner of realistic arcade experiences for grown-ups, not to mention food. The wait for a table here tends to be long, so if you're in the mood for something less complicated, try Champp's Americana, a sports bar with an amazing array of good appetizers and outdoors seating if you want to get away from the television screens. P.F. Chang's China Bistro and Wolfgang Puck's Cafe, both just opposite the Edwards Cinemaplex, are also good choices for lunch or dinner.

The Improv Comedy Club is also a part of the entertaining mix of venues here, as is the Crazy Horse Steakhouse, a great place to see nationally-renown country-western music stars and oldies acts. So even your need for laughter or two-stepping can be satisfied when you visit this sparkling entertainment complex. And if you still need more stimulation, go to Gameworks, a humongous video/virtual reality arcade.

Dining

Chanteclair

18912 MacArthur Boulevard
Information: (949) 752-8001
Hours: Monday through Friday, 11:30 a.m. to 2:30 p.m.
(lunch); Monday through Saturday, 6 to 10 p.m. (dinner).
Reservations recommended.

This restaurant has received national attention for its decor and ambiance (not to mention the food). It is conveniently located right across the street from Orange County's John Wayne Airport. Reservations are needed, but if your are a connoisseur of French cooking with a California twist, you'll be glad you made them.

Prego

18420 Von Karman Avenue
Information: (949) 553-1333
Hours: Monday, 11: 30 a.m. to 10:30 p.m.; Tuesday through
Thursday, 11:30 a.m. to 11 p.m.; Friday, 11:30 a.m. to
11:30 p.m.; Saturday, 5 p.m. to 11:30; Sunday, 5 to 10 p.m.

This popular spot in the midst of Irvine's modest collection of office towers offers Northern Italian specialties such as *zuppe di lenticchie* (lentil soup) and *soncino con anitra* (cold roasted duck breast with goat cheese). The place has a festive atmosphere in addition to great food, so you better make reservations.

Tia Juana's Long Bar

Old Town Irvine
14988 Sand Canyon Avenue
Information: (949) 551-2998
Hours: Tuesday through Saturday, 4 p.m. to 11 p.m.

This nice restaurant is housed inside one of the large, historic buildings of Old Town Irvine. It is also practically on top of the Amtrak railroad tracks. A bell clangs from the "long bar" (70 feet!) every time a train thunders by and shakes the rafters. Tia Juana's food is not your run-of-the-mill Mexican food; that means the menu offers tasty surprises and options beyond burritos. The cocktail hour at the long bar is a big local draw for both young professionals and students from nearby Irvine Valley College. Latin music is played Sunday through Thursday, and pop/rock on Friday and Saturday.

Laguna Hills

This community was born when Leisure World came along in the 1960s. Leisure World is one of the nation's most successful retirement communities, complete with golf course and private gates, spreading in and around the hills just west of the San Diego Freeway (I-5) on either side of El Toro Road. Leisure World was recently incorporated as its own city-within-a-city, and christened Laguna Woods. But we are digressing. Laguna Hills is still it's own city, despite the secession of Leisure World.

Attractions and Special Events

Verizon Wireless Amphitheater
(formerly Irvine Meadows)

8808 Irvine Center Drive
Information: (949) 855-8096

Orange County has only one outdoor concert venue, and it recently acquired the name of a corporate sponsor. Verizon Wireless Amphitheatre is located just south of the San Diego Freeway next to the Wild Rivers aquatic park. It features concerts of pop, rock and classical music. There are three levels of seating, plus "meadow seating" above the reserved seats where listeners can picnic and enjoy the sounds of the Pacific Symphony Orchestra or big-name rock'n'roll bands. Tickets for concerts here or at many other Orange County sites can be purchased at Ticketmaster locations (call 740-2000 for information).

Wild Rivers Water Park
8770 Irvine Center Drive
Information: (949) 768-WILD
Hours: Open daily from mid-May through September
Admission: $23 ages 10 and up; $18 for children under 10

This is Orange County's only waterpark, unless you count the Pacific Ocean. If you've never seen a waterpark, they're "way better" than any municipal swimming pool. Forget cannonballs. Here's where you can plummet down fast chutes of water and fling your body headlong into giant pools and shout "AAAAAAHHHHHHH." This place is designed for letting your kids go crazy. There are also pools and quieter options besides the plunge-and-splash chutes.

At the wave pool called Thunder Cove, Wild Rivers recreates the fun of bodysurfing. While your children are enjoying the thrilling rides, you can float atop a giant inner tube along a meandering stream that flows around a huge wading pool. This was tailor-made for toddlers and those of you interested in working on your tan instead of your adrenaline rush.

For the more adventurous, there is the Abyss and other hair-raising drops down the five-story-high Wild Rivers Mountain. My favorite is the plunge through a pitch-black tunnel that bends and plummets down a large hill. Two side-by-side tunnels let you race your friends to the bottom; the only thing is, you can't see a thing until you emerge at the other end! AAAAAAAHHHHHHHH!!

Wild Rivers is easy to find. Just take the Irvine Center Drive exit south from the San Diego Freeway (I-405). It's about one-half mile on your right, at the same entrance as the Verizon Wireless Amphitheater.

Shopping

Laguna Hills Mall

El Toro Road and Avenida de la Carlota
Information: (949) 586-8282

This mall isn't large, but it is a less crowded alternative to South Coast Plaza a few miles up the 405 Freeway. Sears, J.C. Penney and Macy's are the largest retailers. During October, the Pumpkin City Pumpkin Patch is held in the southeast portion of the parking lot. This Halloween party that lasts for days is extremely popular with kids. There is a tiny train and ponies to ride, farm animals to feed and pet, and live entertainment for the family while you pick out your prize pumpkin amid bales of hay. Call (949) 768-1103 for information.

Next door to Laguna Hills Mall is Oakbrook Village, an outdoor center with Trader Joe's, one of the best grocery chain stores in Southern California. If you haven't been to Trader Joe's before, you'll marvel at their array of unusual domestic and imported groceries and wines at good prices. Many of these items can't be found anywhere else in Orange County.

The Laguna Hills Mall and Oakbrook Village are located directly off the San Diego Freeway (I-5) at the El Toro Road exit. This crossroads is where the communities of Laguna Hills and Lake Forest meet, and in fact the intersections on either side of the freeway at El Toro Road are among the busiest in the county. It can make travel through this area sluggish.

Mediterranean Grocery & Deli

25381-A Alicia Parkway
Information: (949) 770-2007
Hours: Monday through Saturday, 9 a.m. to 8 p.m.;
Sunday, 11 a.m. to 4 p.m.

This may be the only store in south Orange County where you can stock your pantry with delicacies from Persia, Arabia, Armenia, India, Greece and other Middle Eastern and Eastern Europe countries. Tea, cheese, yogurt, rice, dressings, dough—it's a wide variety of imported items that will surely tempt your palate and inspire your cooking. It's located in a nondescript shopping center at the corner of Alicia Parkway and Paseo de Valencia.

Dining

King's Fish House

24001 Avenida de la Carlota
Information: (949) 586-1515
Hours: Serving: Lunch, dinner

Here you'll find excellent seafood at reasonable prices, and the atmosphere is casual. Located in the parking lot of the Laguna Hills Mall at El Toro Road, this establishment has become immensely popular in a short time. If there's too long a wait for a table, do what I do: walk into the bar and eat there instead! The wait is much less, and the food's the same.

Laguna Niguel

The south county communities of Laguna Hills, Mission Viejo and Laguna Niguel don't appear to be much different in character — and they aren't. They all share the rolling slopes of the Saddleback Valley, all have planned residential communities, and all have broad "parkways" to carry commuters quickly to and from work. The housing styles, just as they do in all communities, reflect the different eras in which they were built. Laguna Niguel's skyline is dominated by countless homes that have Spanish tile roofs. At times, while driving along Golden Lantern or Niguel Road, two of the busier parkways in the city, the rooftops seem to undulate in waves across the pretty green landscape. Laguna Niguel has two large, enjoyable regional parks.

Outdoors

Aliso and Wood Canyons Regional Park
Alicia Parkway and Awma Road
Information: (949) 831-2791
Hours: Sunrise to sunset

A huge undeveloped area along the San Joaquin Hills, Aliso and Wood Canyons is ideal for day hikes. From its heights you can see both the Saddleback Valley and the Pacific Ocean. There are biking, hiking and equestrian trails. You may want to consider the bike or horse route, because it takes a few miles to reach the really wild parts of this park. Many archaeological finds have been made here, relics from early days when Indians first hunted, gathered and fished in this part of California. You can seem some of these artifacts at the Orange County Natural History Museum located within the park (see *Attractions* below).

From the San Diego Freeway (I-5), take the Alicia Parkway exit and head west. Just past Aliso Creek Road, the park's main entrance is about two-tenths of a mile on the right—

look for Awma Road, which is unpaved.

One trailhead—the Aliso Summit Trail—can be reached by passing this entrance until you reach Pacific Island Drive, and then turning right and going almost to the top of the hill. Park at the T-intersection of Pacific Island and La Brise. The sign marking the trail is on your right. This two-mile-long ridge trail does not descend into the canyon. On a clear day you can see Catalina Island, Mount Baldy in the San Gabriel Mountains (look northeast), Dana Point to the south and the Saddleback Valley to the east. From this one summit the juxtaposition of blinding-white model homes, rugged mountains and a magnificent ocean vista says it all: this land has a passion that lured people here for centuries. The modern-day irony, of course, is that so many people want to live here that the wild land is disappearing underneath the lawns, patios and garages of south Orange County. Fortunately, parks such as this help preserve the original enchantment.

The warning sign at this trailhead reminds visitors that Aliso and Woods Canyons are natural areas with mountain lions, rattlesnakes, poison oak and rugged terrain. Minors must be supervised and dogs must be on a leash.

Crown Valley Community Park

29751 Crown Valley Parkway
Information: (949) 362-4350
Hours: Daily, sunrise to sunset

This park houses the city's recreation offices, and features an excellent municipal swimming pool with a diving platform. The park is thrust against a green hillside with a landscaped botanical trail. The trail displays acres of drought-resistant plants typical of the Southwest. It's an excellent place to rise above the din of nearby Crown Valley (a busy thoroughfare at any time of day), offering wooden benches where you can relax and contemplate...well, whatever it is you want to contemplate.

Crown Valley Community Park is located between La Paz and Niguel Road on the north side of Crown Valley Parkway.

Laguna Niguel Regional Park

28241 La Paz Road
Information: (949) 831-2791
Fee: $2 day use per auto

Just down the road from the Chet Holifield Federal Building (the "ziggurat") lies a large regional park with a 40-acre lake for fishing and boating. The lake is stocked with bass, catfish and trout. (You'll need a state fishing license unless you are under age 16.)

There are many areas in Laguna Niguel's 174 acres for ball playing, picnicking, jogging, and cycling. There are horseshoe pits here, too. This park is particularly attractive because it butts up against the San Joaquin Hills, providing access to lots of hilly areas for scenic contrast and hiking.

Laguna Niguel also has a remote-control glider plane bluff at the north end of the park, where you're sure to see folks launching their model planes off the short cliff above Alicia Parkway.

The entrance to Laguna Niguel Regional is the first driveway south from the corner of Aliso Creek Road and La Paz. Alternately, you can take the San Diego Freeway to Crown Valley Parkway, head west toward the beach and turn right at La Paz. The park entrance will be on your left.

Attractions and Special Events

Chet Holifield Federal Building

Avila Road and La Paz Road

This is a regional branch office of our federal government, housing some National Archives material and other miscellaneous government documents. It was originally built for the aerospace firm Rockwell International. What makes the structure so distinctive? It's a ziggurat—a stepped pyramid in the style of ancient Babylonia. It is easily the most unusual bit of architecture in South County. To see it, take the San Diego Freeway (I-5) south to La Paz Road, exit and head west toward the ocean. Turn right at Avila Road and you can't miss it.

Orange County Natural History Museum

Aliso and Wood Canyons Regional Park
Information: (949) 487-9155; (www.ocnha.mus.ca.us)

Here you can see exhibits on the many species that are indigenous to this region of California, such as reptiles, insects and birds. Paleontological artifacts from Orange County's prehistoric past are also on display in this facility, housed in a large trailer for the time being. Digs are held regularly in the park for members of the Natural History Association (minimum age to join is 14), and children come here regularly to examine fossils and learn more about the world around them.

From the San Diego Freeway (I-5), take the Alicia Parkway exit and head west. Just past Aliso Creek Road, look for the Aliso and Wood Canyons Regional Park entrance about two-tenths of a mile on the right—look for Awma Road, which is unpaved. The museum is on the park grounds.

Dining

China Sea Restaurant

24050 Camino Del Avion
Information: (949) 489-8168
Hours: Every day, 11:30 a.m. to 2:30 p.m. (lunch),
4:30 p.m. - 9:30 p.m. (dinner), until 10 p.m. Friday and
Saturday

This attractive little restaurant features genuine Mandarin cooking, a style of Chinese food that is definitely distinct from the more familiar Szechwan cuisine served at most Southland Chinese restaurants. The dishes here are simply delicious and the presentation is elegant. Try the Rainbow Shrimp — a speciality — if you can't decide where to begin. The China Sea is located in Monarch Beach Plaza at the corner of Camino Del Avion and Niguel Road.

Lake Forest

Before it was a city, the acreage of Lake Forest was one of the four largest *ranchos* in the Saddleback Valley. The locals still often refer to it by its former name, El Toro. Lake Forest is probably best known for the El Toro Marine Base, closed in 1999. El Toro once boasted the largest air show of any kind in the United States, but no more.

Historical

Heritage Hill Historical Park

25151 Serrano Road
Information: (949) 855-2028
Hours: Wednesday through Sunday, 9 a.m. to 5 p.m.

Heritage Hill, which was the county's first historical park, brings together four buildings from different eras in Saddleback Valley history. Tours of this mini-village are offered at 2 p.m., Wednesday through Friday, with an additional 11 a.m. tour on weekends.

The El Toro Grammar School is a one-room schoolhouse built in 1890 and used for grades one through eight until 1914. The school was then moved from its original site and was used as a Catholic church until 1968. Eventually, it was donated to the county and relocated here.

The Serrano Adobe is the star of this park—the only surviving adobe from the Rancho Canada de Los Alisos of Don Jose Serrano. It is believed to have been constructed around 1863. The Serrano family raised cattle on their rancho, but after a series of droughts their financial fortunes took a turn for the worse and they were forced to sell sections of their land. The Whiting family bought the adobe in 1884, and in 1932 expanded it to its present size. The adobe is now mentioned in *Guide to California State Historic Landmarks*.

The last remaining ranch house from turn-of-the-century

El Toro is the Bennett Ranch House, built in 1908 by the Bennett family, who were citrus pioneers. This structure is typical of the period.

The fourth structure at Heritage Hill is St. George's Episcopal Mission, dating from 1891. When English settlers came to El Toro to grow fruit, this was their house of worship. Many of the interior furnishings, including an oak baptismal font, are original.

Outdoors

Serrano Creek Community Park
Serrano Road

This charming park follows Serrano Creek along Serrano Road between Lake Forest Avenue and Bake Parkway. A huge grove of eucalyptus trees dominate the scenery, their fragrance permeating the walking path. The park is a nice spot for both cyclists and pedestrians. Pets must be on a leash. Heritage Hill Historical Park is at the southern end of this pretty park.

Whiting Ranch Wilderness Park
Portola Hills Parkway near Bake Parkway, Trabuco Canyon
Hours: Daily from sunrise to sunset
Information: (949) 589-4729; Tours: (714) 832-7478

Here are 1,500 acres of woodlands. There are sycamore and oak groves, ponds, rock formations, and rolling hills of grass and canyons. Not only is the scenery pleasing and secluded, it's so close to the hustle and bustle of the city that you don't have to travel very far to get here to relax. It is tailor-made for mountain biking and hiking. A big attraction here is the wildflowers: poppies, Indian paintbrush, sticky monkey flower, mustard, and clover.

Directions: From the San Diego Freeway (I-5), take Lake Forest Drive east five miles to Portola Hills Parkway, turn left and proceed past Bake Parkway to the entrance (approximately one-half mile) on the right.

Dining

Carmel's

23781 El Toro Road
Information: (949) 770-7050
Hours: Open daily 6 a.m. to midnight

Carmel's is my answer to fast-food-style Mexican food that is very tasty. You can eat on the premises and enjoy some Mexican beer with your food, or take-out. The menu isn't large, but the portions are, and everything has a homemade taste. You can even drive-through if you want, but I prefer to go inside where I help myself to generous portions of *pico de gallo* to ladle on my *pollo burrito*. Try the green (*tomatillo*) sauce with a basket of *tacquitos*, or the green chile burrito.

Look for this establishment in the Lake Forest Marketplace parking lot on the northwest corner of Rockfield and El Toro.

Mission Viejo

The land within these city limits originally belonged to two ranchos, Rancho Mission Vieja and Rancho Trabuco. Mission Vieja stretched from the present boundary of Orange and Riverside county to San Juan Capistrano. Rancho Trabuco once incorporated what is now the northern half of Mission Viejo and the Cleveland National Forest. Parts of both were swallowed up into a new ranch owned by Richard O'Neill, who bought the land from the rancheros. This transfer of land was typical during and after the Mexican War.

When Mexico seceded from Spain, the new nation included the lands of Alta ("upper") California—the present state of California—and Baja ("lower") California, the peninsula that is separated from mainland Mexico by the Sea of Cortez. The Mexican governor of California, General Pio Pico, deeded vast portions of land to various Mexican citizens. These were the ranchos. Many ranchos were actually confiscated lands that once belonged to the missions of the Catholic Church. The Franciscan missionaries had been entrusted with this land and were meant in time to turn it over to the local Indian populations. The creation of Mexico changed all that, causing the Indians to receive nothing.

After the Mexican War, the United States annexed Arizona, New Mexico and Alta California. The rancho owners were not immediately displaced, but eventually their property was bought by new settlers from the East, who raised livestock and produce on the land. Sheep were of major importance in the Saddleback Valley, as was citrus fruit. Thus began the spread of the famous orange groves, which eventually gave their name to the region.

Orange County grew slowly during the first half of the 20th century, remaining a rich agricultural county well into the 1950s. During the 1960s, Mission Viejo was one of the prototype planned communities in this part of Orange County. The farmland was cleared to make way for new, affordable family homes. The bungalow style of the post-World War II building boom, familiar to residents in the more populous northern portion of the county, was being replaced by homes that were less boxy, more rancho style, with Spanish tile roofs.

Mission Viejo is a quintessential modern "bedroom" community. The suburban landscape (and nicely landscaped it is) is not designed to attract travelers. There are no theme parks, museums or entertainment complexes. Because it is inland, Mission Viejo has no beaches, either. Consequently, there are few points of visitor interest. However, the local residents have a beautiful lake to enjoy.

Outdoors

Lake Mission Viejo

Marguerite Parkway between Alicia Parkway and
Vista del Lago

One of several "man-made" lakes in Orange County, Lake Mission Viejo is bordered by the Market on the Lake shopping village and residences with their own boat slips. Several restaurants offer dining with a view, and there is a pleasant, 2.5-mile jogging path around this picturesque lake.

Mission Viejo Recreation Center–
Marguerite Complex

27341 Trabuco Circle
Center Information: (949) 768-0981
Swim Office: (949) 380-2552
Hours: Varies with the seasons; call for hours
Marguerite Tennis Center
23840 Marguerite Parkway
Information: (949) 855-6854
Hours: Monday through Friday, 8 a.m. to 12 p.m., and 4
p.m. to 10 p.m.; Saturday and Sunday, 8 a.m. to 8 p.m.

This large recreation complex has excellent tennis and swimming facilities. The fee to play tennis is just $6 for 1.5

hours, and you need not be a resident. The center also has racquetball, handball and volleyball courts for $4 per hour. If you're concerned about its capacity, never fear—there are still more tennis courts just a short drive south at the intersection of Marguerite and Felipe. These courts are also run by the Mission Viejo Recreation Department.

At the Marguerite Complex, the Olympic-sized lap pool and diving area is a true standout. It's used for many regional swim meets and Olympic tryouts. The platform diving structure is so tall it can even be seen behind the tall trees that line Marguerite Parkway.

The tennis facility is at the corner of Trabuco Circle and Marguerite. To go directly to the swimming area, take Marguerite north past Trabuco Circle to Casta del Sol and turn right. The parking lot is on your immediate right. Lockers and child care are available, too.

Shopping

The Shops at Mission Viejo
Crown Valley Parkway and I-5 Freeway

Newly-renovated for the new millennium, this mall has become the new darling of South County. The tenants are a mix of traditional mall shops and the more decidedly *en vogue* designer retailers. Classy home accessory stores are here alongside a healthy assortment of clothiers. Brand new department stores are Saks Fifth Avenue and Nordstrom, joining the stalwarts Macy's and Robinsons-May (the latter expanded to twice its original size). The entire interior got a major facelift, bringing much needed skylights and lighter decor to brighten the entire shopping experience. An extremely comfortable and likable place to stroll for your after-dinner or weekend window shopping.

Dining

Capriccio

25380 Marguerite Parkway
Information: (949) 855-6866
Hours: Monday through Friday, 11:30 a.m. to 2:30 p.m.
(lunch); Monday through Thursday 4 to 9:30 p.m. (dinner);
Friday and Saturday, 4 to 10 p.m.; Sunday, 4 to 9 p.m.

Casual style, good homemade Sicilian-style Italian food (featuring meat, poultry, and pasta), and Italian wines are the hallmarks of this cozy cafe. Restaurants can't get more intimate than this establishment, sandwiched between an ice cream parlor and an auto parts store in the heart of Mission Viejo. If you blink, you'll miss the entrance, and you won't spot it from the street because it's hidden in a strip mall.

From the I-5 freeway, take La Paz Road to Marguerite Parkway, turn right and then left into the Mission Viejo Village Center.

Tortilla Flats

27792 Vista Del Lago
Information: (949) 830-9980
Hours: Daily, 11:30 a.m. to 10 p.m.; Sunday brunch from
10 a.m. to 2 p.m. Serving: Lunch, dinner

Tortilla Flats is a big, festive restaurant both inside and outside, where diners can sit on the edge of Lake Mission Viejo and enjoy traditional California-Mexican cuisine. The building's front is inviting, with its palms, beautiful tile fountain, and profusion of ivy growing up the walls and roof of the "cantina."

Rancho Santa Margarita

This community is, at present, too new to have attracted the offbeat or specialty shops and attractions more prevalent in older communities. Mostly what you will find in Rancho Santa Margarita are housing tracts. The businesses and schools necessary to sustain these new residents are much in evidence, but there's little to draw a visitor except the wonderful view of Saddleback Mountain looming over the community's flat expanse.

Outdoors

Riley Wilderness Park

30952 Oso Parkway, Coto de Caza
Information: (949) 459-1687
Hours: 7 a.m. to 5 p.m. Admission: $2 per vehicle

Most of the wilderness parks in Orange County are very large, but this one is a small, pleasant park that meanders alongside a creek, presenting great butterfly and flower-watching. The park is one more great place to escape suburbia, yet just minutes away from the usual South County amenities.

Tijeras Creek Golf Course

29082 Tijeras Creek Road
Information: (949) 589-9793

A wide-open course with desert appeal. It takes awhile to drive here from the nearest freeway (I-5), but *OC Metro* magazine highly recommends this Ted Robinson-designed course. One duffer describes it as a "fun house." You will probably lose a fair number of balls on your way to the last hole. The course butts up against the wilder portions of Orange County, and sightings of snakes and even mountain lions are possible. Kinda gives new meaning to the term handicap...

San Juan Capistrano

This community is pretty much a must-see when visiting Orange County. But don't let the tourist appeal scare you off: San Juan Capistrano is a nice little town, and if you visit on a weekday, there's plenty of space to park and stroll.

The area along Camino Capistrano from the new Mission Church at the corner of Acjechema, just north of the mission grounds all the way south to Del Obispo Avenue has become a charming walking district of shops and eateries. Many of the buildings are quite old, while others are new (such as Franciscan Plaza, 31781 Camino Capistrano) and designed in the "mission style." All have a charm that makes this great for a stroll on sunny days. There are plenty of gift shops offering antiques, Native American crafts, jewelry, dolls, flowers and other unique gifts.

To reach the heart of San Juan Capistrano (SJC for short), take the San Diego Freeway (I-5) and exit at Ortega Highway. The highway bisects the central part of town if you turn west. Within two blocks you will be right at the city's most famous landmark, the mission.

An alternate way to arrive in San Juan Capistrano is to follow the old Atchison Topeka Santa Fe Railroad line (now Amtrak) that parallels the freeway both north and south of the town center. From the southbound San Diego Freeway, exit at Avery Parkway, turn right and then make an immediate left on Camino Capistrano. If you follow this same road out of San Juan Capistrano, it will take you straight to Capistrano Beach and the ocean.

For a longer excursion, you can leave historic San Juan Capistrano by heading east on Ortega Highway and taking this two-lane mountain road for an hour-and-a-half drive to Lake Elsinore in adjacent Riverside County. Ortega Highway ascends what is probably the most breathtaking mountain pass in all of Orange County. The views of both the ocean and the changing hillsides are spectacular, but if altitude and steep cliffs give you the willies, ask someone else to drive!

Historical

Mission San Juan Capistrano

31882 Camino Capistrano
Information: (949) 248-2048
Hours: Daily, 8:30 a.m. to 5 p.m.
Admission: Adults, $5; children and seniors, $4

Perhaps because it is the oldest—make that the *first*—historic site in all of Orange County, Mission San Juan Capistrano is definitely the most beloved. If you think that the only point of interest here is the swallows, however, you'll be pleasantly surprised. This mission is also a national treasure, as it represents a significant period in the history of North America at a time when California was not yet part of the United States. The explorers serving the Spanish monarchy, who made expeditions by land and sea along the Pacific shores, thought they had found a paradise. They returned again and again to claim more of this land for their country.

Mission San Juan Capistrano was actually founded twice, once in 1775, and then officially on November 1, 1776, by Padre Junipero Serra. Serra was a Franciscan friar who spent his life laboring to do good works among the "heathens" of the New World. The friars took their task very seriously, and their dedication and tenacity is a compelling story. They came to *Alta* ("upper") California with very little assistance from the monarchy that sponsored them, charged with Christianizing the Indians and educating them in European ways. The Spanish monarchy also regarded the colonization of Alta California as an important way to establish territorial sovereignty over what was surely a source of natural wealth, and therefore attractive to other European powers.

With the founding of each mission, Padre Serra and his successors were establishing a chain linked by El Camino Real ("the royal road" or "King's Highway") from San Diego to Sonoma north of San Francisco Bay. The objective was to train Indians to become efficient in agriculture and raising livestock, then gradually bequeath the mission property back to the Indians. *Pueblos* (towns) grew up around or near many of the 21 missions, often creating tension between the Indians and the Spanish settlers. Deadly skirmishes between colonists and Indians were not uncommon, and many Indians gave up emulating the Europeans. However, others thrived under the mission system. They created beautiful crafts, decorated mission walls with their art, and some learned to read and play music. Some were married in the church.

Unfortunately, the mission system did as much to hurt California's Native Indian population as it did to help it. Old World diseases brought death to many villages; friars sometimes punished Indians harshly for transgressions that the Indians did not really understand, and many fled the missions, never to be seen again. As Mexico wrested California from Spain, the new nation began deeding vast tracts of land to its own citizens, stripping the native Indians of what was once regarded as their natural property rights. The missions were neglected, cannibalized for building materials, and ultimately abandoned. Many of them fell into such disrepair that the majority of the structures that visitors see nowadays are restorations or pure recreations of the originals.

The church at Mission San Juan Capistrano was destroyed in 1812 by a devastating earthquake, a catastrophe that affected several other missions in Southern California. Only the church wall behind the altar is standing today. No attempt has been made to recreate the original church structure, which was intended at the time to be the largest of the mission churches. The ruin, however, is quite beautiful in its own right, revealing the architectural style and intentions of its creators and the craft of the Indian laborers who built it. The authentic grounds and buildings lend a wonderful flavor to any visit, even as it experiences ongoing restoration (don't be surprised if you see scaffolding).

Inside the courtyard is a fountain and paths that lead to the church and adjacent buildings. Beautiful landscaping here and in the interior courtyard includes jacarandas, palms, oaks and other trees. Maps provided at the entrance lead visitors on a self-guided tour so they will not miss archaeological points of interest along the way.

Three bells from the period are now hung in a *campanelle*, or bell wall, instead of in a tower atop the nonexistent church. The bells are rung only on special occasions, such as St. Joseph's Day. Inside the adjacent wings of the mission are rooms showing how the Indians, friars and military guards lived. Hide tanning vats and other outdoor work facilities have been restored so that mission life is plainly visualized. Other rooms contain exhibits and artifacts from the Native American and rancho periods of California.

The most peaceful place in the mission is the Serra Chapel, the only remaining building in California where Padre Serra was known to have said mass. It is a beautiful chapel, with continuously lit candles. Note the beautiful *reredos* behind the altar. This 300-year-old, ornately designed gilded wall was brought from Barcelona.

The six-day-long event that celebrates the return of the swallows on March 19 to San Juan Capistrano recently underwent a name change. Instead of the Heritage Festival, it is now called the Fiesta de las Golondrinas (Festival of the Swallows).

This is probably a good time to answer the question: do the swallows always return to San Juan Capistrano on March 19, St. Joseph's Day? The answer is yes, some do. Some arrive before March 19, and some arrive after as well, so March 19 is not a magic day, just a convenient one. The swallows build their mud nests in the walls in and around the mission compound. There are plenty of pigeons, too!

Garcia Adobe

31851-71 Camino Capistrano

This adobe is two blocks south of the mission, and just a few doors from the town's most famous restaurant, El Adobe. The Garcia adobe is unusual in that it has two stories, constructed in the Monterey style. It was built in the 1840s by Manual Garcia, a merchant from Portugal.

Amtrak Depot

26701 Verdugo Street
Amtrak Information: 800-872-7245

This historic depot is nicely preserved, and has been expanded by connecting real railroad cars from the 1930s where you can relax and have a drink while awaiting your train. The depot is located one block west of Camino Capistrano between Anguello Way and Verdugo Street near the Mission.

Los Rios Historic District

Near the Amtrak Depot

Across the tracks west of the Amtrak depot is the Los Rios Historic District. This is the oldest neighborhood in California. Visitors may take a self-guided walking tour of the district and see numerous historic homes. Every Sunday at 1 p.m. a guided tour is given, beginning at El Peon Plaza across the street from the mission. Call San Juan Historical Walking Tours (949-493-8444) for more information.

O'Neill Museum

31831 Los Rios Street
Information: (949) 493-8444
Hours: Tuesday through Friday, 9 a.m. to 12 p.m. and
1 to 4 p.m.; Sunday and Monday, 1 to 3 p.m.
Admission: Donation

One of the homes open to the public in the Los Rios Historic District is this small, Victorian house from the 1880s. This is one of the first wooden (as opposed to adobe) buildings in San Juan Capistrano. It now serves as a museum featuring artifacts from San Juan Capistrano's heritage.

Attractions and Special Events

The Coach House

33157 Camino Capistrano
Information: (949) 496-8930

This popular nightclub headlines some of the more popular names in rock, jazz, fusion, country and folk—both local favorites and international stars, such as B. B. King or Ray Charles. The Coach House has a large, open room with a fun atmosphere. Patrons may have only cocktails or enjoy full dinners. (The menu features basic steak, chicken and fish entrees.) The price of the show varies with the attraction, generally in the $25-per-customer range.

The Coach House is tucked inside a business park south of the main part of town, right off the San Diego Freeway (I-5). Exit at San Juan Creek Road and head south. Watch for Avenida Aeropuerto and turn right.

Dining

Cafe Mozart

31952 Camino Capistrano
Information: (949) 496-0212
Hours: Tuesday through Thursday, 11:30 to 3 p.m. (lunch),
5:30 to 9 p.m. (dinner); Friday and Saturday, open until
10 p.m.

The menu of this quaint indoor/outdoor establishment features European specialties, including wild game. The prices are moderate and the dress is casual. While you're dining, take note of the unusual mosaic mural in the courtyard of this little shopping center. Cafe Mozart is located in the Mercado Village shopping center just a five-minute stroll south of the mission on Camino Capistrano.

El Adobe Restaurant

31891 Camino Capistrano
Information: (949) 493-1163
Hours: Daily until 9:30 p.m.

This popular Mexican restaurant is also an historic landmark. Part of the eatery was the town jail, courthouse and stage depot. Another section was once the home of Antonio Yorba II, one of San Juan Capistrano's early settlers. Traditional Mexican favorite dishes are served daily either inside or on the patio.

L'Hirondelle

31631 Camino Capistrano
Information: (949) 661-0425
Hours: Tuesday through Sunday, 5 to 9 p.m.; Friday and
Saturday until 10 p.m.; Sunday brunch, 11 a.m. to 2 p.m.;
closed Monday

L'Hirondelle is opposite the mission on the west side of Camino Capistrano. The white exterior and wooden-beam interiors are reminiscent of a Belgian country inn. *Civet de lapin, veal cordon bleu, canard a l'orange* and other favorites are prepared daily. There are also Belgian beers and French wines to complement your palate.

Ramos House Cafe

31752 Los Rios Street
(949) 443-1342
Hours: 8 a.m. to 3 p.m., Tuesday through Sunday

This is a wonderful spot for breakfast or brunch, located in the historic district just across the railroad tracks from the Amtrak depot. Chef Humphries, who also lives upstairs in this quaint converted residence, cooks and serves gourmet meals. The setting is quiet — except when the train rolls into the station (but that's for romantic atmosphere anyway). The weather in San Juan Capistrano is so pleasant that you will feel transported to a simpler time when you sip some espresso and taste the fine creations here, all reasonably priced.

Sarducci's

26701 Verdugo Street
Information: (949) 493-9593
Hours: Daily, 8 a.m. to 10 p.m. Serving: Breakfast, lunch, dinner

Sarducci's has a diverse, heady mixture of Italian, Cajun and California specialties on the menu. This restaurant, located in the historic train depot, has a great patio made for relaxing. As most everywhere else in San Juan Capistrano, the outdoor dining is a must, so you may have to wait for a table because the weather is usually delightful. Sarducci's is conveniently located opposite a triple-movie theater complex.

Outdoors

Jones Family Mini Farm

31791 Los Rios Street
Information: (949) 831-6550
Hours: Weekends only, 11 a.m. to 4 p.m.
Admission: Free

If you enjoy the ambiance of a family barnyard, this is your place. The Jones family claims to own the last working farm in the South County, and it's open to the public. On weekends children can ride ponies for $2, and pet the many farm animals roaming about. If you reserve ahead of time, you can take a hay ride through the historic district and end the trip with an old-fashioned barbecue.

San Juan Hills Golf Club

32120 San Juan Creek Road
Information: (949) 837-0361

An inexpensive afternoon of golf, played in a nice location above San Juan Capistrano—what more could one ask for? *The Golf Trekker*® describes this as a "narrow, well bunkered" course. You need ten days advance registration for a tee time.

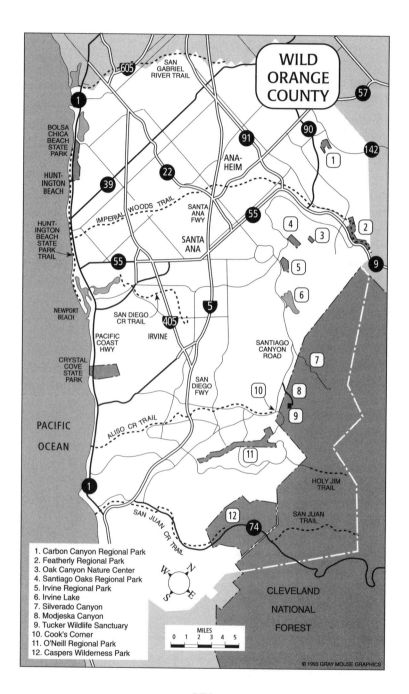

WILD ORANGE COUNTY

1. Carbon Canyon Regional Park
2. Featherly Regional Park
3. Oak Canyon Nature Center
4. Santiago Oaks Regional Park
5. Irvine Regional Park
6. Irvine Lake
7. Silverado Canyon
8. Modjeska Canyon
9. Tucker Wildlife Sanctuary
10. Cook's Corner
11. O'Neill Regional Park
12. Caspers Wilderness Park

© 1993 GRAY MOUSE GRAPHICS

Wild Orange County

Probably one great misconception among people who have never lived here is that Southern California is one uninterrupted urban landscape with Hollywood somewhere in the middle. In fact, the cities and counties that cover Southern California are broken up and divided by many foothills, canyons, and creeks, and harbor real wilderness with excellent opportunities for outdoor recreation.

In the case of Orange County, everything inland from the beach certainly appears dense with residential neighborhoods, shopping centers and business parks. But on closer examination, there are plenty of open spaces left. Along the eastern half of the county, the land butts up against the Santa Ana Mountains with their many canyons and streams. The roads and parks that weave through this part of Orange County provide wonderful scenic diversity.

This chapter includes all the large regional parks located along the eastern edge of Orange County, described in order from north to south. Several regional parks located elsewhere are covered in the other chapters. Cycling trails that crisscross the entire county are listed at the end of the chapter.

Quiet paths lead to a variety of scenery in Orange County

Regional Parks

The county's regional parks are truly wilderness, and no matter how well maintained they may be by the county, they can and do contain unforeseen hazards, including wild animals. When you visit any natural area, keep this in mind: the county's park officials (and the publisher and author of this guide) are not liable for your conduct, for the behavior of wild animals, or even the unpredictable nature of the weather. In other words, by all means enjoy nature, but do it at your own risk. For example, if you came prepared to hike, be sure you follow all the rules of safe hiking in a wilderness area:

- Take along essential gear to ensure your safety:
  Plenty of water
  Protective clothing (to prevent sun and wind burn)
  Extra food
  Pocket knife
  First-aid kit
  Sunglasses and sunblock
  Map and compass
- Don't hike solo
- Pack out your trash
- Be courteous to other hikers

Unless otherwise noted, the county regional parks are open during daylight hours: generally, from 7 a.m. to 9 p.m. (April 1 to October 31), and 7 a.m. to 6 p.m. (November 1 to March 31). There is a $2.00 entry fee per vehicle.

Cleveland National Forest

The Cleveland National Forest, named for former president Grover Cleveland, is one of 22 designated national forests in California. With its 25 lakes and reservoirs stretching south into San Diego County and east into Riverside County, this wilderness is very close to both the Featherly and O'Neill Regional Parks (see below).

The portion of Cleveland National Forest inside Orange County was set aside as a watershed in 1893 to protect the natural vegetation and prevent erosion in the mountains. More than half a million acres of beautiful chaparral and forest were combined into this single forest area in 1908. It protects many endangered species, and is characterized predominantly by its low-lying vegetation, rather than huge groves of trees so often associated with the word "forest."

Two of Cleveland National Forest's campgrounds lie within Orange County: Blue Jay Campground and Upper San Juan Campground.

Blue Jay Campground
Off Ortega Highway (Highway 74)
Reservations: 800-283-CAMP

This campground, located at 3,300 feet above sea level, has piped water, fireplaces, picnic tables and chemical toilets. Pets must be on a leash. The Complete Guide to California Camping says this campground leads to some nice backcountry hiking in the Santa Ana Mountains, as it is near trailheads for the San Juan and Chiquito trails. To reach it,

A Brief Caution

The wilderness trails in Orange County are, without exception, paths that you take at your own risk. Fires, flash floods and mudslides, wild animals, poison oak, hot sun and other forces of nature affect these areas all the time, and they are unforgiving to the hiker or cyclist who is unprepared. Signs are posted advising people who use these trials of the dangers. In particular, there are mountain lions in this region, and they may attack without warning. At all regional parks, a county ranger will give you a brochure with tips on what to do if you encounter a lion.

take Highway 74 to Forest Service Road 6S05 (12 miles west of Lake Elsinore) and follow the signs. Blue Jay is open year-round. Falcon, a smaller campground for groups, is located in the same area.

Upper San Juan Campground

Off Ortega Highway (Highway 74)
Information: (619) 673-6180

Set amid oak trees, this campground is close to trailheads for San Mateo Canyon and the Santa Ana Mountains. It is very popular with hikers. The 18 campsites for tents and motor homes provide piped water, picnic tables, fireplaces and vault toilets. There are no reservations, so it's first-come, first-served; the fee is $7 per vehicle. Located 21 miles north-east of San Juan Capistrano off Highway 74, it is open from April to October.

Carbon Canyon Regional Park

4422 Carbon Canyon Road, Brea
Information: (714) 996-5252

Carbon Canyon used to be the site of an active oil drilling operation, with a town named Olinda. The region went bust around the turn of the century and all that's left of the town is a neighborhood further up the canyon road. There is a state historical marker (#918) located near the ranger station that commemorates the town's past existence.

The equestrian, hiking and biking trails in Carbon Canyon are perfect for a day of exercise in the country. There is a particularly good cycling trail that originates in this park, provided you have a mountain bike. To find the beginning of the trail, park to the left of the park entrance and follow the dirt path farther east that parallels Carbon Canyon Road. Take the first dirt road that forks to the right and follow it past the streambed and orange grove. At the base of a hillside is Telegraph Canyon Trail, which will take you to the summit of Chino Hills State Park, 10,000 acres of wilderness stretching throughout neighboring San Bernardino, Los Angeles, and Riverside counties. From here you can see the beautiful mountains in all directions. This is a 12-mile round trip.

One of Carbon Canyon's more unusual features is a grove of nearly 200 coastal redwoods (Sequoia sempervirens) that was planted in 1975. These dry, sage-covered canyon areas are not the natural home of the redwood tree, but the experiment has worked well in Carbon Canyon. The only thing the park rangers do in the way of extra care is spray the trees occasionally to remove dirt that accumulates from regional smog. Otherwise, the trees haven't required any special assistance to grow and stay healthy. These trees are located at the back of the park, two miles from the park's entrance, where picnic tables, playgrounds, a small lake (stocked with catfish) and some tennis courts can be found.

Directions: Take the 57 Freeway north to the Lambert Road exit and head east. Follow the signs for Highway 142. The entrance is on your right. The park occupies a relatively narrow section along the south side of the highway.

If you were to continue along Highway 142, you would discover a scenic "shortcut" to Chino Hills in San Bernardino County (but that's for another book!). This in itself is a fun drive out of Orange County that avoids the freeway scene.

Featherly Regional Park

24001 Santa Ana Canyon Road, Anaheim
Information: (714) 637-0210

To visit the next stop on our tour, take Highway 142 west to Valencia Avenue and turn left. You're still on Highway 142 at this point. Head south and then turn left at Imperial Highway (Highway 90). Make a left at Yorba Linda Boulevard and proceed east to Featherly Regional Park.

This is an excellent family overnight camping spot in Santa Ana Canyon near the edge of the Cleveland National Forest. It is situated between the Chino foothills to the north and the Santa Ana Mountains to the south. The overnight camping fee is $10 per vehicle, and the usual overnight camping facilities are all here: showers, barbecue pits, playground equipment, hiking trails and an interpretive center.

After visiting Featherly, you can take a scenic tour of the foothill homes and vistas of the Anaheim Hills. Go back to Weir Canyon Road and turn left (south). At Serrano Avenue, turn right, then make another right at Canyon Rim Road. When you reach Nohl Ranch Road, turn left and follow the signs to Oak Canyon Nature Center.

Oak Canyon Nature Center

6700 E. Walnut Canyon Road, Anaheim Hills
Information: (714) 998-8380

A pleasant getaway amid the sprawling growth of the Anaheim Hills subdivision, Oak Canyon has 58 acres of oak stands, a stream and plenty of birds. There are six miles of intersecting trails—some flat, and some steep enough for the adventuresome hiker. There is also a visitor's center with nature displays. This is a good bird watching area.

Oak Canyon is designated as a wilderness preservation area, as opposed to some of the other nature parks in Orange County. Cycling, picnicking and pets (even on a leash) are not allowed. During the summer, evening guided tours through the canyon take place one night a week. Call ahead for information.

Santiago Canyon Road

To reach our next destination, leave the Oak Canyon Nature Center and turn right on Nohl Ranch Road. Proceed west to the Costa Mesa (Highway 55) Freeway and head south. Exit at Katella Avenue and head east. After a name change to "Villa Park Road," this becomes Santiago Canyon Road.

This road bisects the canyon formed by the foothills of the Santa Ana Mountains, and runs parallel to these mountains from the city of Orange to Lake Forest. It links several major Orange County arteries and is a nice back country drive (or ride, if you're cycling). The roads leading to both Silverado and Modjeska Canyons peel off from this route; three regional parks are connected by it: Santiago Oaks, Irvine, and O'Neill.

Santiago Oaks Regional Park

2145 N. Windes Drive, Orange
Information: (714) 538-4400

This park is so close to one of Orange County's suburban neighborhoods that you'd never expect to find it here. That's one of the nicer things about coming here. It's uncrowded.

Once a part of Rancho Santiago de Santa Ana, the area surrounding Santiago Creek was actually inhabited by Gabrieleno Indians for thousands of years. In more recent times, the Butterfield stagecoach ran through this canyon on its way to the budding towns of the future Orange County. Bandits hid in these foothills too, waiting for opportunities to rob unsuspecting travelers. Robber's Roost was so named because it was easy to spot any posse that might be coming after those nineteenth-century outlaws.

One of the first water projects in Orange County, a small dam made from clay that was designed to collect underground water for agricultural use, was constructed here. Rebuilt in 1892 with rock and cement, the dam can still be seen. Santiago Creek, running through the center of this 350-acre park, is the main tributary of the Santa Ana River. This is probably the best place to view the creek before it reaches the flatlands and joins the Santa Ana—which in this century became just another concrete "flood control" channel.

Nature lovers will appreciate the variety of vegetation to be seen here: riparian woodland, coast live oaks, sage scrub, California sycamores, and a Valencia orange grove that is still producing. Mule deer, coyote, bobcat, and more than 130 species of birds range through this lush area. You can enjoy this wonderful wilderness getaway via self-guiding nature trails that wind from the park's nature center (a converted ranch house built in 1938) to high, scenic bluffs such as Rattle-snake Ridge. The park's trails also connect to the Anaheim Hills trail system. The nature center has exhibits on wildlife and an audio-visual center.

Irvine Regional Park

21501 Chapman Avenue, Orange
Information: (714) 633-8074

After you've enjoyed Santiago Oaks, head back to Santiago Canyon Road and turn left. You're now on your way to Irvine Regional Park. This park is located in Santiago Canyon, six miles east of the city of Orange. An old grove of coast live oaks and California sycamores make this, the oldest regional park in the state, a beautiful spot for a picnic.

The 477-acre park was part of a rancho originally owned by the Yorba family. The Irvine family acquired it, and began donating portions of the park to the county in 1897. Among the highlights one must count the new miniature railroad ride that takes dozens of passengers at a time around some of the park's lovely scenery. It's a one-third scale propane locomotive and six cars that can be enjoyed for just $2 a passenger.

Also located in this park is the William Harding Nature Area, a collection of chaparral plants and trees native to the area, planted alongside the park's hiking trail. The park has its own nature center/museum with exhibits on this region's natural flora and fauna. The park is also home to the Orange County Zoo, featuring animals native to the southwest, and a petting corral of domesticated animals.

Rentals for horse and pony rides, tandem bicycles and paddle boats are all available for your enjoyment, and built-in barbecues and sinks are located throughout the park. Biking, hiking and equestrian trails are everywhere, and there are plenty of volleyball courts, softball fields, playgrounds and horseshoe pits. There's even a lake stocked with catfish.

Irvine Lake (Santiago Reservoir)

Off Santiago Canyon Road south of Chapman Avenue
Information: (714) 649-2560
Hours: Daily, 6 a.m. to 4 p.m.; Friday and Saturday until
11 p.m.
Fees: No fishing license is required, but there is a day use
fee of $10 per adult, $8 for children under 12.

Santiago Creek passes through Irvine Regional Park and feeds a reservoir further south. This reservoir is the main attraction of Irvine Lake Park. To find it, drive south on Santiago Canyon Road and look for the entrance on your left.

It should not be confused with Irvine Regional Park's own lake. This large, popular lake covers 660 acres and is stocked with bluegill, catfish, crappie, trout and bass. Live bait is not allowed. There are boat rentals available (call 649-2991 for information), but they don't take reservations. You can launch your own craft, if you have one, for a $5 fee. There's also a bait and tackle shop here in case you forgot anything.

Irvine Lake is stocked regularly with large fish, and catching twelve- and fourteen-pound bass and trout is not uncommon. It is not used for windsurfing, water skiing, tubing, swimming or any other aquatic sport, making it an angler's paradise.

Limestone Canyon

Santiago Canyon Road
Information and Reservations: (714) 832-7478

In May 1993 the Irvine Company opened up 17,000 acres of privately-owned ranch land to the public for the first time in 129 years. The new acreage, which can be toured by reservation only, includes this impressive canyon just west of Santiago Canyon Road.

Over the years the land has suffered much degradation from cattle ranching, but now a new program conducted by the Nature Conservancy has begun to restore it. All the cattle have been removed, and for the first time this century residents and visitors will see beautiful, unspoiled wilderness where grizzly bears and wolves once roamed.

Especially exciting to hikers will be the "sinks," a red sandstone formation in the shape of a huge, 250-foot-deep bowl that was carved by a stream over a million years. The surrounding territory is a woodland of oak and sycamore. The hiking tours are restricted to specific paths, as many areas are undergoing restoration.

Tour space is limited, and the two-hour hikes are only being conducted on Saturdays for groups of 20. You must call the information number between 3 and 5 p.m., Monday through Friday, to make a reservation. The docents who lead the tours are volunteers from the Nature Conservancy. Mountain bike and equestrian tours are also scheduled. Call for tour details and directions to the canyon.

Silverado Canyon

Just a little farther south of Irvine Lake along Santiago Canyon Road is the turn off for Silverado Canyon. When you follow Silverado Canyon Road, you'll discover a unique, back-to-the-woods neighborhood. People who live in Silverado Canyon truly want to get away from it all. The canyons of the Cleveland National Forest are lovely for country drives in the family car. About the only time this canyon is inhospitable is during a heavy rainstorm, when flash floods and mudslides can make it dangerous.

Silverado Canyon was once under a prehistoric ocean; as a result many marine fossils dating from 70 million years ago can be found in the mudstone cliffs that frame Silverado Creek. You can look for fossils in the bluffs along the creek just past the U.S. Forest Service fire station. Silverado Canyon Road eventually dead-ends and the main hiking trail begins. The trail here is 3.4 miles up to 1,900 feet above sea level, ending at the Main Divide Trail and Bedford Peak The round trip to this ridge is nearly seven miles on a steep grade. On a clear day, you won't believe the view — you can see the Pacific Ocean.

Modjeska Canyon

After returning to Santiago Canyon Road, turn left and head south approximately two miles to the next major canyon, Modjeska. When you turn left on Modjeska Canyon Road, you will proceed into a shorter canyon than Silverado. The lifestyle of the local residents and the architecture of their dwellings are similar, however. Modjeska was once a prominent beekeeping area. Today there are two sites of interest in Modjeska Canyon.

Modjeska House was the home of a world-renowned actress, Madame Helena Modjeska, a resident of Orange County at the turn of the century. Madame Modjeska entertained many visitors at her home and gardens, which she called "The Forest of Arden." One of the peaks of Saddleback Mountain is named in her honor. The home, with its five gables, is listed in the National Register of Historic Places, and is open for tours by reservation only (949-855-2028). The house is located at 29042 Modjeska Canyon Road. The 14-1/2 acres here contain the largest grove of redwood trees in the county.

The other site of interest in this canyon is a wildlife sanctuary at the very end of Modjeska Canyon Road.

Tucker Wildlife Sanctuary

29322 Modjeska Canyon Road
Information: 649-2760
Hours: Daily 9 a.m to 4 p.m.
Donation: $1.50

The Tucker Wildlife Sanctuary is a 12-acre preserve operated by the California State Fullerton Foundation. The sanctuary is actually a series of small trails, with flora abundantly labeled (on one trail, the labels are in Braille). Whatever fauna you see on the trails is strictly by chance, but it's out there. A nature center showcases some small reptiles and rodents, and a few taxonomic specimens.

There is a special, glassed-in observation area with bird feeders that attract many varieties of birds, most notably hummingbirds.

If you're interested in adventure, try the 9.5-mile hiking trail that begins here. (That's 9.5 miles in one direction; it's 19 miles if you were to walk all the way in and all the way out.) The trail climbs the mountains for some great views of the Orange County terrain. Restrooms and water are available at the sanctuary, but once on the trail, you're on your own.

Cook's Corner

Corner of Santiago Canyon and Live Oak Canyon Roads
Information: (949) 997-8860
Hours: Daily, 8 a.m. to 2 a.m.

Proceeding back to Santiago Canyon Road, make your way south again and turn left at Live Oak Canyon Road. At this fork in the road is Cook's Corner, Orange County's most famous weekend bikers hangout. On weekends the motorcycles are parked 10-deep in places as visitors and regulars vie for space. Bikers aren't quite what they used to be. Sure, you'll still see plenty of folks with Harley Davidson motorcycles, but now more than ever, "bikers" are clean-cut folks with expensive name-brand machines and designer, color-coordinated leathers. Everyone comes to Cook's for the natural canyon ambiance. Inside this little cafe is a place to shoot pool, order a basket of fries with a pitcher of brew, and listen to live music every evening (usually country-western). Cook's has been operating continuously since 1937.

O'Neill Regional Park

30892 Trabuco Canyon Road, Trabuco Canyon
Information: 858-9365
Admission: $2 vehicle fee, $4 on weekends; call for camping fees.

Continue east on Live Oak Canyon Road to the next large park on our itinerary, O'Neill Regional. This park could easily be missed if you're traveling too fast along El Toro Road/Santiago Canyon Road. There are showers and fire rings for cooking, used for both day use and overnight camping. The park also has some good equestrian trails, and horseback riders may camp here. (Horse trailers are allowed, but you have to bring your own horse.) The park is quite large, meandering along with Trabuco Creek as far south as Mission Viejo. O'Neill also has two self-guided nature walks and a nature center. Be sure to check out the two-mile round-trip hike to Vista Lookout, where you get a great view of the surrounding peaks and even the coastline on a clear day.

Caspers Wilderness Park

33401 Ortega Highway, San Juan Capistrano
Information: (949) 728-0235, 831-2174

When you leave O'Neill Regional, turn right (instead of going back to Cook's Corner) and follow Trabuco Canyon Road to Rancho Santa Margarita, one of Orange County's newest communities. You can then turn right at Santa Margarita Parkway and head back toward South County. To reach the next wilderness area, turn left at Marguerite Parkway and head south to the San Diego Freeway (I-5). Take the on ramp for San Diego and exit at Ortega Highway (Hwy. 74). Turn left and head east back toward the foothills. You're now on your way to Caspers Wilderness Park.

This is Orange County's largest park, and in some ways the most rugged. Nature is definitely untamed in this 7,600-acre expanse. Because of a mountain lion attack on two children in the mid-1980s, anyone under age 18 must be accompanied by an adult, and children are restricted to the picnic areas and visitors center. You must be 18 or over to hike the wilderness trails, and you cannot travel the trails solo. The park permit states that there are certain "inherent dangers" traveling through these canyons and that your safety cannot be guaranteed.

If this sounds frightening, keep in mind that even catching a glimpse of a mountain lion is extremely rare, and there are so many other wonderful sights in this huge park that you will be amply rewarded. Bird watchers love this area. Foxes, bobcats, coyotes, deer and rabbits are also plentiful. Weekend interpretive programs will enhance your enjoyment of the park's geology, wildlife, and Native American history. Thirty miles of trails give visitors an opportunity to really appreciate Orange County's natural beauty before the arrival of settlers. Here you will see chaparral, coastal live oak, cactus, lemonade berry, lupines and sycamores.

Bell Canyon and its trail offer the best tour of the park. Juaneno Indians once pounded oak acorns into ground meal in this canyon. Whenever I walk a trail such as this, I try to imagine what it must have been like to be among the first people to ever explore these beautiful, bountiful lands.

Maps available at the visitors center will help you choose from the many paths that are available in Bell Canyon. Most of the trails stick close to Bell Creek, where black bears used to catch trout (alas, that era is long gone). The longest trail, Oso, is more than six miles in one direction, and leads to a 1,470-foot summit. On a clear day you can spy Los Angeles County and Santa Catalina Island from here.

There is limited overnight camping space. You can also camp here overnight with your horse as long as you have a trailer.

Outdoor Trails

Although many of the regional parks mentioned above have their own cycling, hiking and equestrian trails, I've highlighted a few below that are located in other areas of the county. Some are suitable for only one purpose, such as hiking, while others are used by people on foot, bicycle and horseback.

Aliso Creek Trail

Lake Forest to Laguna Niguel

This 15-plus-mile trail follows a scenic route in the South County area. It begins at the corner of Santiago Canyon Road and Live Oak Canyon Road, where you can pause and refresh yourself at Cook's Corner. The trail winds along Aliso Creek all the way to Laguna Niguel Regional Park. Eventually the completed trail will reach to the beach at South Laguna.

Holy Jim Trail

Trabuco Canyon

This is a ten-mile hiking trail (not a fire road) through Trabuco Canyon in the Cleveland National Forest. This trail is for advanced hikers only. There's no water available on the route, so bring a plentiful supply.

Take El Toro Road in Lake Forest to Live Oak Canyon Road and turn right (this is the fork where Cook's Corner is located). Just past the entrance to O'Neill Regional Park, there are two unpaved roads on the left: Rose Canyon and Trabuco Creek. Take the second one, which is Trabuco Creek Road and is unmarked. Park when you reach another fork in the road and proceed along the left fork on foot. The trail begins here.

Huntington State Beach Park Trail
Along the side of Pacific Coast Highway

A wonderfully long trail from the Newport Beach Pier (on the Balboa Peninsula) stretches to Bolsa Chica Beach State Park. This ten-miles-plus path will give any cyclist or walker all the coastal beach scenery they could ever desire without the worry of dealing with the busy automobile traffic along Pacific Coast Highway.

Imperial Woods Trail (Santa Ana River Bike Trail)

The Imperial Woods is the longest trail in Orange County. It is 30 miles one-way from Huntington Beach to the Riverside County line. The trail is mostly flat, as it follows the Santa Ana river bed for most of its length. There is one detour at Santa Ana Canyon Road. You can access the trail at many cross streets.

The eastern terminus of this cycling, hiking and equestrian path is the Riverside County line. The ocean terminus is Huntington Beach State Park (Brookhurst at PCH).

San Diego Creek Trail
Irvine/Newport Beach

This short bikeway travels through mostly flat country in Irvine, following the San Diego Creek Channel from Irvine Boulevard (near Culver Drive) southwest to Upper Newport Bay at Jamboree Road. The trail passes part of UCI and the San Joaquin Freshwater Marsh Preserve. At Upper Newport Bay you can enjoy some fine birdwatching.

San Gabriel River/Coyote Creek Trail

If you are spending some time in the North County communities of La Palma, Buena Park, Los Alamitos, Cypress or Seal Beach, you should find this trail along the San Gabriel River bed. It provides a pleasant diversion from the densely packed suburban area that is typical at this edge of the county. The trail starts at the 605 Freeway and Katella Avenue and proceeds to Ocean Avenue north of downtown Seal Beach. Stopping at the Seal Beach Pier for a snack and a breath of ocean air is ample reward for all that pedaling.

San Juan Creek Trail

San Juan Capistrano

From the foothills near the Ortega Highway down to Capistrano Beach, this hilly trail will give you spectacular views of South County and the Pacific Ocean. It is primarily for cyclists. Begin at Cook Park (Calle Arroyo and La Novia Avenue) and head southwest to the sea following San Juan Creek. The trail ends at Doheny State Beach in Dana Point.

San Juan Trail

Cleveland National Forest

To reach this trail, drive Ortega Highway (Hwy. 74) from San Juan Capistrano to about three-fourths of a mile past the San Juan ranger station. The trail is tough, but is popular with hikers and mountain bikers just the same. It proceeds northeast from San Juan Hot Springs to the Main Divide Trail inside the Cleveland National Forest. It is 23.2 miles altogether, but there are shorter loop trails. A good reference guide, such as Jerry Schad's Cycling Orange County, would be extra helpful to study before attempting this longer, more arduous type of ride.

Appendix A:
A Glossary of Some Spanish Words

If you're going to be staying in Southern California for any length of time, you should become familiar with some of the Spanish words and phrases that are commonly used. Here are a few for starters:

adobe	(a-DOH-bee) sun-dried brick; synonymous with old structures made from it
agua	(AH-gwa) water
amigo	(a-MEE-go) friend
arroyo	(ah-ROY-o) a watercourse; used in many place names
bonito, bonita	(bo-NEAT-oh, bo-NEAT-ah) pretty
buena, bueno	(BWAY-nah, BWAY-no) good
buenos dias	(BWAY-nos DEE-ahs) good morning
caliente	(kal-YEN-tay) warm, hot, scalding
calle	(kah-yay) street
camino	(ka-MEE-no) road
cantina	(kan-TEE-nah) in American usage: bar, saloon
carne	(KAHR-nay) meat, flesh
carniceria	(kar-ni-se-REE-ah) a market
casa	(ka-sah) house
cerveza	(ser-VAY-sa) beer
comida	(koh-MEE-dah) dinner, meal
de nada	(day-NAH-dah) you're welcome (literally, "think nothing of it")
fiesta	(fee-EHS-tah) party, celebration
gracias	(GRAH-see-us) thanks, thank you; muchas gracias, many thanks

gringo	(GRIHN-goh) slang for anglo or non Hispanic person
hacienda	(ah-see-EHN-dah) large ranch or estate
mesa	(MAY-sah) a flat-topped hill; a table
muy	(MU-WEE) very
ola!	(OH-lah) the word means "wave," but it's used as a casual greeting
palo	(PAL-oh) tree; commonly used in place names
picante	(pi-KAN-tay) hot, piquant
playa	(PLAH-yah) beach, shore
plaza	(PLAH-zah) square, marketplace
¿qué?	(KAY) what?
ranchero	(rahn-CHAY-roh) rancher
rancho	(RAHN-choh) large ranch
raza	(RAH-sa) race; la raza (popular term used by people to denote their Mexican ancestry/heritage)
río	(REE-oh) river
san, santa	(SAHN, SAHN-tah) saint; used in many place names
señor	(say-N'YOHR) mister, sir, gentleman
señora	(say-N'YOHR-ah) madam, lady
señorita	(say-N'YOHR-ee-tah) miss, young lady
sí	(SEE) yes
sierra	(see-EHR-ah) mountain range
via	(VI-yah) way, road, street
vista	(VIS-tah) view
viva!	(VEE-vah) hurrah!

Appendix B:
Recommended Reading

The following books offer more detailed coverage of specific places or activities in Orange County. Look for them at your local library, bookstore, or order them directly from the publishers.

Adventurer's Guide to Dana Point by Doris Walker. 1992. To-The-Point Press, Box 546, Dana Point, CA 92629. An excellent walking guide through Dana Point's past and present.

Beautiful Gardens by Eric A. Johnson and Scott Millard. 1991. Ironwood Press, 2968 W. Ina Road, #285, Tucson, AZ 85741. A colorful pictorial guide to lush gardens in the Southwest, including Southern California.

California Wildlife Viewing Guide by Jeanne L. Clark. 1992. Falcon Press Publishing Co., P.O. Box 1718, Helena, MT 59624. A guide published in cooperation with Defenders of Wildlife, this is one in a series of excellent state-by-state guides to America's wildlife. States with this program have posted road signs depicting a silhouette of binoculars on a brown background to mark wildlife viewing areas.

Cycling Orange County by Jerry Schad. 1991. Centra Publications, P.O. Box 191029, San Diego, CA 92159. A guide to cycling tours throughout Orange County, with illustrated information on the routes, elevations, and difficulty of thirty-one separate riding tours.

The Golf Trekker® Courses of Southern California. Reg. DFP Publications, 1125 Loma Ave., Coronado, CA 92118-2835. A thorough guide to virtually every golf course in five counties and even Baja. Pars, handicaps, green fees, club requirements, course designers, and on-site facilities are all detailed.

A Hundred Years of Yesterdays: A Centennial History of the People of Orange County and Their Communities. Edited by Esther R. Cramer et al. 1988. The Orange County Centennial, Inc. Published in cooperation with the Orange County Register, this large paperback is filled with great photos from Orange County's past, and the stories of the county's pioneers are told city-by-city. It's hard to find, but the county library has it on hand.

In Kid's Guide to Orange County by Susan Hahn Hillgren and Leslie Shattuck McDonald. 1992. MacHill Publications, 923 N. Main St., Orange, CA 92667. A wonderful flipbook (perfect for the kitchen or glove compartment) that contains all kinds of suggestions and places to go to entertain your children.

Lake Recreation in Southern California for Weekenders by Herschell Whitmer. 1991. Herschell Whitmer Associates, P.O. Box 7261, Long Beach, CA 90807. This book lists all the freshwater fishing opportunities you could ever want, from Monterey County in central California to Baja, Mexico.

1000 California Place Names by Erwin G. Gudde. 1959. University of California Press, Berkeley, CA 94720. An interesting dictionary, still available in paperback, that details the meaning and evolution of names given to California's natural surroundings and cities.

Pocket Guide to Orange County Beaches by the California State Coastal Conservancy. Sea Grant Institutional Program/USC. Handy glove-compartment-sized booklet on all the county's beaches and facilities from Seal Beach to San Clemente. Available at state beach park ranger stations.

Whale Watching and Tide Pools by Gregory Lee. 1992.
Renaissance House Publishers, Frederick CO. Gives the
best places along the California shore for tide pool
action and observing the annual gray whale migration
during the winter months.

*California Camping: The Complete Guide to California's
Recreational Areas*, 1992-93 ed. by Tom Stienstra.
Foghorn Press, P.O. Box 77845, San Francisco, CA
94107. A thorough listing of campgrounds and their
facilities throughout the state.

Index

About the Author

Gregory Lee is the nom de plume of Gregory Lee, a 40-something guy who is the alleged author of this, the second edition of THE BEST OF ORANGE COUNTY.

Lee spent his childhood in Santa Ana, when all parents were just like June and Ward Cleaver, fireworks were safe, and daylight-saving time was second only to Christmas, in his estimation. Playing hide-and-seek among the oak trees and orange groves is part of his indelible memories. Early on Lee developed an interest in exploration, mapping out his own neighborhood with colored pencils and even drawing Orange County for his own amusement. His passion for knowing where everything is probably accounts for his obsession with writing this book.

According to the Library of Congress, Lee has written at least two other guidebooks, one about the California missions and the other on the best whale watching and tidepool locations of the California coast. He may have written other books too, but he will deny it. A bachelor's degree in journalism did not lead to a Pulitzer, so Lee abandoned that vocation in a hurry. During his checkered career he has edited more than 100 educational books for young people, on topics ranging from astronauts to zebras. In a parallel universe he is the editor of a science fiction newsletter, Radio Free PKD (a "quarterly), with a total of eight issues in eight years.

Lee is a rabid fan of jazz, basketball, chocolate, warm weather and British sitcoms. When he is not being facetious, Lee works as the left coast sales director for a global manufacturing broker. He lives in — and here's the amazing part — Orange County. Greg, his wife and assorted pets live in Aliso Viejo, where they are busy showing their two grandchildren the best of Orange County.